Unemployment Insurance Reform

Unemployment Insurance Reform

Fixing a Broken System

Stephen A. Wandner
Editor

2018

W.E. Upjohn Institute for Employment Research
Kalamazoo, Michigan

Library of Congress Cataloging-in-Publication Data

Name: Wandner, Stephen A., editor.
Title: Unemployment insurance reform : fixing a broken system / Stephen A. Wandner, editor.
Description: Kalamazoo, Michigan : W.E. Upjohn Institute for Employment Research, [2017] | Series: WE focus series | Includes bibliographical references and index.
Identifiers: LCCN 2017054506 | ISBN 9780880996525 (pbk. : alk. paper) | ISBN 0880996528 (pbk. : alk. paper)
Subjects: LCSH: Unemployment insurance—United States. | Unemployment insurance—Government policy—United States.
Classification: LCC HD7096.U5 U6355 2017 | DDC 368.4/400973—dc23 LC record available at https://lccn.loc.gov/2017054506

The facts presented in this study and the observations and viewpoints expressed are the sole responsibility of the authors. They do not necessarily represent positions of the W.E. Upjohn Institute for Employment Research.

Cover design by Carol A.S. Derks.
Index prepared by Diane Worden.
Printed in the United States of America.
Printed on recycled paper.

For Lawrence E. Weatherford

who directed the U.S. Department of Labor's
successful effort in 1976 to enact major reform
of the Unemployment Insurance program.

Contents

Acknowledgments   ix

1 Why the Unemployment Insurance Program Needs to   1
   Be Reformed
   Stephen A. Wandner

2 UI Reform Proposals in the Fiscal Year 2017 Obama   23
   Budget Request
   Suzanne Simonetta

3 The Employment Service–Unemployment Insurance   65
   Partnership: Origin, Evolution, and Revitalization
   David E. Balducchi and Christopher J. O'Leary

4 State UI Financing Response to the Great Recession   103
   Wayne Vroman

5 Unemployment Insurance Reform: Evidence-Based   131
   Policy Recommendations
   Christopher J. O'Leary and Stephen A. Wandner

6 Conclusions and Needed Reforms   211
   Stephen A. Wandner

Authors   219

Index   221

About the Institute   237

Acknowledgments

The chapters in this book were first presented as papers in November 2016 at the Association for Public Policy and Management's Fall Research Conference. The papers were then revised based on the excellent comments from two discussants, Gary Burtless and Rich Hobbie, and from questions and comments received from the audience during the session.

The most important contribution to this book comes from the authors, all of whom have been students of the Unemployment Insurance program for many years. They share a common belief in the importance of unemployment insurance as a critical component of the American social insurance system, as well as the need for comprehensive reform of the system to assure its effectiveness and efficiency in the 21st century.

—Stephen A. Wandner

Chapter 1

Why the Unemployment Insurance Program Needs to Be Reformed

Stephen A. Wandner
*W.E. Upjohn Institute for Employment Research
and The Urban Institute*

This book examines the Unemployment Insurance (UI) program in the United States from a research and policy perspective. It finds that there is consensus among experts and researchers that the program is broken and needs to be fixed to function as an adequate source of temporary income support to individuals and as a reliable automatic stabilizer in the twenty-first century economy. The chapters are written by experts who review the program as it is supposed to work under federal law and, by contrast, how it actually has been operating in recent years. Based on research evidence, the authors offer prescriptions for restoring the UI program. Chapters 2 and 5 consider a number of different proposals for UI reform proposed by the federal government, private institutions, and individual researchers. In addition, Chapter 5 compares recent reform proposals and presents and analyzes the authors' plan for comprehensive reform.

UI is a form of social insurance that was first enacted in 1935 as a part of the Social Security Act. The program is a federal-state partnership, with the federal government setting a national institutional framework, and the states establishing most of the program specifications through state law and administering day-to-day program operations. For eight decades, the UI program has paid temporary income support to experienced American workers who lose their jobs through no fault of their own. The basic (or "regular") UI program[1] generally pays up to 26 weeks [2] of benefits to eligible workers. Benefit payments usually replace approximately half of a worker's prior wages up to a state determined maximum benefit amount. Compensation is paid weekly and is considered to be adequate if it provides a reasonable level of wage replacement while the unemployed seek reemployment.

Unemployment benefits are paid for by insurance premiums (called "contributions," but in fact, they are a tax) paid by employers on payrolls. Unemployment benefits are designed to be fully paid by employer taxes over time, although the amounts of unemployment benefits paid and unemployment taxes collected are not expected to balance every year because the level of unemployment—and, therefore, benefit payments—is much greater in recessionary times than in more prosperous times. Rather, UI benefit payments and tax revenues are intended to balance over the business cycle.

The UI program's three main goals are to provide:

1) adequate, temporary income support to experienced, unemployed individuals while they search for new employment;

2) a countercyclical stimulus to the American economy when large numbers of workers become unemployed during recessionary periods; and

3) stabilization of employment through the UI experience rating system, which discourages employer layoffs.

Thus, UI is both a social insurance program for individuals and part of the larger macroeconomic policy to limit the harmful effects of economic downturns for individual states and for the United States as a whole. As we will see in this book, it is a complex policy challenge to achieve each of these goals separately and an even more difficult one to achieve them together.

The complexity of the challenge is derived from the number of components of the program that must be in balance. Specifically, if the UI program is to be a self-sustaining, self-adjusting social insurance program, the following must occur:

• The overall *level* of benefits and revenues must balance over time as a result of the financing provisions in state and federal laws (in a static sense).

- Benefits and revenues must both be indexed to wage increases (in a dynamic sense).

- The UI state and federal tax structures need to be structured to adjust automatically so that revenues equal benefit payments over the business cycle.

A number of things must be implemented to create a UI program that remains in balance.

On the benefit side:

- Unemployment benefit levels and durations must be set to ensure an adequate level of wage replacement.

- Unemployment benefits must be adjusted annually to reflect changes in wages that occur in the labor market—to enable UI to provide the same level of wage replacement over time.

On the revenue side:

- The two components of the UI tax system, tax rates and the taxable wage base, must be adequate.

- The taxable wage base must increase annually to accommodate annual increases in UI benefits that reflect increases in wages.

- Tax contributions must vary over the business cycle, increasing after a recession to build up reserves and declining when reserves reach an adequate level to anticipate the next recession.

A SYSTEM OUT OF BALANCE

Balancing the components of the UI program is like keeping all the parts of a clock in working order to make sure it always keeps the right time. Things can go wrong, however, and in recent years, many things have gone wrong with the UI system. On the benefit side, benefits in many states are set below an adequate level and also do not increase as wages increase. On the revenue side, the federal UI wage base has not been increased since 1983, and many states have not increased their state wage bases sufficiently above the federal wage base. Also, state tax rates frequently have not been set high enough to enable states to get through the next recession without running out of reserves, and during economic recoveries, many states resist raising taxes and some lower UI benefits instead.

Thus, the UI program is seriously out of balance in large part because neither unemployment benefits nor UI taxes are indexed to provide adequate benefits or revenues over time. By contrast, the Social Security pension system indexes both benefit levels and the taxable wage base, such that payouts and revenues would be in far better balance than the UI program, if it were not for the drain on program resources from the aging of the U.S. population. Dramatic differences have developed between these two social insurance programs over time despite the fact that both programs started with the same taxable wage base of $3,000. In essence, Social Security has adjusted to changing economic conditions over time, while UI has not.

In response to concerns about the health of the UI system, a number of major UI reform proposals have been released in the past two years. This book reviews and compares several of these proposals.

The authors offer their analyses in the hope that the next serious review of the UI program will consider a wide range of reforms to strengthen the UI program so that it can become more effective and efficient. Given the dramatic changes over the last two decades in the demographics of the U.S. workforce and in work arrangements, it is past time to reform the UI program before the next recession. This evidence-based discussion of reforms will enable federal and state officials to weigh policies so they can provide practical solutions to prevent a recurrence of the problems the program experienced during and after the Great Recession.

UNEMPLOYMENT INSURANCE PUBLIC POLICY: NOT KEEPING UP WITH THE TIMES

The UI program is over 80 years old. When it was enacted in 1935, the United States was in the middle of the Great Depression. As a result, because of concern about potentially overwhelming short-term expenditures, the program that was established was modest in its design—with states paying low weekly benefits for short periods of time—and benefit payments were delayed until 1938 to allow tax collections to build up state reserves in the Unemployment Trust Fund (UTF) in the U.S. Treasury.

With nearly full employment, virtually no unemployment benefits were paid during World War II. In the years after the war, it became clear that the strength of the U.S. economy was such that the UI program could pay more generous benefits for longer periods of unemployment. As a result, states changed their UI laws to increase maximum benefit amounts and lengthen potential durations.

Since the 1970s, however, the federal government has done little to adapt and modernize the UI program through reforms of the federal UI law. In response to most of the postwar recessions, Congress has continued to enact temporary federal extensions of benefits. A permanent Extended Benefit (EB) program was enacted in 1970, but it soon proved to be ineffective because the automatic ("trigger") mechanism to turn the program on and off did not work, and the program has never been fixed. Instead, in response to the ensuing recessions, Congress enacted temporary emergency programs that added to the potential duration of UI benefits.

A major reform of the program was enacted in 1976, but that reform was only partial and it left much undone. Congress authorized two UI study commissions that issued reports in the 1980s and 1990s, but their reform recommendations were ignored.

Under the Social Security Act, individual states are given considerable freedom to determine UI benefit payments eligibility and levels, tax rates, and tax bases. The states have varied widely in the generosity of their unemployment benefit payments and the soundness of their state accounts in the UTF, but over many decades, benefits have generally declined in real terms and benefit financing systems have remained inadequate.

As a result, a general consensus has developed among UI policy experts that the UI system should be reformed for several reasons. These include changing economic conditions, outdated federal statutes that no longer work well, and dysfunction in state programs, which are both underfunded and pay inadequate benefits.

Nevertheless, even though there are serious weaknesses in the UI program, the state UI administrative systems have responded well to recessions. State UI agencies have paid benefits in a reasonably timely and accurate manner, despite the fact that recessionary benefit payments have tended to increase exponentially, and Congress generally has required the states to implement temporary emergency UI programs effective upon enactment.

However, the federal and state UI tax structures have not worked well. Most states have not accumulated adequate reserves to pay benefits during recessions. After recessions, they have only slowly repaid their federal loans and built up their state accounts in the UTF, frequently facing the next recession in a weak fiscal condition. Also, after a recession, many states have reduced benefit levels and durations rather than raised taxes, choosing to lower costs rather than raise revenues. At the same time, federal funding from the Federal Unemployment Tax Act (FUTA) accounts has declined, providing inadequate funding for UI administration, EBs, Employment Service (ES) administration of the UI work test, and provision of reemployment services.

As a result, the current UI system faces a reduced ability to serve individual covered workers who become unemployed through no fault of their own. The percentage of unemployed workers receiving UI benefits has declined to a historic low. In the next recession, a weakened UI system will have a reduced ability to provide a countercyclical stimulus, and the states will not be ready to fund new demands on the system.

The UI program has been extensively studied and evaluated. Public policy analysts have identified problems in the UI system and ways to fix them. The purpose of this book is to highlight what has been learned from the UI research and evaluations and to analyze proposals for the program's reform. This book also includes an update of portions of a two-decade-old UI policy book by O'Leary and Wandner (1997).

FAILURE TO HELP UI RECIPIENTS RETURN TO WORK

The UI system's provision of temporary income support is based on the expectation that UI recipients will receive help to rapidly return to work by receiving information about and referral to job openings, job finding and placement services, and labor market information to assist in their job search. This exposure to job openings is known as the UI Work Test, and it is crucial to assuring that UI recipients are seeking new work as a condition for receipt of weekly unemployment benefits. Historically, ES has provided these services, and the decline of the ES has meant that these functions have badly eroded. The evolution of the relationship between ES and UI is discussed at length in Chapter 3.

In recent decades, UI recipients' need for reemployment services has increased sharply because a large percentage of recipients are permanently laid off, rather than temporarily separated from their previous jobs, and most of them do not have the skills needed to search for work. The provision of Job Search Assistance (also called Reemployment Services) is crucial to facilitating the return to work. Unfortunately, the federal government has provided little new funding for this activity except for a short period during the Great Recession under the American Recovery and Reinvestment Act of 2009, despite the fact that Reemployment Services have been found to be highly cost effective.

WHAT HAS CHANGED? WHY IT IS TIME TO REFORM UI NOW

Above we discussed some systemic problems with the UI program, but part of the reason that UI reform is needed is simply that times have changed, while the UI program has not. The key evolutionary changes that have occurred are changes in the U.S. labor market and in economic conditions. In addition, past program initiatives have not been successful and some current UI rules are outdated, and the previously strong federal-state relationship has deteriorated.

Changing Labor Market and Economic Conditions

From temporary to permanent layoffs

In 1935, the UI program was envisioned as a countercyclical program, providing benefits during the temporary layoff of workers who were expected to be recalled when the economy improved. Since the 1970s, however, temporary layoffs have declined sharply, and permanently laid off workers are likely to need to find new jobs, possibly in new industries or occupations. The UI and ES programs have not fully adapted to the demands of structural, rather than temporary unemployment.

Needs of dislocated workers

As larger numbers of laid off workers have become permanently dislocated, most need reemployment services to help them return to work. The availability of reemployment services, however, has been inadequate. The Workforce Investment Act (and now the Workforce Innovation and Opportunity Act) have a Dislocated Worker program, but funding has been modest. Similarly, the Worker Profiling and Reemployment Services initiative was enacted in 1993 to help dislocated workers but was not funded. Most recently, a Reemployment Services and Eligibility Assessment initiative has been launched, but it too has received inadequate funding.

Long unemployment durations

There has been an upward trend in the duration of unemployment. Dislocated workers are having increasing difficulty finding employment. As a result, UI recipients are in need of income support for longer periods of time. Since the end of the Great Recession, however, a number of states have reduced potential durations of regular benefits below the standard level of 26 weeks. As a result, in times of recession, many unemployed workers will exhaust their entitlement to UI benefits well before they are able to find new jobs.

Changing U.S. labor force

The UI program has not successfully adapted to two major demographic changes in the labor force—the increased labor force participation of women from the end of World War II to the mid-1990s and the increased participation of older workers since the mid-1990s. For example, when a multi-earner family moves when one member finds new employment, the spouse or partner often does not have a job in the new location. In many states, the UI system does not consider the "following" spouse to be eligible for UI benefits. Women and older workers are more likely to work part time, but many states make it difficult for part-time workers to receive UI benefits. The UI and ES programs also have not accommodated the expanding participation of older workers. Their unemployment benefits are sometimes limited, and they are not likely to receive the special types of reemployment services they may require.

Unemployment Insurance Program Failures and Lack of Adaptation

Failure of past provisions and lack of updating

Because UI reform occurs so infrequently, any mistakes made in program design take a long time to correct. For example, the permanent EB trigger mechanism was revealed as faulty—it doesn't turn the program on and off properly—soon after implementation in the 1970s, but it has never been permanently improved.

Many program benefit and taxation provisions also have not adapted well to change. In many cases, the problem is that program parameters have been set using absolute numbers and have not been adjusted to account for wage and price increases. For example, the federal taxable wage base was last increased to $7,000 in 1983 and is now completely inadequate to fund the program in a manner that treats employers and employees equitably. Similarly, many states set their maximum weekly benefit amounts and state taxable wage bases in fixed dollar amounts, and these levels become inadequate over time.

Failure of the federal-state partnership

UI is supposed to be a federal-state partnership, but the partnership has failed in recent decades, both on the federal and state sides. In the Executive Branch, the federal government has gradually given less direction and guidance to the states. For example, in 1950, 1962, 1970, and 1976, the U.S. Department of Labor issued detailed federal guidance regarding conforming state UI legislation, but no similar comprehensive guidance has been issued since 1976. The Congress, too, has declined to enact legislation that helps the UI system adapt to a changing U.S. economy.

With the federal government stepping into the background, in recent decades, the states have been mostly on their own with respect to a wide variety of benefit, financing, and administrative issues. While some states have chosen to adapt to the changing labor-force environment, many have not. States have also been reluctant to respond to the strains of recessions, often reducing benefits after downturns, rather than rebuilding their state UI trust fund accounts by increasing UI taxes to prepare for the next recession. The result has been increasing variation in UI programs among states and a decline in financial resilience and the quality of many program components.

The failure of the federal government and of many states to adapt the program has been a result of political pressures on the UI system resulting in a lack of public policy consensus. Employee groups and public policy analysts typically have called for reform, while employer groups have resisted. It has been employers' organizations that generally have held sway at both the federal and state levels.

POLITICAL CONSTRAINTS ON UI REFORM

Employers have a strong incentive to use their political leverage to oppose UI reform because, in almost all states, they pay the entire UI tax. As a result of employer political leverage, many states have resisted both UI tax increases and increases in benefits that would lead to tax increases. Organized labor generally has not been an effective advocate for legislative efforts to improve UI benefits or provide sufficient tax revenues to pay for the increased benefits.

At the federal level, employers have been successful in resisting increases to the UI taxable wage base and tax rates. As a result, federal UI trust fund accounts frequently have been inadequate to fund federal responsibilities regarding payments for UI and ES administration and EBs. Employers also have resisted federal benefit standards that would provide reasonable qualifying requirements and adequate benefit levels and durations.

Employers also have sought to constrain UI at the state level. They have opposed increases in both taxes and benefits. When state UI revenues have been inadequate to fund benefits in recent recessions, they have pressed for benefit reductions while resisting tax increases.

Today, the federal-state UI system lacks an effective employee constituency in large part because employers pay UI taxes. In order to provide additional state UI revenue to fund the program and to rebalance the political influence between employers and employees in state legislatures, an employee payroll tax would have to be enacted as part of all state UI laws. Because employer resistance to UI reform is likely to continue in the future, one recommendation made in Chapter 5 is that Congress should consider partially or fully funding the UI program with an employee tax. Comprehensive UI reform is unlikely to occur without employee funding of the UI program.

UI REFORM: PAST REFORMS AND STUDY COMMISSIONS

Unemployment Compensation Amendments of 1976

The last comprehensive reform of the UI program was in 1976, following the severe 1974–1975 recession. The Unemployment Compensation Amendments of 1976 made fundamental changes in the UI program, including increasing the kinds and number of workers covered by the program, such that virtually all wage and salary workers in the United States were covered by the program.

However, the 1976 amendments did not address many other benefit and tax issues, so Congress authorized the creation of the National Commission on Unemployment Compensation (NCUC) to examine and recommend further changes to the UI program.

The Commission was composed of representatives from business, labor, and the public. It made a large number of reform recommendations in its final report to Congress (NCUC 1980a) and produced three volumes of sponsored research (NCUC 1980b). No legislation was enacted based on these recommendations.

1981 Amendments

In 1981, a number of changes in federal law were made to reduce federal UI costs. Federal statutory changes included making it more difficult to pay EBs (e.g., eliminating the national trigger, raising the state trigger rate, and adding a minimum work requirement), disqualifying some ex-service members, and tightening child support intercept, federal loan, and Trade Adjustment Assistance provisions.

Advisory Council for Unemployment Compensation

The 1990–1991 recession again revealed weakness in the UI program. In response, as part of the Emergency Unemployment Compensation Act of 1991, Congress established the Advisory Council for Unemployment Compensation (ACUC) to examine approaches to UI reform precipitated by the economic downturn during the 1991 recession. The ACUC sponsored many empirical studies of the UI program—gathered in four volumes of background papers (ACUC 1995b, 1996b), and its three-part final report (ACUC 1994, 1995a, 1996a) recommended numerous reforms to the system. Among the major recommendations were reforms to EB triggers, increasing the UI taxable wage base, encouraging state forward funding of UI benefits, increasing UI-covered employment, increasing UI eligibility, and increasing UI administrative funding. The ACUC recommendations were never considered by the Congress.

The American Recovery and Reinvestment Act of 2009 (ARRA): UI Provisions

The ARRA was enacted in February 2009, over a year into the Great Recession. Congress had already enacted a new Emergency Unemployment Compensation (EUC) program in June 2008. ARRA extended EUC and temporarily increased unemployment benefit levels.

ARRA also tried to improve the availability of UI benefits to unemployed workers by enacting UI Modernization provisions.

States were given a financial incentive to increase initial UI eligibility by enacting alternative base periods, paying benefits to unemployed part-time workers searching for new part-time work, and paying workers leaving work for compelling personal reasons. It also encouraged states to pay an allowance for children and extended regular UI benefits for UI claimants engaged in training. The UI Modernization initiative had modest but uneven success in encouraging expansion of UI eligibility (see Chapter 5).

RECENT REFORM PROPOSALS

There has been a growing realization that the Great Recession has caused continuing problems for the UI program. Some states responded negatively to the recession by cutting benefits in a manner that undermines the purpose of the program to act as both a support to unemployed workers during temporary periods of unemployment and a countercyclical economic stimulus during periods of high unemployment. As a result, a number of organizations have examined the UI program, analyzed its current problems, and recommended new approaches to restore UI to fulfilling its historical programmatic goals.

Obama FY 2017 Budget Proposal

As part of the FY 2017 Presidential Budget request, then President Obama proposed a modest range of reforms to the UI program (White House 2016). These proposals were not considered by the Congress, but they were a recognition that the UI program had not fully recovered from the Great Recession and that major changes should be made to make the program sound (see Chapter 2). The White House 2016 proposal dealt with selective issues and was not meant to be a comprehensive set of reform options.

Proposal by the Center for American Progress–Center on Poverty and Inequality of the Georgetown University Law Center–National Employment Law Project

A combination of three nonprofit organizations—the Center for American Progress, the Center on Poverty and Inequality of the Georgetown University Law Center, and the National Employment Law Project (CAP, CPI, and NELP, together the CGN)—got together and conducted a study of the UI program. In 2016, they issued a report (West et al. 2016) proposing a much wider range of UI reforms than the Obama administration's proposals. The CGN proposal had as its major goal a sharp increase in UI program participation, as measured by greatly increasing the UI recipiency rate, that is, the percentage of all unemployed workers who receive UI benefits. To achieve this goal, CGN recommended the liberalization of a wide range of UI provisions, some of which, if adopted, would create a program that goes beyond insurance principles and would create an unemployment assistance program (see Chapter 5). The CGN proposal represents a comprehensive approach to UI reform, as does the new proposal presented in Chapter 5.

November 2016 White House Meeting on Unemployment Insurance

In its last days, the Obama administration considered the urgent need for UI reform. On November 2, 2016, senior staff from the Council of Economic Advisers, the National Economic Council, the Domestic Policy Council, and the Department of Labor met with outside experts to discuss UI research and policy. The meeting brought together leading researchers and policymakers to address the key components of a modern and effective UI system. The invitation stated: "UI plays several key roles, including providing income support to families experiencing negative income shocks and countering cyclical slowdown through automatic stabilization. As the American economy changes, researchers have an important role to play in understanding the strengths and weaknesses of the UI system. This Convening offers a format for researchers to share evidence-informed solutions and for policymakers to highlight areas where additional research is needed." The discussion covered four topics: "1) Stabilizing Effects of Automatically Triggered Extensions; 2) Shoring Up Finances; 3) Impact of Changing Employer-Employee Relationships; and 4) Ensuring Adequate Benefits." The purpose of the "Convening" appeared to be to set the stage for UI reform during a potential Hillary Clinton administration. The Convening had no effect on public policy.

The National Academy of Social Insurance Examines
UI Reform

The National Academy of Social Insurance (NASI) is an organization dedicated to studying all programs covered by the Social Security Act, including UI. On November 9, 2015, NASI convened a meeting of UI experts, moderated by Stephen Wandner and William Rodgers. The meeting addressed issues including benefit payment (eligibility requirements, disqualifications, recipiency rates, and income replacement rates), benefit financing of regular benefits (taxable wage base and forward funding) and EBs, administrative financing, reemployment services, and work sharing. NASI issued a summary of the proceedings of the meeting (Schreur and Veghte 2016).

In late 2016, NASI also brought together a group of NASI members who are expert with respect to public pensions, health care, and UI. The experts developed papers on public policy dealing with social insurance, which were organized and revised by NASI staff. The result was a discussion of possible social insurance reforms, including those relating to UI. The final report was shared with the Trump administration and was widely distributed (Veghte, Schreur, and Bradley 2017).

SUMMARY OF THE CHAPTERS

The rest of this book consists of four main chapters and a brief summary chapter. In Chapter 2, Suzanne Simonetta first provides substantial background on the UI program and how it operates—information useful for understanding the proposal she discusses as well as others that are discussed in later chapters. She presents the framework of the UI program and how it has been working in states across the country. She reviews the evolution of the program and why some types of reform are needed. She then discusses the components of the reform proposal that was contained in the February 2016 UI legislative proposal in President Obama's Budget Request for Fiscal Year 2017, a proposal that was never considered by the U.S. Congress.

In Chapter 3, David Balducchi and Christopher O'Leary describe the origin and evolution of the partnership between the Employment Service (ES) and UI programs. They start with the policy objectives of the authors of the Wagner-Peyser and Social Security Acts, which established these two programs. They then analyze early actions by policymakers to facilitate inter-program cooperation, as well as policy changes in the ES-UI partnership over time. They turn to reasons for the decline in cooperation starting in the 1980s and explain why service availability has declined continuously since then. Next, the authors examine the changing sources of Wagner-Peyser Act funding, the decline in funding levels, and how funding could be increased. Finally, they suggest ways to revitalize the ES-UI partnership.

Wayne Vroman reviews the policy responses of the states to the Great Recession in Chapter 4. He shows that a substantial portion of the states were unprepared for the Great Recession, and, as a result, most went heavily into debt. He notes that the states could build back their state trust fund accounts either by raising taxes or by reducing benefits. He finds that state responses varied, but a substantial number of states made a slow recovery because they took little action to restore their trust funds. In addition, he analyzes the steps states did take to build back their state trust fund accounts. On the tax side, he shows how success differed, depending on variation in the actions taken by individual states. He also analyzes the actions that a substantial number of states took to make major reductions to their future benefit payments.

In Chapter 5, O'Leary and Wandner review the need for UI reform and the research that supports some of the needed changes to the program. The authors compare two recent UI reform proposals (West et al. 2016; White House 2016) to their own. They call for a comprehensive and consistent reform program that is balanced such that UI benefit payments and tax revenue are balanced and that indexing of both UI benefits and taxes is likely to keep the program both paying adequate benefits and collecting sufficient taxes to pay for those benefits.

Chapter 6 presents a general set of recommendations for comprehensive UI reform, covering the broad range of changes that could yield an adequate and self-sustaining UI program for the twenty-first century. It briefly describes and explains the components of such UI reform with respect to regular and extended benefits, tax policy, and reemployment services.

CONCLUSION

The materials in this book have been developed to provide information for consideration of federal and state UI legislative reform proposals. It provides background information that describes the problems with the current UI and ES programs and why these programs need to be reformed. It also provides a variety of proposals to deal with issues that are currently impeding the UI program from meeting its statutory goals of providing temporary, adequate income support to individuals unemployed through no fault of their own and acting as a macroeconomic stabilizer for the U.S. economy during recessionary periods.

The prospects for reform appear slim in the near term. Interest in UI reform tends to be limited when the economy is going well, and it increases in times of recessions. As unemployment increases, Congress hears from their constituents that the regular UI program is not sufficient and that they want Congress to enact additional weeks of benefits. It is at such times that public policy interest in UI reform surges. It is no accident that the last major reform of UI took place in 1976, soon after the end of the 1974–1975 recession.

The authors offer this book as material and proposals that could be the basis for a discussion of UI reform when interest in the program again increases. We all believe that significant reform is needed now and that putting reforms in place before the next recession would greatly help the United States to more quickly recover from the next recession and unemployed workers get through the next downturn by providing them with improved unemployment benefits and ES resources to help speed their return to productive employment.

Notes

1. The UI program also pays extended benefits—beyond 26 weeks of duration—in times of high unemployment, but most of this chapter discusses the regular UI program. Whereas the regular UI program can be considered a social insurance program, the extended benefits programs cannot.
2. As federal policy after World War II, the U.S. Department of Labor (USDOL) made a wide range of recommendations to states about the contents of their UI laws, including that they should provide claimants with a uniform potential duration of at least 26 weeks of benefits, and that if a state must vary the duration, it should range from 20 weeks to 30 weeks, along with other factors (USDOL 1962, p. 42). The department has not issued similar recommendations on state potential duration of UI benefits since issuing "Unemployment Insurance Legislative Policy: Recommendations for State Legislation, 1962," a "statement of unemployment insurance legislative policy and recommendations for State legislation." That publication was a revision of a 1953 document, *Unemployment Insurance Policy, Benefits-Eligibility*.

References

Advisory Council on Unemployment Compensation. 1994. *Report and Recommendations*. Washington, DC: Advisory Council on Unemployment Compensation (February).

———. 1995a. *Unemployment Insurance in the United States: Benefits, Financing, Coverage–A Report to the President and Congress*. Washington, DC: Advisory Council on Unemployment Compensation (February).

———. 1996a. *Defining Federal and State Roles in Unemployment Insurance–A Report to the President and Congress*. Washington, DC: Advisory Council on Unemployment Compensation (February).

———. 1995b and 1996b. *Advisory Council on Unemployment Compensation: Background Papers, Volumes I, II, III, and IV*. Washington, DC: Advisory Council on Unemployment Compensation.

National Commission Unemployment Compensation. 1980a. *Unemployment Compensation: Final Report*. Washington, DC: National Commission on Unemployment Compensation.

———. 1980b. *Unemployment Compensation Studies and Research, Volumes 1, 2, and 3*. Washington, DC: National Commission on Unemployment Compensation.

O'Leary, Christopher J., and Stephen A. Wandner, eds. 1997. *Unemployment Insurance in the United States: Analysis of Policy Issues*. Kalamazoo, MI: W.E. Upjohn Institute for Employment Research.

Schreur, Elliot, and Benjamin W. Veghte. 2016. "The Current State of Unemployment Insurance: Challenges and Prospects." Unemployment Insurance Brief No. 3. Washington, DC: National Academy of Social Insurance. https://www.nasi.org/sites/default/files/research/The_Current _State_of_Unemploymen_%20Insurance_Challenges_and_Prospects.pdf (accessed September 29, 2017).

U.S. Department of Labor. 1962. *Unemployment Insurance Legislative Policy: Recommendations for State Legislation*. BES No. U-22. Washington, DC: Bureau of Employment Security. https://workforcesecurity .doleta.gov/dmstree/pl/brown_book.pdf (accessed May 22, 2018).

Veghte, Benjamin, Elliot Schreur, and Alexandra L. Bradley, eds. 2017. *Report to the New Leadership and the American People on Social Security and Inequality*. Washington, DC: National Academy of Social Insurance. https://www.nasi.org/sites/default/files/research/Report_to_New _Leadership_American_People_web.pdf (accessed September 29, 2017).

West, Rachel, Indivar Dutta-Gupta, Kali Grant, Melissa Boteach, Claire McKenna, and Judy Conti. 2016. "Strengthening Unemployment Protections in America: Modernizing Unemployment Insurance and Establishing a Jobseekers Allowance." Washington, DC: Center for American Progress.

https://cdn.americanprogress.org/wp-content/uploads/2016/05/31134245/
UI_JSAreport.pdf (accessed September 29, 2017).

White House. 2016. *Congressional Budget Justification: Employment and
Training Administration, State Unemployment Insurance and Employment Service Operations.* Washington, DC: U.S. Department of Labor.
https://www.dol.gov/sites/default/files/documents/general/budget/CBJ
-2017-V1-08.pdf (accessed September 29, 2017).

Chapter 2

UI Reform Proposals in the Fiscal Year 2017 Obama Budget Request

Suzanne Simonetta

U.S. Department of Labor

The experience of the Great Depression, with unemployment rates reaching 25 percent in 1933, had a devastating impact at both the individual and societal level, making it abundantly clear that the United States needed to establish an unemployment insurance (UI) program (Haber and Murray 1966). It was during this crisis that the political will was found to enact legislation enabling UI in the Social Security Act of 1935.

The Great Recession was unquestionably the worst economic downturn the United States faced since the Great Depression (Goodman and Mance 2011). The experience of the Great Recession demonstrated the UI program's success at mitigating individual economic insecurity (Gabe and Whittaker 2012) and providing macroeconomic stabilization (Kekre 2016). However, even though some of the problems outlined below developed over many decades, they were greatly exacerbated during and after the Great Recession and threatened the program's ability to effectively function as a meaningful social insurance program. While these programmatic challenges are serious when the economy is growing, the weakening of the social safety net for jobless workers and their families could have devastating consequences for local and state economies, as well as the national economy, during the next economic downturn.

Building on the lessons learned from the past and looking to the future, the fiscal year (FY) 2017 Obama Budget contained a set of UI reform proposals aimed at addressing many of these challenges in order for all states to have a robust, meaningful, and genuine UI program with adequate resources in reserve to provide unemployed

23

workers with sufficient benefits as they seek new jobs. This chapter provides an overview of the UI program, defines the problems that were the basis for the UI reform proposals in the FY 2017 Obama Budget, describes those proposals, and explains how they were intended to remedy the problems.

OVERVIEW OF UNEMPLOYMENT INSURANCE[1]

UI is designed to provide partial, temporary income support to individuals who are unemployed through no fault of their own. This program is a federal-state partnership (USDOL 2017a) based on federal law, but it is administered by states under state law. Unless there is an explicit requirement or prohibition in federal law, states have great latitude to establish the parameters of their UI programs. For this reason, there is much variation among the states with respect to qualification and eligibility requirements, weekly benefit amounts, number of weeks of benefits, disqualification provisions, taxable wages, tax rates, and many other key policy areas (Employment and Training Administration [ETA] n.d.-a).

Eligibility

Determining benefit eligibility is a multi-step process. First, UI applicants must have sufficient recent labor market attachment, measured by work experience, to qualify for UI benefits. New entrants to the labor market, reentrants after a withdrawal from the labor market, the self-employed, and genuine independent contractors are not eligible for UI because they have not recently worked in covered employment positions. In general, prior to becoming unemployed, applicants must have earned sufficient amounts working in covered employment during at least two calendar quarters in a 12-month period to qualify for benefits.[2] Traditionally, states would examine earnings during the first four of the most recently completed five calendar quarters when making what is called a "monetary determination." Recognizing that using this period of time (i.e., the "base period") as a basis for establishing UI eligibility does not take into account up to the most recent six months of an individual's work history, many states have begun to use an alternative base period that examines earnings during the most recent four completed calendar quarters when making a monetary determination (Mastri et al. 2016).[3]

Next, a determination must be made that the applicant was separated from employment (i.e., became unemployed) through no fault of their own. The classic example of this is when an employer lays someone off because work is no longer available. However, under certain circumstances, if an individual quits or the employer fires an individual they may still be eligible for benefits. Every state's UI law defines what constitutes good cause for quitting (ETA 2016a). While all states include good cause connected with work, many states also include certain personal reasons in their definition. Similarly, although there are many reasons an employer may decide to fire an employee, individuals generally would be disqualified from receiving UI benefits only if they were fired for work-related misconduct.

After the initial eligibility determination is made, applicants must demonstrate their continued attachment to the labor market by meeting a set of ongoing eligibility requirements each week that they claim benefits. These include being able to work, being available for work, and actively seeking work. Reflecting workforce behavior from decades ago, even if individuals earned/worked enough in part-time employment to qualify for benefits, many states continue to require individuals to be available for and seek full-time work to be eligible for benefits due to the presumption that individuals who work part time do not have a genuine attachment to the labor market.

Financing

The UI program is funded primarily through federal and state taxes assessed on employers.[4] In general, the Federal Unemployment

Tax Act (FUTA) effective tax rate is 0.6 percent (ETA 2016b)[5] on the first $7,000 of workers' earnings (Griffin 1999).[6] The full FUTA tax is 6.0 percent, but employers get a credit of up to 5.4 percent if the state's UI law conforms to federal UI law and the state has no long-term outstanding federal advances (loans) to pay benefits. FUTA revenue is primarily used to pay for states' costs in administering the program, benefit costs for certain programs that extend (provide additional weeks of) benefits, and for advances to states that run out of funds to pay UI benefits.

State unemployment tax revenue is used to pay for "regular" benefits—typically up to 26 weeks of benefits are payable to individuals when they become unemployed. Some states provide a uniform number of weeks of benefits to all jobless workers who qualify. Other states provide a variable number of weeks of benefits whereby individuals with earnings throughout the base period will be eligible for more weeks of benefits than individuals with earnings during only a small part of the base period. The unemployment tax rates and the amount of wages that are subject to state unemployment taxation vary significantly among the states. In addition, in all states, the state unemployment tax rate assigned in a given year varies from employer to employer based on the employer's experience with unemployment (i.e., "experience rating"). Employer accounts are "charged" for benefit payments made to their former employees, and these charges are factored in when determining employer tax rates in subsequent years. In general, employers that have more former employees who receive UI benefits pay higher state unemployment taxes than employers with lower UI benefit costs associated with their former employees.

The range of applicable state unemployment tax rates varies from year to year depending on the reserves the state has in its account in the Unemployment Trust Fund (UTF) to pay future benefits. When the economy is strong, trust fund balances increase because there are more employers paying taxes on more employees' wages while fewer benefit payments are made. If the state's trust fund account balance exceeds certain levels, the range of applicable rates decreases in the following year because less revenue needs to be raised. When the economy declines, trust fund balances decrease because benefit payments go up as layoffs increase and tax revenue decreases as fewer employers pay unemployment taxes on the wages of fewer employees. If the state's trust fund account balance goes below specified levels, the range of applicable rates increases in the next year so that more funds will be collected to pay for benefits. Thus, not only will state unemployment tax rates vary from employer to employer based on their experience with unemployment, rates also will vary from year to year based on the state's reserves in the UTF.

Advances

Unemployment Insurance is, as its name implies, a social insurance program paid as a matter of right to all individuals who meet its requirements. If a state runs out of funds to pay benefits, the state may borrow from the federal government[7] to continue to meet its obligations to all eligible unemployed workers. Federal advances accrue interest under certain circumstances. Since states may not use trust fund dollars to pay this interest, many states assess a separate tax on employers to cover this cost. Also, in general, should a state have outstanding federal advances as of January 1 on two consecutive calendar years, its employers' FUTA tax credit will begin to be reduced, with the resulting additional revenue being used to pay back the federal debt.[8] States may avoid the credit reduction or reduce it if certain requirements are met.[9] In short, sustained insolvency results in marked increases in employers' total unemployment-related costs— the schedule of applicable state tax rate increases and/or a solvency add-on tax may be triggered, additional state taxes to pay interest may be assessed, and net federal unemployment taxes may increase to pay down the outstanding federal advances to the state to pay benefits.

Solvency

Maintaining sufficient reserves of benefit funding is essential to mitigate the likelihood of large fluctuations in employers' state UI tax liability from year to year, with especially large increases needed if the economy is recovering from a recession. Hence, states are encouraged to forward-fund their accounts in the UTF (U.S. Advisory Council on Unemployment Compensation 1996). The average high cost multiple (AHCM) measures state solvency. Using data from the most recent three recessions to determine high benefit costs in a state, the AHCM measures how long the state could pay benefits when benefit payment levels are high given the state's current balance in the UTF. Although it is recommended that states maintain trust fund balances sufficient to pay benefits for one year at recessionary levels, there is no federal requirement concerning state solvency.[10] Because states have great latitude when designing their UI tax structures and the revenues they are expected to yield, some states have opted to follow more of a "pay as you go" model that keeps employer taxes low but does not generate enough revenue to build significant reserves for use during the next economic downturn. As explained above, this can result in greater volatility in the state and federal unemployment tax payments that employers are required to make.

Extended Benefits

Recognizing that during recessionary periods regular state UI benefits provide insufficient income support for many unemployed workers, the federal-state Extended Benefits (EB) program is intended to provide for additional weeks of UI benefits when unemployment is high and rising.[11] Benefit costs are shared equally by the state and federal government.[12] EB is "triggered" when states' unemployment rates exceed certain levels and are higher than they had been in recent years. All states must have an EB trigger based on the insured unemployment rate (IUR), which is based on data concerning individuals who are currently receiving regular UI benefits. To trigger on, the 13-week IUR must be at least 5 percent and be at least 120 percent of the rate for the equivalent 13-week period in each of the preceding two calendar years. Under the IUR trigger, individuals may receive up to 13 additional weeks of benefits. If a state uses an optional total unemployment rate (TUR) trigger, which uses the Bureau of Labor Statistics' (BLS) household survey data about individuals who are not working and have looked for work during the last four weeks, individuals may receive up to 13 or 20 weeks of additional benefits, depending on the state's TUR. Up to 13 weeks of benefits would be available if the state's three-month TUR is at least 6.5 percent and at least 110 percent of the rate for the corresponding three-month period in either of the two previous calendar years. A total of up to 20 weeks of benefits would be available if the state's three-month TUR is at least 8.0 percent and the rate meets the 110 percent "lookback" requirement. Because these triggers are not very responsive to economic downturns and states historically have not been triggering EB during recessions (or not triggering on soon enough), especially via the IUR trigger, special federal programs have been created to provide additional weeks of benefits to unemployed workers.

Reemployment

Although providing benefits to individuals unemployed through no fault of their own is the overall mission of the UI program, there has been an explicit acknowledgment of the importance of helping individuals who receive UI benefits to become reemployed since the program's inception. Whereas some workers maintain their attachment to their jobs (i.e., they are on a temporary layoff), most do not. It is for this reason that federal law requires UI payments to be made through public Employment Offices.[13] Thus, in the past, when unemployed workers had to go in person to apply for UI benefits, those who were not job attached would be referred for assistance finding work to the Employment Service, which was colocated with local UI offices. As UI claims taking moved out of local offices in the 1990s and was increasingly handled over the phone or via the Internet, the connection to public Employment Offices weakened in some states. To strengthen this connection, several strategies have been implemented, including the development of the UI Reemployment and Eligibility Assessment (REA) program. Since 2005, funds have been appropriated to the U.S. Department of Labor (USDOL) to enable states to address the individual reemployment needs of UI claimants, and to prevent and detect improper benefit payments by reviewing their eligibility for benefits (ETA 2016c). The results have been positive with respect to reducing the number of weeks claimed and compensated, the likelihood of exhausting UI benefits, and improper payments (Benus et al. 2008). Due to its early successes, REA funding was increased. The program was renamed Reemployment Services and Eligibility Assessments (RESEA), which reflects a narrower focus on individuals who are most likely to be long-term unemployed (and on those who transitioned out of the military). Recognizing the need for increased reemployment services for these individuals, RESEA funding may now be used for this purpose. In February 2018, explicit permanent statutory authority for RESEA was included in the Bipartisan Budget Act of 2018.

Short-Time Compensation

When tackling the problem of unemployment, increasing emphasis has been given to implementing strategies that avoid layoffs. Starting in 1982, federal UI law permitted states to experiment with short-time compensation (STC), also known as work sharing, which provides a partial UI weekly payment to certain individuals whose work hours were reduced.[14] This is noteworthy because such individuals normally wouldn't be eligible for any weekly UI payment because they earned too much money. Authority to run STC programs became permanent in 1992.[15] While not all states operate STC programs, there has been increasing recognition of its value. By reducing hours of work for a group of employees rather than laying off a portion of them, employers maintain their skilled workforce and no one loses their job. The workers meanwhile experience a smaller reduction in their earnings because they receive a reduced UI payment. For these reasons, STC is considered a win-win situation.[16,17] Interest in STC heightened during the Great Recession, and the Middle Class Tax Relief and Job Creation Act of 2012 included several provisions designed to encourage more states to enact STC laws and for existing STC states to expand their programs (ETA n.d.-b). These provisions include two measures: 1) reimbursing states for up to three years of STC benefit costs, and 2) providing grants to states for implementation or improved administration of STC programs and for promotion of and enrollment of employers in STC programs. Sixteen states received grant funds totaling $46,154,004. As a result of these offerings, the STC program has grown and strengthened (Bennicci and Wandner 2015).

Integrity

An operational area that has received increasing attention and emphasis in recent years concerns integrity.[18] This is a broad undertaking that includes efforts to ensure that employers are paying the proper amount of unemployment taxes as well as efforts to prevent, detect, and recover improper benefit payments. These efforts have been central to the UI program for quite some time, but new challenges have arisen as the claim-taking process moved out of local offices due to advances in technology. These technological advances, however, have also provided more tools to help states in their efforts to combat these challenges. For example, states cross-match claim information with information in their state directories of new hires for the purpose of finding individuals who continue to claim UI benefits after they return to work. In addition, under certain limited circumstances, states may recover improper UI benefit payments by offsetting federal income tax refunds due to the individual.

DATA: A SNAPSHOT OF THE PROGRAM[19]

The UI reform proposals in the FY 2017 Obama Budget addressed several key policy areas: solvency, benefit adequacy, extended benefits, reemployment, short-time compensation, and integrity. Before discussing the specifics of these proposals, it is essential to provide both the high-level context and a broad description of the state of the UI program, which help define the problems that the proposals were designed to address.

Unemployment

Unemployment is a lagging indicator, so the national TUR peaked in June 2009 as the Great Recession ended (Figure 2.1). As economic recovery continued, job growth exceeded and TUR dropped below prerecessionary levels. These data are quite compelling, but they do not tell the entire story (BLS 2009).

Figure 2.1 Job Growth and Unemployment, 2007 to 2016

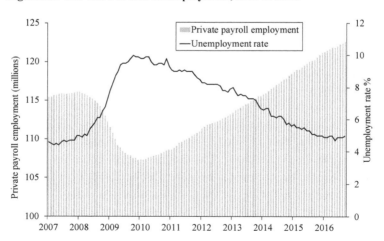

SOURCE: USDOL/BLS data.

Although the economy continued growing and there were increasing opportunities for workers, significant challenges remained. For example, consistent with changes at the national level, TUR declined in most states (Figure 2.2), but it remained markedly higher than the national average in some states. In addition, long-term unemployment remained a persistent challenge (Ghayad 2013) even as economic recovery continued (Figure 2.3). For example, in September 2016, 24.9 percent of the unemployed (2.0 million people) had been unemployed for more than 27 weeks.

UI Benefits

Consistent with the long-term unemployment data, the average number of weeks an individual receives UI benefits (i.e., "duration")

Figure 2.2 Unemployment Rates by State

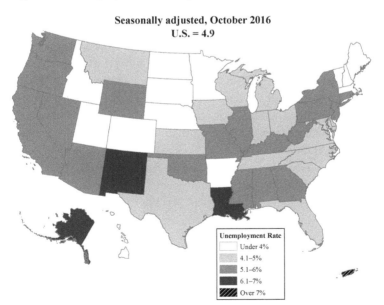

NOTE: Inset maps not to scale.

Figure 2.3   Incidence of Long-Term Unemployment (more than 27 weeks)

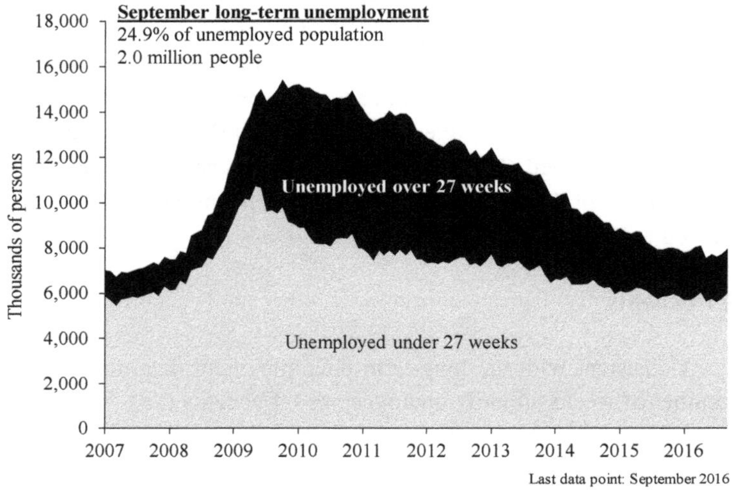

Last data point: September 2016

SOURCE: USDOL/BLS data.

increased. Historically, the average duration of UI benefit receipt has varied consistently with changes in TUR, but the average duration of UI benefit receipt did not decline as much as would have been expected when TUR declined (Figure 2.4). There are many possible reasons for this, including insufficient job growth, proportionately more permanent layoffs, and a mismatch between worker skills and emerging employer needs.

When an individual initially establishes eligibility for UI benefits, the state UI agency issues a "first payment." As expected, the number of first payments has varied, consistent with changes in TUR (Figure 2.5). However, increasingly, the percentage of individuals who were eligible for and claimed UI benefits (i.e., claimants) and who received everything to which they were entitled (i.e., they "exhausted" benefits) did not track with changes in TUR and exceeded the exhaustion rates of prior recessions (Figure 2.6). This was probably due to both

Figure 2.4 Average Duration on UI in the Regular Program

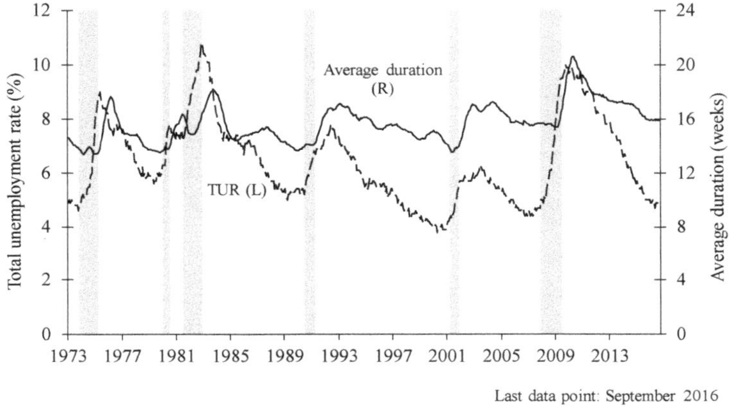

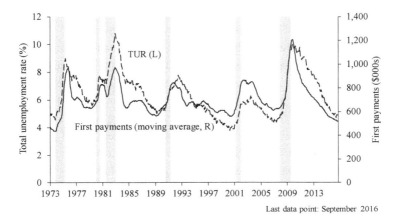

Last data point: September 2016

NOTE: The gray shaded areas represent recessions.
SOURCE: USDOL/OUI and USDOL/BLS data.

Figure 2.5 People Receiving First Payments in the Regular UI Program

Last data point: September 2016

NOTE: The gray shaded areas represent recessions.
SOURCE: USDOL/OUI and USDOL/BLS data.

Figure 2.6   Exhaustion Rate in the Regular Program

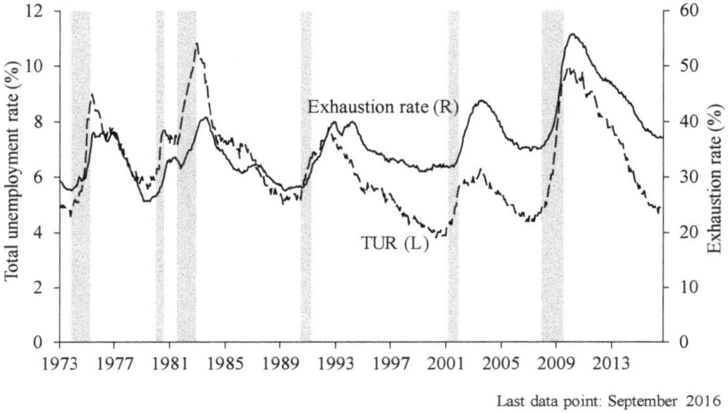

Last data point: September 2016

NOTE: The gray shaded areas represent recessions.
SOURCE: USDOL/OUI and USDOL/BLS data.

the increase in long-term unemployment and the fact that, with the maximum number of weeks of UI benefits having been cut in several states (see Table 2.1), individuals exhausted benefits earlier in their unemployment spell than they previously would have.

Evidence of the declining role of the program can be found when comparing UI claims data with the size of the civilian labor force and the TUR. The number of weeks of UI benefits claimed is expected to vary cyclically as TUR rises and falls. However, it would also be expected that, as the civilian labor force increases and with everything else being equal, the number of weeks of regular UI benefits claimed would increase because the pool of workers who may lose their jobs is increasing. However, as Figure 2.7 shows, this has not been the case. The trend in weeks of regular UI benefits claimed, other than the spikes during recessionary periods, is flat. Overall, the number of weeks claimed remained constant while the civilian labor force increased.

Table 2.1 Summary of Changes to Benefit Duration in Selected States

State	Effective	Previous maximum (weeks)	New maximum (weeks)
AR	7/27/11	26	25
	7/15/15	25	20
FL	1/1/12	26	12–23[a]
GA	7/1/12	26	14–20[a]
ID	7/1/16	26	20–26[a]
IL	1/1/12	26	25[b]
KS	1/1/14	26	16–26[a]
MI	1/15/12	26	20
MO	4/17/11	26	20
	1/16/16	20	13–20[a]
NC	7/1/13	26	12–20[a]
PA	1/1/13	16 or 26	18–26[c]
SC	6/19/11	26	20

[a] The number of weeks is tied to the unemployment rate.

[b] In Illinois, the number of weeks for 2012 was reduced to 25. For 2013, both the taxable wage base and the duration would have remained in place unless the state generated sufficient revenue to overcome a 2011 loss to the unemployment fund. Since Illinois generated sufficient revenue to overcome the loss, the benefit cut to 25 weeks only applied to 2012. The number of weeks increased to 26 weeks in January 2013 and has not changed.

[c] The number of weeks of benefits is equal to the number of credit weeks, up to a maximum of 26. Claimants with fewer than 18 credit weeks are not entitled to any benefits.

SOURCE: USDOL, Division of Legislation.

When data about the percentage of unemployed workers who received UI benefits (i.e., the "recipiency rate") are examined, it becomes increasingly evident that, over time, fewer unemployed workers have been accessing UI benefits when they lose their jobs (Figure 2.8). As noted earlier, not everyone who loses their job is eligible for benefits. It would be expected that when the economy is in a downturn, layoffs become the dominant form of unemployment, and proportionately fewer individuals will become unemployed because they were fired for misconduct connected with work or because they

Figure 2.7 Weeks Claimed, Civilian Labor Force, and Total Unemployment Rate (TUR)

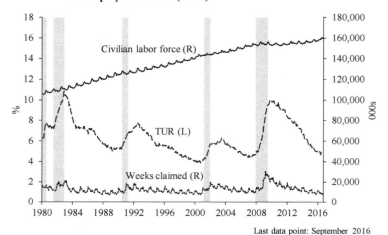

Last data point: September 2016

NOTE: The gray shaded areas represent recessions.
SOURCE: USDOL/OUI and USDOL/BLS data.

Figure 2.8 UI Recipiency Rates, All Programs (Insured Unemployed/ Total Unemployed)

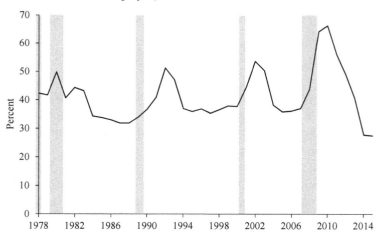

NOTE: The gray shaded areas represent recessions.

quit their jobs without good cause. Thus, recipiency rates would increase during recessions because proportionately more individuals become unemployed because they were laid off (i.e., because of a lack of work). However, as shown in Figure 2.8, the UI recipiency rate nationwide plummeted to less than 30 percent and was lower than it had been at similar points during economic recoveries in recent decades.

State-level data are even more striking. Because states have much discretion with respect to determining who is potentially eligible for UI benefits, it is not surprising that there is huge variation among the states with respect to recipiency rates. As shown in Figure 2.9, in the second quarter of calendar year 2016, the range of recipiency rates among the states went from less than 10 percent to more than 65 percent, with a national average of 28.6 percent.

Figure 2.9 Recipiency Rates by State (Insured Unemployed/Total Unemployed), Second Quarter 2016

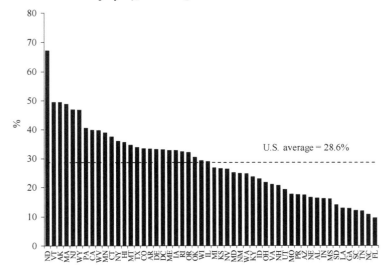

SOURCE: USDOL/OUI and USDOL/BLS data.

UI Taxes and Solvency

The UI program is intended to operate counter-cyclically, with benefit payments increasing during economic downturns and funding reserves being built up when unemployment is low. Figure 2.10 shows how state tax rates, contributions (taxes) collected, and benefits paid varied since 2000 and the impact these factors had on trust fund balances. During the Great Recession, when trust fund balances were negative, most states borrowed from the federal government. In total, 36 states borrowed and the peak amount of the advances was $47.2 billion (Figure 2.11).

The primary reason for this impact on the trust fund was the severity of the Great Recession—some states would have become insolvent no matter how well they prepared in advance. However,

Figure 2.10 Contributions Collected, Regular Benefits Paid, Tax Rate on Taxable Wages, and Year End Net Reserve Balance (UTF), 2000 to 2015

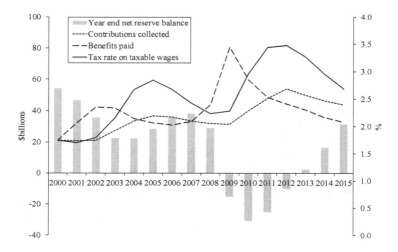

SOURCE: USDOL/OUI, USDOL/BLS, U.S. Bureau of Public Debt data.

Figure 2.11 Federal UI Advances to States during the Great Recession

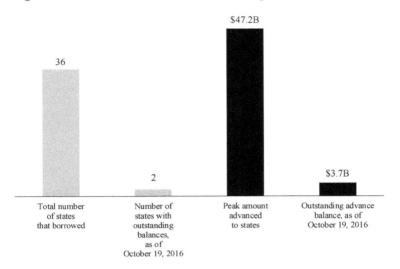

SOURCE: USDOL/OUI, USDOL/BLS, U.S. Bureau of Public Debt data.

the data demonstrate that had more states achieved an adequate level of solvency beforehand, fewer states would have run out of benefit funds and borrowing levels would have been much lower for the states whose economies were hard hit by the recession. The AHCM is the federal measure of state solvency, where an AHCM of 1.0 means that a state has a trust fund balance sufficient to pay benefits for one year during a recessionary period.[20] Only about one-third of the states had an AHCM of at least 1.0 when the recession began (Figure 2.12). There were a few states that met this solvency standard that still borrowed from the federal government to pay UI benefits, but most of the states that borrowed did not meet the standard (Figure 2.13).

Between the economic recovery and the actions states took to increase revenue and decrease expenditures, there have been marked improvements in solvency in recent years. However, as of 2015 a couple of states still had outstanding UI debt, and most states (includ-

Figure 2.12 Average High Cost Multiple by State in 2007

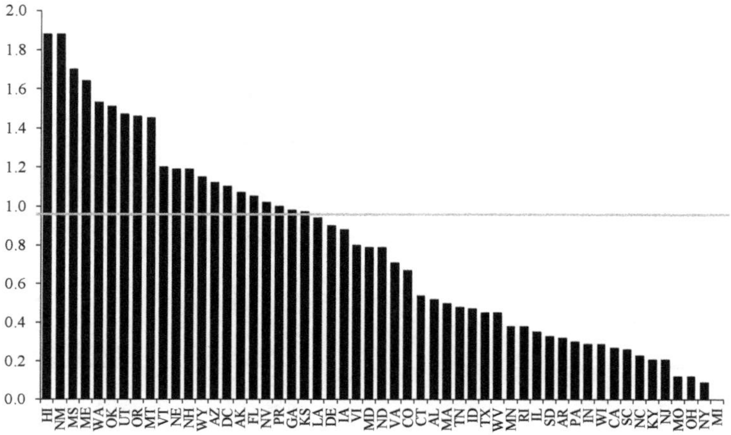

NOTE: An AHCM of 1.0 (the gray line) means that a state has a trust fund balance sufficient to pay benefits for one year during a recessionary period.
SOURCE: USDOL/OUI data.

ing all large states) did not have an AHCM of at least 1.0, calling into question their readiness for the next recession (Figure 2.14).

UI Benefit Adequacy

Although there are no federal standards regarding the adequacy of UI benefits, there has been a long-standing recommendation that the weekly benefit amount (WBA) replace at least 50 percent of lost earnings over a six-month period, with a maximum WBA equal to two-thirds of the state's average weekly wage (AWW) (U.S. Advisory Council on Unemployment Compensation 1996). At the national level, not only has that recommendation not been met during the last 40 years, there is a long-term declining trend in the replacement rate (Figure 2.15).

Another way to examine benefit adequacy is to examine recipiency rates (Figures 2.8 and 2.9). Of the many factors that influence

Figure 2.13   States Borrowing from the Federal Government to Pay UI Benefits During the Great Recession

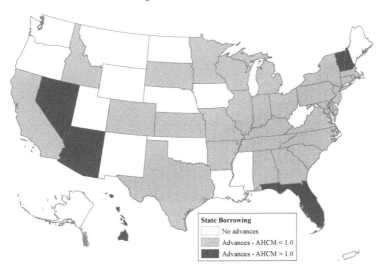

NOTE: AHCM: Average high cost multiple. Inset maps not to scale.

this rate, UI eligibility requirements, disqualification provisions, and the number of weeks of benefits available are among the most important. In recent years, several states enacted laws (ETA n.d.-c) that restrict access to the program in a multitude of ways, including raising qualifying earnings requirements, broadening the scope of what constitutes misconduct connected with work, and increasing the requirements needed to overcome a disqualification and reestablish eligibility for UI benefits. In addition, several states cut the maximum number of weeks of UI benefits (Table 2.1). In the past, states generally offered up to 26 weeks of benefits. About one-quarter of the states now offer fewer than 26 weeks. In several states, the maximum available depends on the unemployment rate. For example, in North Carolina, as few as 12 weeks of benefits will be available under certain circumstances.

Figure 2.14 Average High Cost Multiple by State in 2015

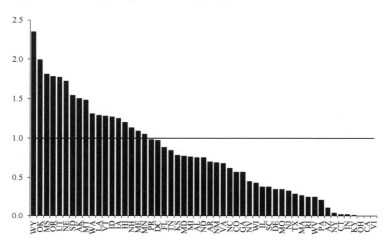

NOTE: An AHCM of 1.0 (the gray line) means that a state has a trust fund balance sufficient to pay benefits for one year during a recessionary period.
SOURCE: USDOL/OUI data.

As should be evident from the above discussion, the UI program has deviated from historical standards and its original goals, resulting in an erosion of the social safety net for jobless workers. The proposals detailed in the following section were designed to address several of the most important causes of these problems.

BUDGET PROPOSALS AND ANALYSIS[21]

Solvency

From the brief examination of the data in the previous section, it should be clear that states are not prepared for the next recession because they don't have sufficient funds to pay benefits when demands are high. Most states' UTF accounts do not meet the federal

Figure 2.15 Average Weekly Benefit, Average Weekly Wage, and UI Replacement Rate, 1970 to 2015

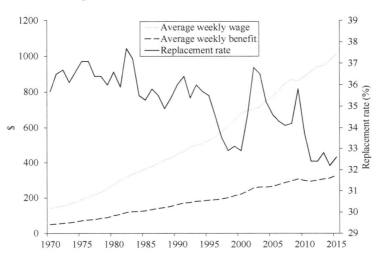

SOURCE: USDOL/OUI data.

solvency recommendation. The FY 2017 Obama Budget recognized the importance of states having sufficient reserves to pay benefits, to avoid borrowing, and to avoid large increases in employer taxes when economic conditions are weak or recovering, so it included a set of legislative proposals to address solvency. First, in 2017, it would have restored the 0.2 percent FUTA surtax, which would help the federal accounts in the UTF pay their outstanding debts. For example, as of November 10, 2016, the Extended Unemployment Compensation Account owed $7.2 billion to the General Fund of the U.S. Treasury and $7.5 billion to the Federal Unemployment Account. Since the amount of wages subject to unemployment taxation at the state level is closely related to the corresponding amount at the federal level, there was also a proposal to increase the federal taxable wage base to $40,000 in 2018 (at present, it is $7,000) and to index it to inflation in subsequent years. By itself, this would have a limited effect on state solvency, but it was expected that the change would encourage states to take action to improve their solvency. However, it would have more equitably allocated the tax burden among employers. When a taxable wage base is low, employers with more low-wage or part-time workers pay unemployment taxes on a larger portion of employee earnings than employers with more high-wage or full-time workers.

An additional proposal would have required states to impose a minimum tax per employee equal to 0.175 percent of taxable wages, thereby spreading the cost of UI more widely among all employers.[22] At present, many states allow a significant portion of employers with the best unemployment "experience" to pay a zero tax rate. Not only does this hamper efforts to improve solvency, but it undermines the fundamental principle of insurance—paying a premium to insure against the risk of an event occurring, in this case, the risk of unemployment. As it is for other types of insurance, premiums reflect the likelihood of an event happening. However, contributions are made on behalf of everyone covered by the insurance because everyone has the benefit of potential access to funds if the insured event occurs.

Another proposal to help states attain solvency in the FY 2017 budget was to reduce the FUTA credit available to employers when a state had an AHCM of less than 0.5 on January 1 in two consecutive years, with the additional amounts paid being used to bolster the state's account in the UTF. This process would be similar to that used to reduce FUTA credit to help states pay back their outstanding advances to pay UI benefits.

To avoid a massive federal tax increase when the federal taxable wage base increases, the proposal would have decreased the effective FUTA tax rate to 0.167 percent. However, FUTA revenue would have gradually increased over time as the federal taxable wage base increased after indexing. This would have mitigated the likelihood of future borrowing from the General Fund of the U.S. Treasury, because the administrative and benefits costs paid from the federal accounts in the UTF would increase over time as well.

Benefit Adequacy

As described above, UI claims have plummeted. They have reached the lowest level since the 1970s. For example, in October 2016, initial claims were below 300,000 for more than 85 consecutive weeks—the longest streak since 1970 (USDOL 2016). Although much of the reduction in claims is due to improving economic conditions, actions by several states to cut benefits and restrict eligibility also were factors. For this reason, the FY 2017 Obama Budget included a set of proposals designed to expand access to UI benefits and services. First, it would have established the following federal requirements:

- States must provide at least 26 weeks of benefits for the regular program.[23]

- States must adopt the following three provisions for which UI Modernization incentive payments were made available under the American Recovery and Reinvestment Act (ARRA):

    1) Use an alternative base period.

    2) Allow benefits to individuals who seek part-time employment.

    3) Allow unemployed workers to be eligible for benefits if they leave their jobs for family reasons.

Increasing the number of weeks of benefits back to the historic norm is important because it takes time for an individual to find a job, even in a good economy. Moreover, it is beneficial to both the individual worker and the economy as a whole if workers are able to take the time to find jobs that align well with their skills, education, and experience. These workers would be able to increase their contributions to society, as well as better provide for themselves and their families. Additional weeks of UI benefits would also result in increased macroeconomic stabilization.

To understand the importance of the alternative base period proposal, it is important to note the history and evolution of monetary
determinations. Before employers began reporting their employees'
quarterly earnings to the states (ETA 1984), the UI base period used to
determine whether an individual earned enough to qualify for benefits
was generally the most recent 52 weeks before the individual filed a
claim. Although this procedure was more administratively challenging because states had to contact employers to get this information
about each individual applying for UI benefits, it more accurately
captured the individual's recent attachment to the workforce. When
states transitioned to establishing eligibility based on quarterly wage
reports, administrative necessity forced states to use more remote
work experience when making this determination. Before electronic
reporting was possible, employers had to mail paper copies of wage
information. Given the lag between when a calendar quarter ended
and when the state could reasonably expect to have wage information
from most employers, states opted to consider wages earned during
the first four of the most recent five completed calendar quarters. As
technology has advanced and employers report increasingly sooner
after the end of the calendar quarter, this administrative constraint
has largely disappeared. Therefore, administrative issues such as this
should no longer be the deciding factor for a UI benefit eligibility
requirement. Using the most recent available reported earnings data
more accurately measures a worker's present attachment to the workforce and should be the basis for determining who qualifies for UI
benefits (Carr 2016). As of 2016, 37 states, the District of Columbia,
Puerto Rico, and the U.S. Virgin Islands already used alternative base
periods when making monetary determinations (ETA 2016b).

   The remaining proposed requirements were designed to help the
UI program better reflect the twenty-first century economy. In the
1930s, the single breadwinner model was typical for most families—
very different from today's conditions. With that construct in mind,
and with the intent to design a program that provided benefits only
to individuals who became and remained unemployed involuntarily,

individuals who left their jobs for personal reasons or who were only working part time were not considered to be genuinely attached to the labor force. While the risk that is insured by the UI program today remains the same—involuntary unemployment—the way in which that concept is defined should be reexamined. In particular, with an increasing number of two-earner families, the meaning of labor-force attachment has changed. For example, it is hard to argue that quitting a job to move across the country when a spouse's job necessitates the move is voluntary. Maintaining a family unit is paramount and does not equate with a decision to leave the workforce. In this type of circumstance, since the individual's employer did not cause the unemployment, the UI benefits paid may be "non-charged" (i.e., won't be taken into account when determining the employer's state unemployment tax rate).[24] However, denying benefits to such individuals would be inconsistent with the goals of the UI programs and the values of our society.

Similarly, regardless of economic necessity or overall preference, the demands of family life or older workers' transition to retirement[25] often require some individuals to work part time. This does not automatically equate with a weak or casual connection to the workforce. For this reason, if individuals earn enough to qualify for UI benefits and meet all other requirements, making them ineligible because they are only available for part-time work also would be out of line with the principles upon which the UI program is based (Michaelides and Mueser 2009).

The FY 2017 Obama Budget also provided for a new $5 billion Modernization Fund. To become eligible for its share of funds, a state would have had to:

- allow for broader federal access to wage records;
- adopt employer electronic filing and/or increased penalties for employer nonreporting; and
- have a definition of "misconduct" that conforms to a USDOL model.

In recent years, UI wage records are increasingly being used to evaluate and measure the performance of a vast array of public programs. Evidence-based decision making regarding investment of public funds requires access to high-quality, comprehensive data, which is why the first two prerequisites were chosen.

When determining whether individuals became unemployed through no fault of their own, the state must decide whether the reason an employee was fired was "misconduct connected with work," which would disqualify them from receiving benefits—typically for their entire spell of unemployment. Although there are many reasons why an employer may legitimately and legally fire a worker, only a small subset of those reasons would constitute misconduct connected with work. Historically, states generally defined misconduct connected with work narrowly in line with the definition in *Boynton Cab Co. V. Neubeck*, 237 Wis. 249 (Wis. 1941):

> [T]he intended meaning of the term "misconduct". . . is limited to conduct evincing such willful or wanton disregard of an employer's interests as is found in deliberate violations or disregard of standards of behavior which the employer has the right to expect of his employee, or in carelessness or negligence of such degree or recurrence as to manifest equal culpability, wrongful intent or evil design, or to show an intentional and substantial disregard of the employer's interests or the employee's duties and obligations to his employer. On the other hand, mere inefficiency, unsatisfactory conduct, failure in good performance as the result of inability or incapacity, inadvertencies or ordinary negligence in isolated instances, or good-faith errors in judgment or discretion are not to be deemed "misconduct" within the meaning of the statute.

Some states have significantly broadened the definition of misconduct connected with work, which has had the effect of disqualifying more workers from receiving UI benefits. To be eligible for its share of the Modernization Fund, a state's definition would have to conform to the federal definition.

In addition to the prerequisite requirements, to receive a Modernization Fund payment, states would have had to adopt one benefit expansion and two pro-work reforms. The benefit expansions were:

1) allow more individuals to receive UI benefits while participating in training;

2) provide a maximum WBA equal to at least two-thirds of the state's AWW during the most recent 12 months; or

3) improve eligibility for temporary workers.

Recognizing that training may increase the likelihood of reemployment and the quality of the job obtained, federal UI law prohibits states from making individuals ineligible because they are not available for work or actively seeking work while they are in training approved by a state agency.[26] States would have sole authority to determine which types of training to approve for this purpose, but this proposal would have given states an incentive to expand the scope of training they approve.

The formula established in many states' UI laws to determine the WBA is generally designed to replace one-half of a worker's weekly wage (ETA 2016c). This amount helps jobless workers meet the necessities of life without providing a disincentive to work (Chetty 2008). However, regardless of the WBA the formula would generate based on an individual's wage history, the maximum amount is capped. In some states, the maximum WBA is a fixed amount that can only be changed by enacting a state law. In other states, the maximum WBA changes each year because it is set as a specified percentage of the AWW. Ensuring that the maximum WBA increases are consistent with increases to the state AWW avoids an erosion of benefits, particularly for middle income workers.

Some states establish additional requirements in order for temporary workers to be eligible for UI benefits. The FY2017 Obama Budget was designed to ensure that such requirements didn't become a barrier to temporary workers getting benefits.

States would have had to adopt two of the following five pro-work reforms to qualify for an incentive payment:

1) progressively more intense reemployment service delivery as duration of benefit receipt lengthens;

2) improved reemployment services for UI claimants;

3) subsidized temporary work programs;

4) relocation assistance coupled with individual case management, in-person career counseling, provision of customized information about job opportunities, and referrals to suitable work; or

5) improved data systems for workforce and education program performance, research, and evaluation purposes.

From its inception, the UI program has been closely tied to the U.S. Employment Service[27] because, unless workers are on a temporary layoff, it is imperative to help them find jobs, which is the rationale for the first two options. The next two options represent alternative ways to help individuals find work—via temporary work programs and relocation. The last pro-work choice was premised on workforce and education programs becoming more effective at giving people the knowledge and skills they needed to become reemployed if data were used more effectively when evaluating, researching, and assessing the performance of these programs.

Extended Benefits

EB does not function effectively because it doesn't trigger on soon enough (or at all) in states with high unemployment. Since its inception in 1970, special federal programs providing additional weeks of benefits were created during each major downturn and were effective during the periods 1972 to 1973, 1975 to 1978, 1982 to 1985, 1991 to 1994, 2002 to 2004, and, most recently, 2008 to 2013 (ETA n.d.-d). Implementing these temporary federal programs poses several challenges. Foremost of these, it takes too long. It takes several months for sufficient economic information to become available to demonstrate need and design an extension program; legislation to be drafted, passed by Congress, and enacted into law; the USDOL to develop operating instructions and guidance; and the states to implement the new program. In addition, in these temporary federal programs, some portion of the benefits is generally available in all states, rather than targeting all benefits only to the states experiencing higher unemployment. Moreover, without knowing the program parameters of a new extension, states do not have sufficient time to prepare to implement and administer these special federal programs, which leads to further delays, public confusion, and occasionally errors. In short, while providing vital benefits to jobless workers and their families, these ad hoc programs do not provide for efficient and timely macroeconomic stabilization.

To obviate the need for hurried enactment of temporary federal UI extension programs, the FY 2017 Obama Budget included a proposal to reform the EB program. Specifically, it would have:

- Provided for four 13-week tiers of benefits, with availability depending on the state's TUR.

- Provided permanent 100 percent federal funding of EB with nonrepayable advances from the General Fund if there were insufficient amounts in the federal account in the UTF.

- Established new TUR trigger thresholds of 6.5, 7.5, 8.5, and 9.5 percent. These thresholds would have been met if the state's TUR met or exceeded one of those levels or if the total of the state's TUR and the change in the TUR from a comparable period in one of the previous two years equaled or exceeded one of those levels.

- Required reemployment services and eligibility assessments for all EB claimants.

These proposals drew largely on experience from the Great Recession—not just with EB, but also with the Emergency Unemployment Compensation (EUC) program (ETA n.d.-e). At its peak, EUC was a four-tiered program providing up to 53 weeks of benefits, depending on the state's TUR. After the federal account ran out of funds to pay for EUC, it was paid with funds from General Revenue that did not have to be repaid.[28] The triggers changed over time. Most recently, Tier 1 had no trigger, and Tier 2 triggered on in states with a three-month TUR of at least 6.0 percent. For Tier 3, the rate was at least 7.0 percent, and for Tier 4, it was 9.0 percent.

The EB triggers failed for several reasons. First, even with the TUR-based triggers, it took too long for EB to become available in many states. The EUC program was first enacted in June 2008, six months after the Great Recession began.[29] In January 2009, most states still hadn't triggered onto EB—more than one year after the recession began (ETA n.d.-f). Related to this concern is that too few states had a TUR trigger in their laws before the recession began. One of the most important EB-related provisions in ARRA was temporary 100 percent federal funding of EB.[30] As a result of the 100 percent federal funding, 29 states amended their EB laws to provide for temporary TUR triggers conditioned on 100 percent federal funding. The final negative consequence of the design of the EB triggers is the fact that states with sustained high unemployment eventually triggered off EB. To remain on EB, a state's TUR must not only meet or exceed certain levels, but the rate had to be higher than it had been during comparable periods in the prior year or two. With the impact of the Great Recession lasting for such a long time, the unemployment rates in some states, while high, were not higher than they had been during the previous two years. Even though federal law was amended to allow states to use a three-year "lookback," and 33 states amended their laws to provide for it, the longer lookback eventually became insufficient, and this component resulted in EB no longer being available to long-term unemployed workers in states with sustained high unemployment (ETA 2012).

Recognizing the importance of helping individuals find jobs, in particular the long-term unemployed, and ensuring that they continue to meet all eligibility requirements, the EUC program was modified in 2012 to require all new EUC claimants to receive reemployment services, and reemployment and eligibility assessments (ETA n.d.-g). This is the reason the EB proposals in the FY 2017 Obama Budget would have required reemployment services and eligibility assessments for all EB claimants.

Reemployment

The increases in long-term unemployment, average duration, and exhaustion rates demonstrate the need for strategies designed to assist with reemployment efforts for individuals who become unemployed. Building on the initiative that began in 2005 in a few states and national implementation in 2012 for individuals receiving EUC, the FY 2017 Obama Budget proposed making the RESEA program a permanently authorized program that would have required all states to participate and would have provided enhanced funding to enable more individuals to be served. For the regular UI program, the one-third of new claimants who would have been identified[31] as the most likely to be long-term unemployed and in need of reemployment services would have been required to participate in RESEAs as a condition of eligibility for UI benefits.

Recognizing the importance of helping transitioning veterans find employment in the civilian labor force, the FY 2017 Obama Budget also proposed requiring all new claimants for the Unemployment Compensation for Ex-Servicemembers program[32] to participate in RESEAs as a condition of eligibility for UI benefits.

The FY 2017 budget included another proposal designed to encourage reemployment—wage insurance. Particularly for workers transitioning to new occupations, new jobs might pay significantly less than the jobs individuals had prior to becoming unemployed. To provide a safety net to such workers and to encourage their swift reemployment, this wage insurance proposal would have been avail-able to individuals who had been working for at least three years with their prior employer. If their new job paid less than $50,000 per year, workers would have received a payment equal to half the difference between their prior and new annual wage, up to $10,000 over a period of two years.

Short-Time Compensation

The experience during the Great Recession highlighted the importance of helping workers to keep their jobs. While many states did avail themselves of the STC-related funding opportunities in the Middle Class Tax Relief and Job Creation Act of 2012, and a few states created new STC programs, not all did. Although there are a variety of explanations, one of the most meaningful is timing. To implement a new program requires an extensive time commitment. In 2012 and 2013, states had limited capacity to take on new initia-tives, given the high workload and the complex modifications to the EUC program that they had to administer, among other reasons. Since economic conditions improved significantly after recovery from the Great Recession, states were in a much better position to consider commencing STC programs or improving existing ones. For this rea-son, the FY 2017 Obama Budget included proposals to give states an additional two years of federal reimbursement of STC benefit costs and two more years to apply for and receive STC grants. In addition, there was a proposal to make state STC benefit costs subject to 50 percent federal reimbursement whenever the state triggered on the EB program.

Integrity

Despite states' best efforts, many challenges remain to prevent improper payments. The FY 2017 Obama Budget included a set of highly technical proposals related to benefit integrity that built on recent enactments. They were designed to provide states with additional resources to dedicate to this purpose and to ensure that states used all of the tools at their disposal to combat this issue. Specifically, they would have:

- allowed states that contracted out all information technology functions to use the Treasury Offset Program for benefit overpayment recovery;

- required states to use an electronic system to transmit information with employers to obtain information needed to determine benefit eligibility;

- required states to use the National Directory of New Hires to find individuals who continued to claim benefits after returning to work and to require penalties on employers that did not report their new hires;

- allowed the USDOL to require that states whose poor program performance required creation of corrective action plans to dedicate specified amounts of their administrative grants to implementing those plans, and to provide awards or incentives to states with excellent performance;

- required states to use UI penalty and interest funds for UI administration with a portion dedicated to program integrity activities;

- required states to cross-match UI claim information with the Prisoner Update Processing System to find individuals who were claiming benefits while incarcerated; and

- allowed states to use up to 5 percent of recovered overpayments or delinquent employer contributions collected for integrity purposes rather than for future benefit payments.

CONCLUSION

As is evident from this brief description and analysis, the FY 2017 Obama Budget included an ambitious set of UI legislative proposals that focused on many of the most profoundly meaningful aspects of the program. Opinions will certainly vary about those proposals from both a substantive policy perspective as well as from an ideological perspective. However, when considering UI's philosophical underpinnings, it should be clear that many of these proposals could bring the current UI program into better alignment with its foundational principles, given the economic, societal, and technological changes that have occurred during the more than 80 years since the inception of the UI program in 1935. Moreover, by raising the profile of some crucial issues and setting forth a comprehensive plan for addressing them, public dialogue and debate might yet be encouraged and result in permanent positive reforms to the UI program.

Notes

The opinions expressed in this chapter are the author's alone. They do not purport to reflect the official position or views of the U.S. Department of Labor. Many thanks are given to Daniel Hays in the Division of Legislation of the U.S. Department of Labor's Office of Unemployment Insurance for his assistance with research. Thanks also to Ed Dullaghan in the Division of Fiscal and Actuarial Services of the U.S. Department of Labor's Office of Unemployment Insurance for creating and updating all of the figures.

1. Although this overview addresses many key aspects of the UI program, it mainly focuses on the aspects of the program pertinent to the reform proposals discussed in this paper. It is not comprehensive and is intended to provide the information necessary to understand the issues that presently exist and how the proposals were intended to address them.
2. Washington State does not determine UI eligibility based on earning wages equal to or exceeding a specified amount. Instead, state law requires an individual to have at least 680 hours of base period employment.

3. Following the enactment of the American Recovery and Reinvestment Act, 23 states enacted new or modified existing alternative base periods.

4. Alaska, New Jersey, and Pennsylvania levy nominal UI taxes on workers under certain limited circumstances. In Alaska, the tax rate is equal to 27 percent of the average benefit cost rate, but not less than 0.5 percent or more than 1.0 percent of taxable wages. In New Jersey, the tax rate is 0.3825 percent. Depending on the adequacy of the fund balance in a given year, Pennsylvania employees pay contributions ranging from 0.0 percent to 0.08 percent of total gross covered wages earned in employment.

5. Until June 2011, the FUTA tax was 6.2 percent and the effective FUTA tax rate was 0.8 percent. A 0.2 percent "surtax" was originally added in 1985 to help the federal accounts in the Unemployment Trust Fund (UTF) pay back their advances from the General Fund of the U.S. Treasury. Between advances to states and federal benefit spending during the Great Recession, the federal accounts in the UTF ran out of funds and had to borrow to meet all obligations.

6. At the onset of the program, the FUTA tax was 1.0 percent on total wages with an effective rate of 0.1 percent. In 1939, the FUTA taxable wage base was set at $3,000, which exceeded the annual wages of 98 percent of workers. According to USDOL estimates, FUTA taxable wages in 2015 represented less than 17 percent of total wages in the United States.

7. States may use other state funds or may borrow from other sources to pay UI benefits. During the Great Recession, Colorado, Illinois, Michigan, Nevada, Pennsylvania, and Texas borrowed via bonding. On December 31, 2013, the outstanding bond amount for these states was $9.725 billion.

8. If on November 10 of the year in which on a second consecutive January 1 a state has a remaining outstanding Title XII advance balance, the state's FUTA credits will begin to be reduced in the subsequent year to repay the outstanding debt.

9. The state must apply for and be found eligible for relief from tax credit reduction in the form of avoidance or a cap on reduction (26 U.S.C. 3302 and Social Security Act, Section 901(d)(1)).

10. There is an incentive in 20 C.F.R. 606.32 for states to maintain a solvent account in the UTF. Without meeting the funding goals prescribed by this regulation, any Title XII advance that a state receives is interest accruing.

11. The program was created in the Federal-State Extended Unemployment Compensation Act of 1970.

12. FUTA revenue in the Extended Unemployment Compensation Account is used for this purpose.

13. See section 3304(a)(1) of the Federal Unemployment Tax Act and section 303(a)(2) of the Social Security Act.
14. See P.L. 97-248, 96 STAT.409.
15. See P.L. 102-318, 106 STAT.298.
16. It is important to note that the workers who would not have been laid off (typically those with most seniority) experience a reduction in their income that they otherwise wouldn't have. However, the fact that most states require labor union approval of STC plans if the workplace is subject to a collective bargaining agreement demonstrates the overall support for STC because it helps workers (typically the most junior) avoid becoming unemployed. Anecdotal evidence indicates that workplace morale often improves when an agreement is reached to avoid layoffs by reducing hours and offering STC.
17. STC payments are treated like unemployment compensation (UC) payments. Thus, they are deducted from an individual's maximum benefit amount during a given benefit year, which would reduce the number of weeks of UC available should the individual later become unemployed. Similarly, under permanent law, STC payments are "charged" to employers' accounts for purposes of determining their experience-rated state UC tax rate in the same way UC payments are charged.
18. Federal laws and executive orders establish requirements for reducing improper payments in Federal programs. For additional information, see http://www.oui.doleta.gov/unemploy/improp_pay.asp (accessed March 24, 2018).
19. The figures contained in this section were prepared by staff in the Division of Fiscal and Actuarial Services utilizing ETA and BLS data.
20. The AHCM is calculated by dividing the Calendar Year Reserve Ratio (or "Trust Fund Balance as a percent of Taxable Wages") by the Average High Cost Rate.
21. The material in this section draws on USDOL (2017b).
22. To a certain extent, this is an inherent design feature of insurance. It generally is not expected that premiums would cover the full cost of the benefits. However, it is widely acknowledged that excessive levels of socialized costs due to ineffective charging and insufficient maximum tax rates to reflect employer experience with unemployment result in some employers paying for a smaller portion of benefits than others. Also, it is important to note that for UI purposes, certain entities are permitted to self-insure. State or local governmental entities, 501(c)(3) nonprofit organizations, and Indian tribes may opt to reimburse benefit costs rather than be assessed a contribution rate.
23. Regular benefits are paid at the beginning of a spell of unemployment. This is in contrast to programs like EB, which are available to individu-

als who exhaust entitlement to regular benefits in states whose unemployment rate exceeds certain levels.

24. Consistent with the insurance principle of the UI program, states have been allowed to have "non-charged" UI benefit payments when the employer is not at fault for the spell of unemployment. A typical reason has been when benefit payments are made to individuals who quit for good personal cause.

25. Older workers increasingly are taking part-time "bridge jobs" after they leave their career jobs and before they fully retire.

26. Federal Unemployment Tax Act, Section 3304(a)(8).

27. Since enactment of the Workforce Investment Act of 1998, the Employment Service has been incorporated into the one-stop career center system. For additional information, see http://research.upjohn.org/cgi/viewcontent.cgi?article=1032&context=reports (accessed March 24, 2018).

28. Although it was expected that the proposal to improve federal solvency would generally obviate the need for General Revenue, during severe recessions that might not have been the case, and such funds would have become available under this EB proposal.

29. P.L. 119-252, http://www.oui.doleta.gov/dmstree/pl/pl_110-252.pdf (accessed March 24, 2018).

30. Although EUC eventually was funded with General Revenue, federal EB costs continued to be funded by FUTA revenue in the EUC Account. When those funds were depleted, the federal accounts in the UTF borrowed from the U.S. Treasury to meet its obligations.

31. Federal law presently requires states to operate the worker profiling and reemployment services program, which identifies claimants likely to exhaust benefits and need reemployment services to find work, and requires such individuals to participate in those services as a condition of UI eligibility.

32. Since state UI programs do not cover individuals who work for the federal government, there are separate federal UI programs to provide benefits to such workers when they become unemployed. States administer these programs under an agreement with the USDOL. One such program is Unemployment Compensation for Ex-Servicemembers.

References

Bennicci, Frank, and Stephen A. Wandner. 2015. *Short-Time Compensation after Enactment of the Middle Class Tax Relief and Job Creation Act of 2012: A Qualitative Assessment of the Short-Time Compensation Program.* Report from the Secretary of Labor to Congress. Washington, DC: U.S. Department of Labor.

Benus, Jacob, Eileen Poe-Yamagata, Ying Wang, and Etan Blass. 2008. "Reemployment Eligibility Assessment (REA) Study: FY2005 Initiative." ETA Occasional Paper 2008-02. Washington, DC: U.S. Department of Labor, Employment and Training Administration.

Bureau of Labor Statistics. 2009. "Ranks of Discouraged Workers and Others Marginally Attached to the Labor Force Rise during Recession." *Issues in Labor Statistics* April: 1–3.

Carr, Catherine. 2016. "Moving Women out of Poverty: A Call to Action for Legal Aid." *Impact: Collected Essays on Expanding Access to Justice* 2: 66–71. http://digitalcommons.nyls.edu/impact_center/11/ (accessed November 17, 2017).

Chetty, Raj. 2008. "Moral Hazard versus Liquidity and Optimal Unemployment Insurance." *Journal of Political Economy* 116(2): 173–234.

Employment and Training Administration (ETA). 1984. Amendments Made by P.L. 98-369 (The Deficit Reduction Act of 1984), Which Affect the Federal-State Unemployment Compensation Program. Unemployment Insurance Program Letter No. 01-85. Washington, DC: U.S. Department of Labor. https://workforcesecurity.doleta.gov/dmstree/uipl/uipl85/uipl_0185.htm (accessed November 17, 2017).

———. 2012. Trigger Notice 2012-20, State Extended Benefit (E.B.) Indicators under P.L. 112-96. Washington, DC: U.S. Department of Labor. http://oui.doleta.gov/unemploy/trigger/2012/trig_060312.html (accessed November 17, 2017).

———. 2016a. *2016 Comparison of State Unemployment Insurance Laws: Nonmonetary Eligibility.* Washington, DC: U.S. Department of Labor. https://workforcesecurity.doleta.gov/unemploy/pdf/uilawcompar/2016/nonmonetary.pdf (accessed November 17, 2017).

———. 2016b. *2016 Comparison of State Unemployment Insurance Laws: Financing.* Washington, DC: U.S. Department of Labor. https://workforcesecurity.doleta.gov/unemploy/pdf/uilawcompar/2016/financing.pdf (accessed November 17, 2017).

———. 2016c. Unemployment Insurance Program Letter No. 7-16. Washington, DC: U.S. Department of Labor, ETA. https://wdr.doleta.gov/directives/attach/UIPL/UIPL_07-16.pdf (accessed November 17, 2017).

———. n.d.-a. Significant Provisions of State UI Laws. Washington,

DC: U.S. Department of Labor. https://workforcesecurity.doleta.gov/
unemploy/statelaws.asp#sigprouilaws (accessed November 17, 2017).
———. n.d.-b. Short-Time Compensation. Fact sheet. Washington, DC: U.S.
Department of Labor. https://ows.doleta.gov/unemploy/docs/stc_fact_
sheet.pdf (accessed November 17, 2017).
———. n.d.-c. State Law Information. Washington, DC: U.S. Department of
Labor. https://ows.doleta.gov/unemploy/statelaws.asp#reports (accessed
November 17, 2017).
———. n.d.-d. Temporary Federal Benefit Extension Programs. Washington, DC: U.S. Department of Labor. https://ows.doleta.gov/unemploy/
spec_ext_ben_table.asp (accessed November 17, 2017).
———. n.d.-e. Emergency Unemployment Compensation 2008 (EUC) Program. Washington, DC: U.S. Department of Labor. https://ows.doleta
.gov/unemploy/pdf/euc08.pdf (accessed November 17, 2017).
———. n.d.-f. Trigger Notice 2008-51, State Extended Benefit (E.B.)
Indicators under P.L. 102-318. Washington, DC: U.S. Department of
Labor, Employment and Training Administration. http://oui.doleta.gov/
unemploy/trigger/2009/trig_010409.html (accessed November 17, 2017).
———. n.d.-g. Middle Class Tax Relief and Job Creation Act of 2012: Reemployment Services (RES) and Reemployment and Eligibility Assessments (REAs). Fact sheet. Washington, DC: U.S. Department of
Labor. https://ows.doleta.gov/unemploy/pdf/Factsheet_RES&REA.pdf
(accessed November 17, 2017).
Gabe, Thomas, and Julie M. Whittaker. 2012. "Antipoverty Effects of Unemployment Insurance." CRS Report R41777. Washington, DC: Congressio-
nal Research Service. https://fas.org/sgp/crs/misc/R41777.pdf (accessed
November 17, 2017).
Ghayad, Rand. 2013. "The Jobless Trap." Unpublished paper. Boston: North-
eastern University.
Goodman, Christopher J., and Steven M. Mance. 2011. "Employment Loss
and the 2007–09 Recession: An Overview." *Monthly Labor Review*
(April): 4–11.
Griffin, Maureen Ann. 1999. "Payroll Tax, Federal." In *The Encyclopedia of
Taxation and Tax Policy*, Joseph J. Cordes, Robert D. Ebel, and Jane G.
Gravelle, eds. Washington, DC: Urban Institute Press, pp. 320–322. http://
www.urban.org/sites/default/files/alfresco/publication-pdfs/1000540-
Payroll-Tax-Federal.PDF (accessed November 17, 2017).
Haber, William, and Merrill G. Murray. 1966. *Unemployment Insurance in
the American Economy*. Homewood, IL: Richard D. Irwin, Inc.
Kekre, Rohan. 2016. "Unemployment Insurance in Macroeconomic Stabili-
zation." Unpublished paper. Cambridge, MA: Department of Economics,
Harvard University.

Mastri, Annalisa, Wayne Vroman, Karen Needels, and Walter Nicholson. 2016. *States' Decisions to Adopt Unemployment Compensation Provisions of the American Recovery and Reinvestment Act: Final Report.* Princeton, NJ: Mathematica Policy Research.

Michaelides, Marios, and Peter Mueser. 2009. *UI Benefits Study: Recent Changes in the Characteristics of Unemployed Workers.* Columbia, MD: IMPAQ International.

U.S. Advisory Council on Unemployment Compensation. 1996. *Collected Findings and Recommendations 1994–1996.* Recommendation 1995-2. Washington, DC: U.S. Advisory Council on Unemployment Compensation. http://research.upjohn.org/cgi/viewcontent.cgi?article=1000&conte xt=externalpapers (accessed November 17, 2017).

U.S. Department of Labor. 2016. *Unemployment Insurance Weekly Claims.* News release, October 20. https://ows.doleta.gov/press/2016/102016.pdf (accessed November 17, 2017).

———. 2017a. "Unemployment Compensation: Federal-State Partnership." Washington, DC: Office of Unemployment Insurance. https://workforce security.doleta.gov/unemploy/pdf/partnership.pdf (accessed November 17, 2017).

———. 2017b. Congressional Budget Justification: Employment and Training Administration, State Unemployment Insurance and Employment Service Operations. Washington, DC: USDOL. https://www.dol.gov/sites/ default/files/documents/general/budget/CBJ-2017-V1-08.pdf (accessed November 17, 2017).

Chapter 3

The Employment Service–Unemployment Insurance Partnership

Origin, Evolution, and Revitalization

David E. Balducchi
Consultant

Christopher J. O'Leary
W.E. Upjohn Institute for Employment Research

This chapter traces the evolution of the partnership between the Employment Service (ES) and Unemployment Insurance (UI) programs in the United States from its origins. Using primary sources, we analyze the early actions of federal policymakers to facilitate cooperation between the two programs to meet economic exigencies, grapple with political cronyism, and surmount legal barriers. We also discuss factors that caused changes in the ES-UI partnership over time. We identify reasons that cooperation started eroding in the 1980s, and explain why there has been a continuous decline in service availability ever since. Reviewing evidence on the effectiveness of in-person employment services for UI beneficiaries, we suggest ways to revitalize the ES-UI partnership. We explore the source of Wagner-Peyser Act funding, how it was formalized, then eroded, and how it can be renewed.

The public ES and UI programs are essential to maintaining robust American labor markets. Established by the Wagner-Peyser Act of 1933 and the Social Security Act of 1935, respectively, these programs were the first permanent federal laws addressing the problem of unemployment in an American industrial society where workers were separated from the sustenance provided by the land. Both programs were structured to expand economic security using an approach to federalism that instituted a federal-state cooperative system. The federal government provides grants-in-aid (referred to as "grants") to states to administer the UI and ES programs under state laws. With these programs, workers who lose their jobs involuntarily are provided temporary partial wage replacement to help support themselves and their families while looking for new jobs, and employment services are provided to speed the return to work.[1] Employers benefit from the UI program by keeping skilled workers attached to their businesses during periods of slack product demand.[2] They also benefit from the ES program by having a reliable means of canvassing local registries for qualified new workers and ensuring that UI beneficiaries are actively seeking work. By emphasizing reemployment for beneficiaries, the social insurance character of UI is maintained and the moral hazard risk is reduced—that is, the risk that payment of cash benefits during periods of joblessness might unnecessarily prolong unemployment.

Four broad topics are explored in this chapter. First, we describe the origin and evolution of the ES-UI partnership and the decisive efforts undertaken to unify the two programs at the federal and state levels. Second, we explain how the partnership matured as policymakers sought to secure adequate funding to support the national system of public employment offices (now referred to as American Job Centers [AJCs]) through cycles of policy preferences. Third, focusing primarily on ES, we show how the partnership has acquired added service mandates over the past four decades despite chronic reductions in ES resources. These reductions in real funding have curtailed staff-assisted assessments (interviewing, testing, and counseling), job search assistance (JSA), and job finding and placement services, as well as diluted ES-UI coordination.[3] We explain that while technology has offered enormous job finding capabilities, it often has not worked for many long-term UI claimants, who are exhausting unemployment benefits at higher rates before securing new work. We summarize several research studies providing evidence that offering employment services for UI claimants is highly cost effective. Finally, we suggest policy remedies to revitalize the ES-UI partnership based on the proposals of others and our own research, thoughts, and experience with the programs.

ORIGIN AND EVOLUTION OF THE ES-UI PARTNERSHIP

The initial impetus for a social security program in the United States emerged in the Progressive Era of the early twentieth century. During the Great Depression of the 1930s, key elements of social insurance were enacted into federal law. A national network of public employment offices was established, along with a UI program for partial income replacement to the unemployed that provided a safety net for jobless workers (Reich 2010, p. 44). Curt Harding, an early policymaker of the Utah Employment Security Agency, summed up the economic security history of that period, saying it "was part of a reform that was needed in order that the free enterprise system might continue" (USDOL 1985, p. 1). While some European countries nationalized industries and others expanded public assistance to the needy, the United States took a different approach to establishing a social insurance system. Within the panoply of other New Deal reforms and programs, the introduction of ES and UI programs, dubbed "employment security" programs, helped sustain American capitalism.[4]

In the late 1930s, federal ES and UI policymakers sought to operate as partners out of necessity. A report from the Committee on Economic Security (CES), prepared by a White House working group, is the seminal document on social insurance policy in the United States.[5] Baldwin (1993, pp. 31–32) observes that the 1935 CES report recommended a program of employment assurance before suggesting a UI program. In Baldwin's view, this was an attempt to emphasize reemployment after job loss and resulted in ES offices being designated as the points of service for UI claimants.[6] Thus, the expectation of continued public support for reemployment efforts during periods of UI receipt gave birth to the ES-UI partnership.

BEGINNINGS OF THE ES AND FUNDING

Ordered by President Franklin D. Roosevelt in 1933 to immediately revitalize the federal U.S. Employment Service (USES), which was originally set up in 1918 to staff the buildup of defense industries in the first world war (O'Leary and Eberts 2008, p. 2), U.S. Department of Labor (USDOL) Secretary Frances Perkins instructed staff members to begin helping states enact ES laws consistent with the Wagner-Peyser Act. State agencies were established and became affiliated with the USES system, using federal ES grants to support operations (Perkins 1946, p. 179).

Under the Wagner-Peyser Act, the network of ES offices was administered by states and funded by the federal and state governments on a 50-50 matching basis. During the initial stage of USES growth, recruitment of unemployed workers to fill job openings for public works projects[7] necessitated setting up temporary federal reemployment offices (called National Reemployment Service [NRS] offices). These offices were financed 100 percent by the federal government. To supervise the national buildup of NRS offices, a separate division of NRS was organized within USES (USDOL 1953, p. 12).

As states affiliated with USES and received Wagner-Peyser Act ES grants, NRS offices were either closed or transferred to state administration. In December 1933, there were 158 ES offices and 3,270 NRS offices nationwide. By June 1938, the balance was reversed, with 1,263 ES offices and only 188 NRS offices. From 1933 until the early part of fiscal year (FY) 1938, the ES system was financed by five different sources. The biggest source was NRS allotments from federal public works appropriations, but there were also state and local government appropriations, Wagner-Peyser Act ES grants, and facilities or staffing contributions from local governments (USDOL 1953, p. 13).

RECESSION OF 1937–1938 SPURS ES-UI PARTNERSHIP

Unemployment declined in 1934, the year after President Roosevelt took office, but recovery from the Great Depression was not continuous.[8] A new economic downturn started in May 1937 and lasted until June 1938. Unemployment reached 20 percent, with 11 million unemployed in 1938 (Burns 1956, p. 324; Waiwood 2013). The economic recession of 1937–1938 had an enormous impact on the emerging federal-state ES and UI programs. The Social Security Board, which administered the nascent UI program, and USDOL, which administered the fledgling ES system, began discussions to gather resources to help states expand the network of ES offices.[9]

The CES report had advised states to pay unemployment benefits only through ES offices pursuant to provisions in the Wagner-Peyser Act (CES 1935, p. 19),[10] and immediately after the Social Security Board was organized, it accepted that advice (Blaustein 1993, p. 156). The Board believed that idled claimants should be offered publicly posted job openings. It also sought to bolster the public image of UI as an earned entitlement rather than a dole involving a means test and therefore opted not to pay benefits out of state welfare offices. That decision flowed from an overarching New Deal policy that sought to establish permanent federal-state programs to ameliorate unemployment, and findings from the CES report, which saw unemployment benefits as a temporary income support paid only when suitable jobs were not available. These are foundational elements of social insurance distinct from relief. Every state provided for ES offices to administer UI payments.

USDOL and the Social Security Board agreed in 1937 that an expanded system of ES offices was needed to meet the demands of

the UI program. Expansion came after intense discussion among policymakers involving valid misgivings. Some USDOL policymakers
believed too rapid a buildup of state ES offices could lead to hiring
incompetent ES staff, which could result in bias and a lack of professionalism in administration and have severe adverse public consequences. This perspective was not without merit, given the patronage
systems operating in many local and state governments at that time.

After state ES laws[11] were enacted, Secretary Perkins's hand-
picked director of USES, Frank Persons, proceeded cautiously to
partner with some states.[12] There were nine states in 1937 where affiliation with USES was withheld and distribution of Wagner-Peyser
Act ES grants and the closing of NRS offices were delayed, in most
instances because of political issues surrounding the administration
of ES agencies (USDOL 1937a).[13] For example, in Massachusetts,
where the ES director was an appointee of Governor James Curley,
Director Persons believed the Massachusetts appointee was too weak
to resist patronage pressures (McKinley and Frase 1970, p. 295).[14]
Most striking was that, of the 35 states affiliated with USES in 1936,
only nine were attempting to provide services statewide.[15] The other
26 states had not yet set up ES offices outside large cities (USDOL
1953, p. 12).

Frank Persons and others argued against consolidated ES and
UI activities because it might be harmful to placement activities and
hinder participation by employers. Although there was sympathy for
this view, it was ultimately not shared by Secretary Perkins and the
Social Security Board (McKinley and Frase 1970, pp. 298, 305). The
relationship between ES and UI raised a host of new policy issues in
public administration. These issues necessitated an exchange of viewpoints among remarkably capable New Deal public officials.

Policymakers understood that the UI provisions of the Social
Security Act would radically expand the mission and volume of ES
operations. The policy dilemma facing USDOL and the Social Security Board in 1937 was that the Wagner-Peyser Act did not authorize
money for UI activities or the carrying out of UI activities by the

state ES (USDOL 1937b, p. 5). However, the Social Security Act did permit the funding and conducting of UI activities by the state ES. The administrative challenges were to obtain agreement between the secretary and the Board on how to connect federal ES and UI funds, and then figure out how states were to coordinate ES and UI functions within ES offices. Meeting the challenges required a formal collaboration between two federal agencies, USDOL and the Social Security Board, to successfully enlarge the national network of ES offices and coordinate the UI and ES programs.

POLITICAL CONTEXT AND AGREEMENT OF 1937[16]

Getting government executive agencies to collaborate is always a challenge. Perhaps more so in this instance because when Congress enacted the Social Security Act, it authorized the Board as an independent agency, outside USDOL. According to Perkins, legislators made the Board independent because they did not want USDOL to acquire additional responsibilities and resources (Perkins 1946, p. 300).

Therefore, the political context for the agreement included the following:

- The 1937–1938 recession was causing unemployment to rise again, and there were fears of another structural breakdown. Thirty-two states were to start paying unemployment benefits in 1938 (USDOL 1937b).[17] Payment of UI benefits in each state required establishing standard administrative procedures for determining eligibility, paying benefits, and certifying that claimants had conducted job searches.

- The recession produced rising political pressure to increase access to services for the jobless. There were large service gaps in helping the unemployed file UI claims and locate work, and Wagner-Peyser Act ES funds alone could not expand service capacity for the burgeoning UI program (McKinley and Frase 1970, p. 306). The fledgling ES system required rapid establishment and expansion of ES offices statewide in each state.

- A novel financial relationship between two federal agencies, USDOL and the Board, was essential for the success of the untested federal-state ES and UI programs.

A policy agreement, dated March 30, 1937, between Secretary Perkins and Board Chair Arthur Altmeyer established coordination and integration of the functions between the two federal agencies. The agreement created a type of "unified service and financing pact," but it did not govern state operations. According to the agreement, two federal agencies, the Bureau of Unemployment Compensation (within the Board) and USES (within USDOL), were to

- "act as if they were a single agency" with respect to all matters affecting state ES agencies, including state plans funded under the Wagner-Peyser Act and the Social Security Act (USDOL 1937c, 1953, p. 19);

- expand state ES offices and prepare for the payment of UI benefits (USDOL 1937b);

- regard the state agency ES and UI systems as a "unified service" (USDOL 1937d, e); and

- use UI grants under Title III of the Social Security Act to expand public ES offices, administer benefit payments, and maintain standards of USES (e.g., merit standards); such UI grants were in addition to ES grants (USDOL 1937d).

The Board interpreted the requirements of the Social Security Act to allow UI grants to support ES. This interpretation was based on the intent of the CES report and the Board's subsequent selection of state ES offices to administer UI payments (Haber and Murray 1966, p. 104).[18] An opinion from the Comptroller General of the United States in July 1937 affirmed the Board's decision (Atkinson, Odencrantz, and Deming 1938, p. 55). USDOL and the Board required states to appropriate funds to match Wagner-Peyser Act ES grants before they could receive UI grants.[19]

The Secretary-Board Agreement formalized the ES-UI partnership. It was an improvised interdepartmental arrangement, which allowed UI grants to supplement ES grants and state resources to build and maintain a national ES system.[20] Under the Secretary-Board Agreement, both ES and UI services were provided jointly in ES offices. While ES and UI functions were unified at a single point of service, ES and UI grants were not comingled. Both USDOL and the Board made federal grants available during FYs 1936 to 1938 to establish and maintain ES offices and to coordinate ES and UI activities. During 1938, 9.2 million initial UI claims were filed, and ES made 2.7 million nonagricultural job placements (Haber and Kruger 1964, p. 29). By the end of FY 1939, the plan to expand ES offices was completed in the 48 states, District of Columbia, and territories of Alaska and Hawaii (USDOL 1953, p. 13).[21]

FINANCING AND ORGANIZING THE PARTNERSHIP

The Wagner-Peyser Act provided ES grants to states, which they were required to match, to administer state ES systems. Title III of the Social Security Act provided nonmatching UI grants (and still does) to states to administer state UI laws and, as a result of the Secretary-Board Agreement, to finance the ES system.[22] Between 1938 and 1941 about 85 to 90 percent of the costs for administering ES offices were financed through UI grants. Overall, between 90 and 95 percent of the entire costs of maintaining all state ES office systems were financed by the federal government under the Wagner-Peyser Act and the Social Security Act. Between January 1942 and November 1946, war-time mobilization of civilian labor required federalization of the state ES systems, and the total cost of administering ES offices was paid from federal general revenues. When Congress returned the ES to federal-state administration after the war, it waived the state ES matching requirement. The 1947 Labor-Federal Security Appropriation Act and subsequent laws (Friedman 1948, p. 17) provided 100 percent federal funding of ES administrative costs until 1950, when the Wagner-Peyser Act was amended to permanently eliminate the matching provision.[23]

Locating the ES and UI programs in USDOL to overcome federal and state structural barriers to fortify the two programs' partnership proved challenging during the Truman administration.[24] Ultimately, in August 1949, under Reorganization Plan No. 2, the Bureau of Employment Security that had responsibility for both programs was permanently transferred from the Federal Security Agency to USDOL (USDOL 1955, p. 53).

EARMARKING REVENUES FOR EMPLOYMENT SECURITY

Struggles in obtaining adequate appropriations for ES and UI after World War II led to legislative proposals starting in 1949 to earmark the Federal Unemployment Tax Act (FUTA) receipts solely for the purpose of employment security—that is, ES and UI. Earmarked funds were thought to be less susceptible to budget manipulations. Not until the Employment Security Administrative Financing Act of 1954 (P.L. 83-567) was the proposal enacted into law to earmark FUTA receipts. However, FUTA receipts continued to be deposited in general revenues of the U.S. Treasury, and appropriations for ES and UI administration continued to be paid from general revenues. The 1954 law did provide, however, that excess tax receipts (revenues over expenditures) at the end of each FY were to be credited to the Unemployment Trust Fund (UTF) (Haber and Murray 1966, pp. 404–405).

Since the 1954 amendments, administrative grants for both ES and UI have been financed from FUTA revenues. In the ensuing years, however, USDOL budget requests for ES and UI administrative grants continued to be cut by Congress. Thus, in 1959, the Eisenhower administration proposed yet another change in the law that would require Congress to finance employment security administration directly from the UTF. Amounts equal to FUTA revenues could then be placed in the UTF, from which the grants to states could be appropriated with an adequate balance maintained as a reserve. The president's budget message for FY 1961 argued that "employment security programs would be financed in essentially the same way as other major social insurance programs" (Federal Reserve Archive 1960).

During the Eisenhower presidency, many of the early architects of the federal and state ES and UI programs remained active in policy making. Based on their experiences, they sought to strengthen the ES-UI partnership into the future. Congress approved the proposed Eisenhower reform with overwhelming bipartisan support; the Social Security Amendments of 1960 were enacted on September 13, 1960.[25]

Title V of the 1960 amendments, the Employment Security Administrative Financing Amendments, established a new federal Employment Security Administration Account (ESAA) within the UTF.[26] Under the law, FUTA payroll taxes paid by employers to the U.S. Treasury are deposited in the ESAA, and about 20 percent of those receipts today are allotted to the Extended Unemployment Compensation Account (established in 1970). Funds to administer state ES and UI programs are expended directly from ESAA, rather than from the general revenue fund (Miller 1997, p. 359).

The 1960 amendments transformed the fiscal federalism of the ES and UI programs. Since then, FUTA revenues have not only been earmarked, but they go directly into the UTF and also come out of the UTF as ES and UI grants. Federal ES and UI laws, federal-state grant agreements, and state operating plans set forth conditions for administration of the grants. The 1954 and 1960 revisions to the UTF remain in place, and over time, have safeguarded the framework of the ES-UI partnership.

CHANGES IN THE LABOR FORCE

The role of the ES expanded in the second half of the twentieth century to serve more of the economically disadvantaged, who had little or no previous work experience and difficulty entering the labor market. Because added funding for ES was needed to serve the disadvantaged, advocates began to consider new ES funding sources and arrangements. They argued for the use of monies from federal general revenues to augment ES appropriations and expand service capacity. During mid-century, the national effort to enact the first large-scale public job training program also emerged.[27] Ruttenberg and Gutchless (1970, p. 73) typified the sentiments of some job training advocates, observing: "Trust fund financing has provided a continuity and stability that was essential to the steady development of the employment service." They and others argued that grant funds from FUTA should be used to assist job seekers with prior attachment to the labor force, and that additional grant funds to serve the disadvantaged and other groups should be drawn from federal general revenues to finance some ES administration.

The 1970 Employment Security Amendments (P.L. 97-373) provided that the ES grants include a "mix" of monies from FUTA and general revenues. Based upon USDOL policies to meet statutory requirements, the percentage of FUTA monies in the mix is determined by the percentage of persons in UI-covered employment. In 1973, the source of funding for ES grants was 85 percent from FUTA and 15 percent from general revenues. A series of changes in this formula followed. In 1975, the grant mix was set at 86 percent from FUTA and 14 percent from general revenue. In 1976, the proportions were changed to 87 percent and 13 percent, respectively. In 1978, the proportions were adjusted to 92 percent from FUTA and 8 percent from general revenue. Before the summer of 1980, the proportions were again revised to 97 percent from FUTA and 3 percent from general revenues, and they have remained unchanged since then (Lubin 1980, p. 877).

Over the next 30 years, national policy shifted about whether UI and ES services should be delivered jointly or separately at local offices. In 1980, a report by the National Commission on Unemployment Compensation (NCUC) made recommendations to revitalize the ES-UI partnership by enhancing the ES program. The report specified that for ES to serve as the prime federal and state labor exchange and provide job search and work test services to UI claimants, the Wagner-Peyser Act ES grants to states had to be increased. To accomplish essential ES objectives, the report proposed that annual federal grants be sufficient to fund at least four ES staff positions for each 10,000 local members of the civilian labor force (NCUC 1980, pp. 137, 141). No action by the president or Congress was ever taken on these NCUC policy recommendations.[28]

ES AND UI AS INTERDEPENDENT PROGRAMS

From FY 1994 through FY 2000, under the "One-Stop" initiative, states received supplemental USDOL grants totaling $825 million to consolidate fragmented workforce development delivery systems. Interestingly, one of the federal principles for the states' receipt of the new funding was *integrated services* (Balducchi, Johnson, and Gritz 1997, p. 476; Balducchi and Pasternak 2001, p. 145),[29] and the meaning of *integrated services* became a source of policy differences within USDOL because it concerned how local offices would be funded. Unlike the position held by federal UI policymakers in 1937, this time federal UI policymakers did not want state UI agencies to assume large costs for the upkeep of the consolidated One-Stop centers that housed multiple program partners. USDOL UI policymakers who previously had been reluctant to sponsor new telephone and Internet claims processes, changed position to avert a potential UI resource grab by One-Stop operators. USDOL began distributing supplemental UI grants to states for new telephone and Internet technologies, which resulted in relocating the vast majority of state UI staff out of local offices and into detached call centers. Currently, most UI staff members are not located in physical AJCs, although states are required to provide access to claims services at these centers (Wandner 2010, pp. 198–199).

With implementation of the One-Stop grant initiative, the Clinton administration next sought to enshrine in law the One-Stop approach in the delivery of workforce development programs. Codified in the Workforce Investment Act (WIA) of 1998, this reform brought together the ES, UI, and job training systems into a single One-Stop delivery system, without reapportioning state control of ES and UI programs and local control of job training programs (Balducchi and Pasternak 2001, p. 156).

The ES-UI partnership weakened during the WIA era (1998–2014), mostly because of inadequate funding for the ES program under the Wagner-Peyser Act. This happened despite the introduction of new federal programs requiring ES-UI cooperation to assist the increasing numbers of dislocated UI beneficiaries. These included the Worker Profiling and Reemployment Services[30] (WPRS) program (1994), and the Reemployment and Eligibility Assessment initiative (2005), which was replaced in 2015 by the Reemployment Services and Eligibility Assessment (RESEA)[31] program. Over the past four decades, the president's annual budget requests have been insufficient to provide adequate Wagner-Peyser Act ES grants to states,[32] and subsequent underfunding by Congress has widened the fissure between ES and UI program activities.

Despite these challenges, the union of ES and UI remains intact in federal statutes, and the operating procedures of the ES-UI partnership are still faithful to its founding principles (USDOL 1955, p. 12), which

- guarantee that impartial services will be delivered by competent state government professionals who are free of patronage or private interests;

- pledge that the prospect of suitable jobs will be found for UI claimants as soon as possible, so that in many cases the payment of benefits will be unnecessary;

- assure cooperation between staff members performing job finding and placement, and those performing claims activities to satisfy state laws requiring that UI beneficiaries must be able and available to work or they may be disqualified if they refuse suitable work without good cause;

- state that when a claimant has refused a referral or a job based upon a referral, ES must report the facts to the UI claims staff to determine whether a benefit disqualification should be imposed; and

- assure employers that claimants who are required to do so fulfill their responsibility to seek work and that employers have a reliable means to obtain qualified workers.

The Workforce Innovation and Opportunity Act (WIOA) of 2014 retained the WIA's One-Stop concept along with the distribution of authority for ES and job training between state and local entities. However, WIOA did collapse the WIA categories of core and intensive services into the single category of "career services." Career services are typically the same as Wagner-Peyser Act ES services. The key differences between the structure of ES and WIOA are that ES is under the administrative control of state workforce agencies, where resources can be reassigned within states, and services are mostly delivered by merit-based government employees, retaining the assurance of impartiality sought by the founders of the ES and UI programs. Grants (derived largely from FUTA) are awarded for administering ES services throughout each state, with distinct responsibilities for UI claimants. Thus, ES funds enable governors to align statewide economic development with recruitment and job placement services without destabilizing local WIOA resources in any area. In contrast, grants (derived from general revenue) for administering WIOA career services and job training are mostly under the control of local workforce development boards, and WIOA services are delivered by private and public employees.

EVIDENCE OF COST-EFFECTIVENESS

In this section, we examine selected studies evaluating the cost-effectiveness of ES programs. Syntheses of the best evidence about the cost-effectiveness of ES for UI beneficiaries may be found in O'Leary (2006) and Wandner (2010). Studies since the 1980s have shown that many dislocated, experienced workers actually only require adequate unemployment benefits and JSA to return to employment (Corson et al. 1989; Jacobson et al. 2004; Johnson et al. 1983). In addition, random trials testing strategies to renew linkages between ES and UI have estimated that closer cooperation results in shorter unemployment durations and lower UI benefit payment costs (Corson, Long, and Nicholson 1985).

These results mean that conservation of UTF reserves through reduced joblessness can be achieved by providing job finding and placement services and exposing UI claimants to suitable jobs. This is particularly true for younger and dislocated UI claimants. Analyzing data from Washington State, Lachowska, Meral, and Woodbury (2016) find that for dislocated UI claimants the work test reduced time to reemployment by one to two quarters and increased post-UI job tenure by about two quarters.[33]

Other evidence can be found in several USDOL-sponsored studies. A demonstration in Wisconsin (Almandsmith, Adams, and Bos 2006) tested a services regimen that included joint ES-UI staff interviews with UI claimants, JSA, UI eligibility reviews, and staff-assisted job referrals. Using a quasi-experimental methodology, the researchers found that UI durations were shortened by 0.9 week, relative to the comparison group of other UI claimants. More evidence of effective ES activities comes from three evaluations of reemployment and eligibility assessments (REA) involving random trials (Benus et al. 2008). In Nevada, REA led to significantly shorter UI durations and lower benefit amounts where treatment group UI claimants collected 3.13 fewer weeks and $873 lower total benefit amounts than their non-treatment peers (Michaelides et al. 2012; Poe-Yamagata et al. 2011).[34]

INADEQUATE ES FUNDING AND ITS CONSEQUENCES

Because of chronic underfunding of the Wagner-Peyser Act ES grants to states, the types of effective, staff-assisted ES services needed to return the unemployed or underemployed to work are not always available at the AJCs.[35] These grants have been underfunded in spite of research showing that assessment, JSA, and job finding and placement services can be highly cost-effective ways of reducing joblessness.

Since program year (PY) 1984, Wagner-Peyser Act ES grants to states have remained stagnant or decreased in nominal terms.[36] Additionally, the Tax Equity and Fiscal Responsibility Act of 1982 capped a shift in federal policy that tightened rather than expanded access to UI benefits. This was manifested in tougher initial and continuing eligibility conditions at the state level (Blaustein 1993, pp. 262–263).[37] This shift was the result of federal fiscal policies that promoted reduction in the size of government, opposition to tax increases, and devolvement of social programs to states. Resistance by some states to tax hikes in recent years also has resulted in unprecedented reductions in unemployment benefit durations. The potential federal funding of ES-UI programs was further squeezed with the drop in 2011 of the FUTA tax rate from 0.8 percent to 0.6 percent. Likewise, the federal UI wage base, the wage cap per employee used to calculate employers' tax contributions to support the ES-UI programs, has remained at $7,000 since January 1, 1983. After enactment of the Social Security Amendments of 1939, laws to increase the federal UI wage base to support these vital programs have been enacted only three times, all under Republican administrations, in 1970 (P.L. 91-373), 1976 (P.L. 94-566), and 1982 (P. L. 97-248).[38]

The tightening of state UI eligibility conditions and reduction in funds for ES services occurred in a period of enormous technological advancements. This leap in technology enabled states to move to high volume mainframe and distributed computer processing and Internet services without workload disruptions. Sometimes, particularly in rural areas, this gave a false impression that access through computer-assisted services always resulted in effective service interventions (Dunham et al. 2005). With federal budget constraints and the rampant use of technology-based self-services, there has been precipitous erosion in staff-assisted ES job finding and placement services. Moreover, utilization of technology-based services appears to have expanded during the Great Recession. According to state workforce agency administrators, more than 80 percent of the 45 respondents to a 2012 National Association of State Workforce Agencies (NASWA) survey funded by the Urban Institute (Wandner 2015, pp. 156, 163) reported that they had increased rather than cut computer-assisted services. Throughout this period, regular UI average durations and exhaustion rates have been trending upward, suggesting a possible cause and effect.

From 1993 until the first decade of the twenty-first century, the WPRS program required states, as an unfunded mandate, to provide additional reemployment services to UI claimants likely to exhaust benefits. As a consequence, ES services in states were widely underfunded and WPRS claimants underserved.[39]

Both the executive and legislative branches of the federal government have contributed to the underfunding of the ES program in recent decades. Neither the president's annual budget requests to Congress, nor separate Congressional appropriation actions have provided adequate funding. FUTA provides a statutory mechanism to fully fund ES services, and funds are contained in the UTF for this purpose, but it has not been adequately used to support the program. On the other hand, since 1962, there have been five major federal job training laws enacted, including WIOA most recently, and each incarnation has included changes to state and local delivery arrangements.[40] Every one of the five public job training programs has been funded from general revenues with discretionary Congressional appropriations. Public job training has received policy attention and funding; but it is not an entitlement, nor does it have a statutory funding mechanism. In contrast, the Wagner-Peyser Act ES program, which has an existing institutional structure for funding, has regularly lacked sufficient funds despite the fact that they have already been paid for by employers through FUTA taxes.

Most industrialized nations provide a free public employment service as a right to all citizens. Indeed, these developed nations and many middle-income nations are signatories to the 1948 International Labor Organization (ILO) Convention 88 on public employment services (ILO 1948). Convention 88 asserts that all labor force members should have the right to free labor market information and job matching services as a means to social participation. Although the United States is not a signatory to ILO Convention 88, it has respected the principle of the convention that all nations "shall maintain or ensure the maintenance of a free public employment service" (ILO 1948, article 1). President Eisenhower asserted, "[S]tate employment security offices are important for a smoothly operating free labor market in a growing economy" (Federal Reserve Archive 1960). Through the ES, the United States provides a public exchange at no cost to job seekers. Furthermore, the ES has a statutory funding mechanism to ensure Americans have access to a free public employment service. However, the mechanism has not worked well in recent years. Policy action should be taken to ensure adequate funding under FUTA. Additional factors for ES budget formulation might be established by USDOL to improve justifications to the Office of Management and Budget and Congress for increases in annual appropriations.[41] In an American society where work is the avenue to self-sufficiency, a free and effective public labor exchange should be available to all job seekers.

Because Wagner-Peyser Act ES grant funds to states have declined in nominal terms since PY 1984, their real value through PY 2015 has dropped by more than half (Figure 3.1). For 2015, it would have taken funding of $1.47 billion to have maintained the 1984 real level of spending.[42] Workers and employers need to be more aware of the role ES contributes to the smooth functioning of the labor market and to the integrity of the UI program. Some states have taken limited measures to make up for portions of these ES grant shortfalls by augmenting federal funding through special assessments or by tapping UI funds. As of 2015, 30 states have provided supplementary ES funding (USDOL 2016a, Table 2-17, pp. 2-31 to 2-32). In addition, based on the annual NASWA survey of state workforce agencies, state supplementary spending on ES totaled more than $150 million (NASWA 2016). This is compelling evidence that state workforce agency administrators value ES programs for their customers.

Figure 3.1 Wagner-Peyser Funding for Employment Services in Millions of Nominal and Real Dollars, 1984 to 2015 (1984 = 100)

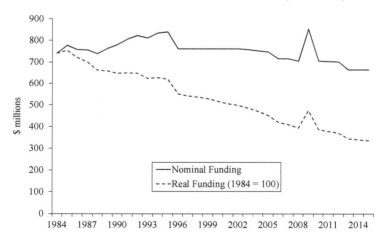

SOURCE: BEA (2015), USDOL (2014, 2015a,b).

OPPORTUNITY FOR ES-UI
PARTNERSHIP REVITALIZATION

Over the years, the ES-UI partnership has ebbed and flowed. Historically about 40 percent of the ES registrants for services have been UI claimants. In the Great Recession, the highest number of ES registrants in any year was 22,447,124 in PY 2009, and of those, 10,712,573 were UI claimants, totaling 47.7 percent of all registered ES job seekers (USDOL 2009).

Workforce changes over several decades and new work arrangements, including in today's so-called gig labor market, have resulted in more workers being at risk for joblessness. Currently, fewer than one in three unemployed workers receive unemployment benefits, and a record high 38 percent of workers exhaust benefits. After the Great Recession, nine states (Arkansas, Florida, Georgia, Illinois, Kansas, Michigan, Missouri, North Carolina, and South Carolina)—mostly as a result of debt due to inadequate benefit financing—reduced their maximum unemployment benefit durations to less than 26 weeks, ranging from 12 to 25 weeks.[43] The number of weeks available in four of those states (Georgia, Florida, Kansas, and North Carolina) is based on a sliding scale governed by the states' unemployment rates (The White House 2016).

The decisions by some states to reduce UI benefit durations have adverse effects on both claimants and job seekers who have exhausted unemployment benefits. Reductions in UI receipt by unemployed workers will not reduce the number of job seekers who need ES services. Business downturns or dislocations will cause many claimants in states with reduced durations of benefits to exhaust benefits, but many will continue to be job seekers who need an array of job finding and placement services. Shortened maximum durations of UI make provision of early ES services even more important. For example, in PY 2014, UI claimants accounted for 37.3 percent of all job seekers registered with ES—a 10 percentage point decline from PY 2009 (USDOL 2014). Although much of this decline may be attributed to improved economic conditions, if additional states reduce their maximum duration of benefits, the percentage gap between UI claimants and ES job seekers may widen, but the necessity of providing employment services to UI exhaustees will remain.

POLICIES TO REVITALIZE THE ES-UI PARTNERSHIP

In June 2016, the Center for American Progress (CAP), the National Employment Law Project (NELP), and the Center on Poverty and Inequality (CPI) of the Georgetown University Law Center proposed improvements in unemployment protections for workers and enhancements of the ES-UI partnership. They called for a $1 billion increase in Wagner-Peyser Act ES grants and a $535 million increase in RESEA above the 2017 presidential budget request (West et al. 2016, pp. 20–21).

If the current administration is successful in stimulating aggregate demand through tax reform or other measures, then domestic labor demand also is likely to increase. Many businesses with job openings will require some staff-assisted ES recruitment services. This possible surge in labor demand is an ideal time for policymakers to revitalize the ES-UI partnership. We offer four policies for consideration.

Increase Annual Wagner-Peyser Act ES Grants to States

In FY 1981, regular Wagner-Peyser Act ES grants totaled $781.4 million. That year ES grants served 16.5 million job seekers (USDOL 1982, pp. 48–49). Had ES received only increases in annual funding that maintained the real level of funding over the years, the amount would have been $1.47 billion in FY 2015 instead of the $664 million appropriated by Congress. We therefore support the funding increases proposed by CAP, NELP, and CPI.

In a report issued by the Brookings Institution, Jacobson (2009, p. 25) estimates a cost of $383 per UI claimant to institute call-in

notifications and provide JSA services. Adjusting for annual inflation, the cost rises to $430 per UI claimant in 2016. Based on his-
toric usage, $430 seems to be a reliable estimate for the average cost
per UI claimant to receive staff-assisted assessment and job search
services.[44] Using the $430 amount, the proposed $1 billion in added
Wagner-Peyser Act ES grants could provide job search activities to
an added 2.3 million UI claimants (or the long-term jobless who have
exhausted their unemployment benefits). In FY 2015, for example,
only 16 percent of UI claimants were scheduled for RES or RESEA
eligibility and job search services (USDOL 2016b, p. 37). Using PY
2014 national ES data, 5,411,656 UI claimants were registered with
ES, and of those, 1,845,036 received job search activities (USDOL
2014). An additional $1 billion could have increased the receipt of job
search activities for UI claimants from 34.1 percent to 77 percent.[45]

Furthermore, amendments to the Wagner-Peyser Act in WIOA
in 2014 expanded ES assistance to UI claimants, added work test
responsibilities to include making eligibility assessments, and broadened ES referrals and assistance to training and employment opportunities.[46] Logically, additional ES responsibilities should give rise
to increases in annual Wagner-Peyser Act ES grants to states, but no
increases in ES grants to states have thus far been proposed.

**Raise and Index the FUTA Taxable Wage Base and Make the ES
Grants Budget Mandatory**

Americans should have a right to a vibrant and free public
employment service. We propose restoring the funding capacity of
the Wagner-Peyser Act ES program by raising and indexing the FUTA
taxable wage base as well as moving the Congressional allocation
derived from funds in the ESAA for state ES grants from the discretionary to the mandatory side of the federal budget.

To secure additional Wagner-Peyser Act ES financing, the FUTA
wage base could be tied to one-third of the Social Security taxable
wage base or set equal to the average weekly wage in UI covered

employment. Either rule would secure the foundation for Wagner-Peyser Act ES grant financing and help insulate it from the politics of the budgetary request and appropriation processes.

Create a Contingency Fund for the Wagner-Peyser Act ES Program

Starting in FY 1950, the federal budget for state UI grants has included a contingency fund to cover state workload expenditures above the expected level. Supplementary grants to states from this fund are based on the number of UI claims filed, claims paid, and state salary increases above the expected level (USDOL 1957, p. 6). USDOL should create a companion ES contingency fund so that as UI workloads climb, so does ES funding under the Wagner-Peyser Act in order to serve the additional ES workload.

Establishing an ES contingency fund would ensure that as state UI workloads go up, funds above budgetary levels for Wagner-Peyser Act ES services would also rise proportionally. These additional ES funds would be provided to serve added UI claimants and provide to them cost-effective, staff-assisted ES job finding and placement services. Also, such funds could be used to administer increased work test activities and referrals to appropriate training. A federal-state work group should be formed to design and test an ES contingency model to determine its effectiveness and exportability.

Increase Uniformity of State UI Provisions

Reforms of the Social Security Act and FUTA and state UI financing rules will be more successful if UI eligibility provisions that are truly national in scope become federal conformity requirements where states are compelled to enact companion laws.[47] Examples include not disqualifying individuals for benefits who leave work to care for immediate family members who are ill or disabled, or to accompany spouses who are relocating, and program alternatives such as short-time compensation and self-employment assistance.

This will ensure that conditions for receipt of benefits are uniform and lessen the advantage of one state over another as a cost of doing business. Likewise, such federal policy mandates will advance national economic security outcomes, increase recipiency, strengthen the ES and UI partnership as an economic stabilizer, and expand labor mobility and the equal treatment of workers.

SUMMING UP

The ES-UI partnership is rooted in permanent authorizing statutes, an identical fund source, common rules for state administration, and interdependent practices to guard against improper payments and to expose claimants to suitable job openings. This partnership is central to the success of the public workforce system. Over the past several decades, the ES has been consistently underfunded, thereby weakening the ES-UI partnership, despite research evidence that demonstrates its value to reducing unemployment durations. During recent recessions, federal policies have increased emergency unemployment benefits and job training, but they have by and large ignored long-term underfunding of Wagner-Peyser Act ES grants, and Congress has been inattentive to the adequacy of ES finances. Similarly, state governors and interest groups have not advocated for ES funding sufficiently to revitalize the ES-UI partnership.

In this chapter, we explored the origin and objectives of the ES-UI partnership. We reviewed the early actions by ES and UI framers to forge an interdependent relationship between the two programs. At the outset, creative financing and strict rules for professionalism were required to properly launch and maintain employment security programs. A statutory system for cooperation and financing was set by 1960, but it has atrophied—along with the ES and UI partnership—mostly because of inattention and underfunding of the ES program. We also reviewed research that demonstrates the effectiveness of ES and the reliance of the ES and UI programs on each other to satisfy social insurance principles. We described how amendments to the Wagner-Peyser Act in WIOA broadened ES activities, and we proposed a path to revitalizing the long-standing ES-UI partnership.

Notes

We thank Michael Miller, Suzanne Simonetta, and Stephen Wandner for their suggestions; Jess Aragon, Richard McHugh, Robert Pavosevich, and Ronald Wilus for their support; and Julie Balster, Robert Johnston, and the staff of the Wirtz Library at the U.S. Department of Labor for help in locating primary source materials. Particular thanks to the late Bill Haltigan for sharing the little-known McKinley and Frase book containing contemporaneous accounts of early Social Security personalities and disputes. Any errors of fact or judgment are solely our responsibility. Only our own views are expressed, and they are not necessarily those of the W.E. Upjohn Institute for Employment Research, U.S. Department of Labor, or any other organization.

1. The ES provides employment services without cost to job seekers—both UI beneficiaries and other individuals.
2. Preventing unemployment was one of the original objectives of the UI policymakers, and maintaining employer–employee attachments by preventing dispersal of an employer's workforce was the practical policy enunciated by USDOL (Blaustein 1993, pp. 43–64).
3. On average, just over half of UI claimants each year obtain at least one staff-assisted ES service (West et al. 2016, p. 15).
4. The term *employment security* was the invention of Arthur Altmeyer, chairman of the Social Security Board. President Roosevelt's Reorganization Plan No. 1 of 1939 created the Federal Security Agency. Within the agency, a new bureau was formed containing the Social Security Board and the U.S. Employment Service. Altmeyer named it the Bureau of Employment Security to unite the ES and UI programs (Blaustein 1993, pp. 175–176). *Employment security* is likely a derivative of *social security* and *economic security* (the original term used by Roosevelt to introduce social insurance).
5. The president initiated CES to study social insurance at the suggestion of the Secretary of Labor (Perkins 1946, p. 279). The membership included the Secretaries of Labor, Agriculture, and Treasury, the Attorney General, and Federal Relief Administrator.
6. See also Balducchi (2011) for an analysis of CES's recommendations.
7. These projects were launched under the National Industrial Recovery

Act, Public Works Administration, Civil Works Administration, and in 1935, Works Progress Administration.

8. This section draws from Friedman (1948).

9. Of the over 30 states in March 1936 that had affiliated with USES, only 11 had matched funds to the upper limit of federal Wagner-Peyser Act ES grants available to them (McKinley and Frase 1970, p. 302).

10. The Social Security Act requires that benefits must "be paid through public employment offices or such other agencies as the Social Security Board may approve." There was little early resistance to the Board's mandate. In one instance, the South Dakota legislature adjourned in early 1939 without appropriating funds to match the Wagner-Peyser Act ES grant. The state proposed to pay unemployment benefits through the state welfare offices instead of state ES offices. The Board withheld South Dakota's UI administrative grant until the state came into compliance. By September, the legislature provided matching funds for the Wagner-Peyser Act, state ES offices were reopened, and the UI grant resumed (Rubin 1983, p. 175).

11. State ES laws included authorization for or appropriation of matching funds. Legislative acceptance of the Wagner-Peyser Act was included in the UI laws of Kansas, Maine, Maryland, Michigan, Mississippi, Montana, South Carolina, Utah, Washington, and Wyoming (USDOL 1937a).

12. Incrementalism is a trait of federalism. Stepwise adoption of ES by states and USDOL validation was a harbinger for later ES-UI policy initiatives. For example, the national WPRS system was enacted into federal law in 1993 and required concomitant state compliance. Not until June 1996 did all states implement WPRS systems (Robinson 1996, p. 11).

13. The states were Massachusetts, Pennsylvania, Ohio, Virginia, Illinois, Missouri, Oklahoma, Minnesota, and Colorado.

14. From the outset, a professional cadre of employees of state government was indispensable to avert favoritism or corruption by private interests in classifying and referring job seekers. After state ES laws were enacted, USDOL continued to uphold standards of professionalism. The Iowa ES agency in March 1935 was warned that not adhering to merit standards would jeopardize its Wagner-Peyser Act ES grant. In August 1935, USDOL suspended Missouri's Wagner-Peyser Act ES grant for violation of merit staffing standards. It wasn't until 1998 in Michigan that another state's Wagner-Peyser Act ES grant was suspended for violating federal standards (Balducchi and Pasternak 2004; *Michigan v. Herman* 1998).

15. By May 1937, 44 states had adopted UI laws.

16. We refer to this agreement as the Secretary-Board Agreement.

17. Thirty-two was the number of states used in memoranda prepared by the Social Security Board. In fact, benefits became payable in 22 states in January, with an additional eight states by the end of 1938 (USDOL 2017). The Social Security Act delayed initial UI payments in each state for two years to build reserves. In August 1936, Wisconsin became the first state to pay unemployment benefits.

18. The Board also cited testimony of January 21, 1935, of Edwin Witte, executive director of CES, before the House Ways and Means Committee (McKinley and Frase 1970, p. 302).

19. A technical resolution adopted in May 1937 governed the operating mechanics of the Secretary-Board Agreement (USDOL 1937d).

20. A UI grant for the ES was first made to Wisconsin in 1936 and to other states in mid-1937 (Atkinson, Odencrantz, and Deming 1938, p. 197).

21. For the two FYs, 1938 and 1939, the Board increased its share of the total costs of the ES from 60 percent ($14.3 million) in FY 1938 to 80 percent ($25 million) in FY 1939 (Haber and Joseph 1939, p. 29).

22. Parts of this section are drawn from U.S. Congress (1950).

23. The cost to states for administering ES offices from 1933 through 1950 in the years when matching was required never exceeded 10 percent (U.S. Congress 1950). Federal law has never prohibited supplementation of funds by states to support the ES system.

24. In July 1946, the Social Security Board was abolished. Its functions, including UI administration, were transferred to the new Social Security Administration in the Federal Security Agency (FSA). During the presidential campaign of 1948, over President Truman's veto, Congress transferred the ES program from USDOL to FSA. Thus, the USES and UI programs were combined in the Bureau of Employment Security, but not in USDOL.

25. In contrast to recent partisanship in tax policy, HR 12580 (P.L. 86-778) also raised the federal payroll tax from 3.0 to 3.1 percent without a change to the allowable 2.7 percent offset (USDOL 1985, p. 48). The bill sponsored by a Republican administration received 369 House votes to approve, with 236 Democrats voting for it. In the Senate, the bill received 74 votes to approve, including 43 Democrat votes (Social Security Administration 2016). In 2017, a tax under FUTA was levied on employers at a rate of 6.0 percent on wages up to $7,000 a year paid to an employee. The law provides a credit against federal tax liability of up to 5.4 percent to employers who pay state UI taxes. Thus, employers pay an effective federal tax rate of 0.6 percent, or a maximum of $42 per covered employee per year.

26. Sections 901(a) and (c) and 903 (c), Social Security Act (42 U.S.C. 1103).

27. The rise of automation as a means of production began to trigger dis-

location of workers. The needs of the dislocated and disadvantaged prompted the birth of public job training. Under the Manpower Development and Training Act (MDTA) of 1962, ES and UI played vital roles. The state ES screened and referred job seekers to training institutions, and UI administered MDTA allowance payments (Wandner, Balducchi, and O'Leary 2015).

28. In 1982, James Rosbrow, executive director of NCUC, told an author of this chapter that the report's recommendations were not acted upon because of the publication's timing. It was issued during the 1980 presidential election, and the outcome of that election resulted in a rollback of federal policy making (Rosbrow 1982).

29. Supplemental USDOL grants for the development of state One-Stop delivery systems were authorized under the Wagner-Peyser Act, but the source of funds was general revenue. The other One-Stop principles were universality, customer choice, and performance-driven/outcomes based.

30. *Reemployment services* is defined as employment services for individuals who have work experience and seek new work.

31. The RESEA program requires UI claimants to report in person to AJCs and receive one-on-one reviews of eligibility for UI, assessing their ability and availability for work, and referrals to reemployment services or training. When the WPRS program was launched in March 1994, the inclusion of UI eligibility reviews was considered, but obtaining funding and setting up the framework would have delayed state implementation. Eligibility reviews, thus, were not included in the original WPRS process (USDOL 1994). Later efforts to introduce such reviews lacked policy support, until the launch of the REA initiative. However, the ultimate aims of WPRS and RESEA are similar—reduced duration and faster job placement. In FY 2015, USDOL merged aspects of the two efforts. Claimants determined most likely to exhaust benefits under state WPRS systems and veterans receiving unemployment benefits are the primary groups directed to RESEA. For a discussion of other aspects of the WPRS and RESEA, see Wandner (2010) and USDOL (2015a).

32. Grants for the ES refer to annual formula grants, which support staffing and infrastructure of state labor exchange operations. They are distinct from episodic federal grants for reemployment services under the RESEA program.

33. The work test is an ES responsibility under the Wagner-Peyser Act, section 7(a)(3)(F). Provision of the work test is not in WIOA. The Middle Class Tax Relief and Job Creation Act of 2012 amended the Social Security Act at section 303(a)(12) to require that UI claimants be able to work, available for work, and actively seeking work.

34. Material in this section was derived from Wandner, Balducchi, and O'Leary (2015). Some research suggests that shorter unemployment durations result from the threat of requiring participation in services rather than due to the value of the services. For example, Johnson and Klepinger (1994) asserted that responses to enhanced work search supports in a Tacoma experiment happened after assignment but before service participation; Black et al. (2003) found a similar response after Kentucky UI beneficiaries were assigned to WPRS. However, the cited Nevada experiment provided persuasive evidence that the reemployment services in REA had strong positive effects separate from any threat effect of the eligibility assessment.

35. One result of underfunding has been cutbacks by some states of physical local offices and staff-assisted ES services. For example, since 2011 the governor of Iowa has closed 36 offices and reduced state workforce agency staff by 27 percent, which makes it hard "to provide employment services to individual job seekers" (*Des Moines Register* 2017).

36. Appropriations for ES and UI had been funded on the basis of FYs, and they jointly developed annual state plans of service. Amendments to the Wagner-Peyser Act in 1982 (P.L. 97-300) required appropriations for ES in FY 1985 and thereafter to be made available for obligation on a PY basis, and the joint development of state ES plans of service with agencies of the Job Training and Partnership Act. The PY begins July 1 of the calendar year and ends June 30 of the following year. Beginning in 1976, the FY begins October 1 of the calendar year and ends September 30. https://www.gpo.gov/fdsys/pkg/STATUTE-96/pdf/STATUTE -96-Pg1322.pdf (accessed May 23, 2017).

37. See https://history.nih.gov/research/downloads/PL97-248.pdf (accessed February 15, 2017).

38. In 1939, two federal laws were enacted that affect the ES-UI partnership. P.L. 76-1, untitled, transferred Title IX of the Social Security Act to the Internal Revenue Code, Chapter 23, FUTA. The Social Security Amendments (P.L. 76-379) limited the tax base under FUTA to the first $3,000 of a covered worker's earnings (USDOL 1986, p. 43).

39. In 1997, USDOL staff began drafting internal papers arguing for increases in Wagner-Peyser Act ES funds to serve dislocated UI claimants. Separate approvals were required from Employment and Training Administration, other offices in USDOL, the Office of Management and Budget (for inclusion in the President's annual budget request), and Congress. It took three years to gain concurrences. For PYs 2001–2005, Congress added $35 million to the Wagner-Peyser Act ES appropriation to serve WPRS UI claimants, but these funds were inadequate. Subsequently, the George W. Bush administration abandoned supplementation

and cut Wagner-Peyser Act ES grants. In 2009, the Obama administration, under the American Recovery and Reinvestment Act, achieved
a one-time increase in Wagner-Peyser Act ES grants of $400 million,
available through PY 2010, which included $250 million targeted for
reemployment services to UI claimants.

40. O'Leary, Straits, and Wandner (2004) review the first four federal job
training laws.

41. Section 901(d) (4) of the Social Security Act establishes the factors for
requesting funds for Wagner-Peyser Act ES grants. These factors include
"the relationship between employment subject to state laws and the total
labor force in the United States, the number of claimants and the number of job applicants, and such other factors as he finds relevant." Thus,
federal law permits development of modernized factors to strengthen the
case for increased ES grants.

42. The implicit price deflator value for 2015 was 197.97, with the base year
1984 equal to 100.00. The nominal 1984 level of funding for Wagner-
Peyser Act programs was $740 million.

43. In 2013, Illinois resumed a 26-week maximum UI duration.

44. The ES provides job finding and placement services to all job seekers
who ask for them. In PY 2014, the cost per individual for ES was $45.74.
This rate included individuals receiving self-service through virtual tools
and those receiving staff-assisted ES services (USDOL 2016b, p. 53).

45. The actual 1,845,036 UI claimants in receipt of job search activities
added to an estimated 2,325,000 UI claimants in receipt of job search
activities totals 4,107,036 UI claimants.

46. Sections 7(a)(3)(F) and (G) of the Wagner-Peyser Act.

47. The National Governors Association's principles of state-federal relations endorse federal action for problems that are truly national in scope
(National Governors Association 2017).

References

Almandsmith, Sherry, Lorena Ortiz Adams, and Han Bos. 2006. "Evaluation
of the Strengthening the Connections between Unemployment Insurance
and the One-Stop Delivery Systems Demonstration Projects in Wisconsin." Employment and Training Administration Occasional Paper No.
2006–11. Washington, DC: U.S. Department of Labor.

Atkinson, Raymond C., Louise C. Odencrantz, and Ben Deming. 1938. *Public Employment Service in the United States*. Chicago: Public Administration Service.

Balducchi, David E. 2011. "Iowans Harry Hopkins and Henry A. Wallace

Helped Craft Social Security Act's Blueprint." *Iowa Heritage Illustrated*. Des Moines, IA: State Historical Society of Iowa.

Balducchi, David E., Terry R. Johnson, and R. Mark Gritz. 1997. "The Role of the Employment Service." In *Unemployment Insurance in the United States: Analysis of Policy Issues*, Christopher J. O'Leary and Stephen A. Wandner, eds. Kalamazoo, MI: W.E. Upjohn Institute for Employment Research, pp. 457–503.

Balducchi, David E., and Alison J. Pasternak 2001. "One-Stop Statecraft: Restructuring Workforce Development Programs in the United States." In *Labour Market Policies and the Public Employment Service: Proceedings of the Prague Conference, July 2000*. Paris: Organisation for Economic Co-operation and Development, pp. 141–167.

———. "Federal-State Relations in Labor Exchange Policy." 2004. In *Labor Exchange Policy in the United States*, David E. Balducchi, Randall W. Eberts, and Christopher J. O'Leary, eds. Kalamazoo, MI: W.E. Upjohn Institute for Employment Research, pp. 33–71.

Baldwin, Marc. 1993. "Benefit Recipiency Rates and the Federal/State Unemployment Insurance Program: Explaining and Reversing Decline." PhD diss., Massachusetts Institute of Technology.

Benus, Jacob M., Etan Blass, Eileen Poe-Yamagata, and Ying Wang. 2008. "Reemployment and Eligibility Assessment (REA) Study: Final Report." Employment and Training Administration Occasional Paper 2008-2. Washington, DC: U.S. Department of Labor.

Black, Dan, Jeffrey Smith, Mark Berger, and Brett Noel. 2003. "Is the Threat of Reemployment Services More Effective than the Services Themselves? Experimental Evidence from the UI System." *American Economic Review* 93(4): 1317–1327.

Blaustein, Saul J. 1993. *Unemployment Insurance in the United States: The First Half-Century*. Kalamazoo, MI: W.E. Upjohn Institute for Employment Research.

Bureau of Economic Analysis. 2015. "Implicit Price Deflator 1984-2015, National Income and Product Account Tables." Washington, DC: U.S. Department of Commerce. https://www.bea.gov/national/nipaweb/DownSS2.asp (accessed September 29, 2017).

Burns, James MacGregor. 1956. *Roosevelt the Lion and the Fox*. New York: W.S. Konecky Associates and Harcourt Brace.

Committee on Economic Security. 1935. *Report to the President*. Washington, DC: Government Printing Office.

Corson, Walter, David Long, and Walter Nicholson. 1985. "Evaluation of the Charleston Placement and Work Test Demonstration." Unemployment Insurance Occasional Paper No. 85-2. Washington, DC: U.S. Department of Labor, Employment and Training Administration.

Corson, Walter, Paul T. Decker, Sherri M. Dunstan, Anne R. Gordon, Patricia

Anderson, and John Homrighausen. 1989. "New Jersey Unemployment Insurance Reemployment Demonstration Project." Unemployment Insurance Occasional Paper No. 89-3. Washington, DC: U.S. Department of Labor, Employment and Training Administration.

Des Moines Register. 2017. "Branstad's Legacy Is Dissing, Dismissing Public Workers." February 23. http://www.desmoinesregister.com/story/opinion/editorials/2017/02/23/editorialbranstads-legacy-dissing-dismissing-public-workers/98226516/ (accessed February 24, 2017).

Dunham, Kate, Annelies Goger, Jennifer Henderson-Frakes, and Nichole Tucker. 2005. "Workforce Development in Rural Areas; Change in Access, Service, Delivery, and Partnerships." ETA Occasional Paper No. 2005-07. Washington, DC: U.S. Department of Labor, Employment and Training Administration.

Federal Reserve Archive. 1960. Budget of the United States, Ending June 30, 1961. Message of the President, p. M 60. Washington, DC: Government Printing Office. https://fraser.stlouisfed.org/title/54#!19004 (accessed July 26, 2016).

Friedman, Gladys R. 1948. "Reorganization Plan No. 1 of 1948: Legislative History and Background." *Social Security Bulletin* 11(5): 15–21. https://www.ssa.gov/policy/docs/ssb/v11n5/v11n5p15.pdf#nameddest=article (accessed July 6, 2016).

Haber, William, and J. J. Joseph. 1939. "Unemployment Compensation." *Annals of the American Academy of Political and Social Science*, March 1: 22–37.

Haber, William, and Daniel H. Kruger. 1964. *The Role of the United States Employment Services in a Changing Economy.* Kalamazoo, MI: W.E. Upjohn Institute for Employment Research.

Haber, William, and Merrill G. Murray. 1966. *Unemployment Insurance in the American Economy: An Historical Review and Analysis.* Homewood, IL: Richard D. Irwin.

International Labor Organization (ILO). 1948. "Employment Service Convention, 1948 (No. 88)." Geneva: International Labor Organization.

Jacobson, Louis, Ian Petta, Amy Shimshak, and Regina Yudd. 2004. "Evaluation of Labor Exchange in the One-Stop Delivery System Environment." ETA Occasional Paper No. 2004-09. Washington, DC: U.S. Department of Labor, Employment and Training Administration.

Jacobson, Louis. 2009. *Strengthening One-Stop Centers: Helping More Unemployed Workers Find Jobs and Build Skills.* Washington, DC: The Hamilton Project, Brookings Institution.

Johnson, Terry R., Katherine P. Dickinson, Richard W. West, Susan E. McNicholl, Jennifer M. Pfiester, Alex L. Stagner, and Betty J. Harris. 1983. *A National Evaluation of the Impact of the United States Employment Service.* Washington, DC: U.S. Department of Labor, Employment and Training Administration.

Johnson, Terry R., and Daniel H. Klepinger. 1994. "Experimental Evidence on Unemployment Insurance Work-Search Policies." *Journal of Human Resources* 29(3): 695–717.

Lachowska, Marta, Merve Meral, and Stephen A. Woodbury. 2016. "Effects of the Unemployment Insurance Work Test on Long-Term Employment Outcomes." *Labour Economics* 41(3): 246–265.

Lubin, Carol R. 1980. "The Employment Service Role in Unemployment Compensation." In *Unemployment Compensation: Studies and Research*, vol. 3. Washington, DC: National Commission on Unemployment Compensation, pp. 869–906.

McKinley, Charles M., and Robert W. Frase. 1970. *Launching Social Security, A Capture and Record Account 1935–1937*. Madison, WI: University of Wisconsin Press.

Michaelides, Marios, Eileen Poe-Yamagata, Jacob Benus, and Dharmendra Tirumalasetti. 2012. "Impact of the Reemployment and Eligibility Assessment (REA) Initiative in Nevada." Employment and Training Administration Occasional Paper No. 2012-08. Washington, DC: U.S. Department of Labor, Employment and Training Administration.

Michigan v. Herman. 1998. "Whether States Are Required to Employ Merit Staffing in the Delivery of Employment Services under the Wagner-Peyser Act." No. 5:98CV-16. U.S. District Court for the Western District of Michigan, May 15, 1998. 81 F. Supp. 2d 840.

Miller, Mike. 1997. "Appendix to Chapter 8, the Role of Federal Financing in the Unemployment Insurance System." In *Unemployment Insurance in the United States: Analysis of Policy Issues*, Christopher J. O'Leary and Stephen A. Wandner, eds. Kalamazoo, MI: W.E. Upjohn Institute for Employment Research, pp. 355–361.

National Association of State Workforce Agencies (NASWA). 2016. *State Supplemental Funding Survey: Results for the State Supplemental Fund Survey for FY 2015*. Washington, DC: NASWA.

National Commission on Unemployment Compensation (NCUC). 1980. *Unemployment Compensation: Final Report*. Arlington, VA: National Commission on Unemployment Compensation.

National Governors Association. 2017. *Principles of State-Federal Relations*. Washington, DC: National Governors Association. https://www.nga.org/cms/home/federal-relations/nga-policy-positions/pageecpolicies/col2-content/main-content-list/principles-for-state-federal-rel.html (accessed February 18, 2017).

O'Leary, Christopher J. 2006. "State UI Job Search Rules and Reemployment Services." *Monthly Labor Review* 129(6): 27–37.

O'Leary, Christopher J., and Randall W. Eberts. 2008. "The Wagner-Peyser

Act and U.S. Employment Service: Seventy-Five Years of Matching Job Seekers and Employers." Prepared for the Center for Employment Security Education and Research, National Association of State Workforce Agencies. Kalamazoo, MI: W. E. Upjohn Institute for Employment Research.

O'Leary, Christopher J., Robert A. Straits, and Stephen A. Wandner. 2004. "U.S. Job Training: Types, Participants, and History." In *Job Training Policy in the United States*, Christopher J. O'Leary, Robert A. Straits, and Stephen A. Wandner, eds. Kalamazoo, MI: W.E. Upjohn Institute for Employment Research, pp. 1–20.

Perkins, Frances. 1946. *The Roosevelt I Knew*. New York: Viking.

Poe-Yamagata, Jacob Benus, Nicholas Bill, Hugh Carrington, Marios Michaelides, and Ted Shen. 2011. "The Impact of the Reemployment and Eligibility Assessment (REA) Initiative." Employment and Training Administration Occasional Paper No. 2012-08. Washington, DC: U.S. Department of Labor, Employment and Training Administration.

Reich, Robert B. 2010. *After-Shock: The Next Economy and America's Future*. New York: Alfred A. Knopf.

Robinson, John M. 1996. "Worker Profiling and Reemployment Services National Colloquium, Keynote Address, Partners in Reemployment." In *Worker Profiling and Reemployment Services Systems, National WPRS Colloquium, June 1996: Selected Papers and Materials*, David E. Balducchi, ed. Washington, DC: U.S. Department of Labor, Employment and Training Administration, pp. 11–16.

Rosbrow, James. 1982. Interview of James Rosbrow by David E. Balducchi, September 21.

Rubin, Murray. 1983. *Federal State Relations in Unemployment Insurance*. Kalamazoo, MI: W.E. Upjohn Institute for Employment Research.

Ruttenberg, Stanley H., and Jocelyn Gutchless. 1970. *The Federal-State Employment Service: A Critique*. Policy Studies in Employment and Welfare Number 5. General Editors: Sar A. Levitan and Garth L. Mangum. Baltimore: John Hopkins University Press.

Social Security Administration. 2016. Vote Tallies. 1960 Amendments. https://www.ssa.gov/history/tally1960.html (accessed December 20, 2017).

U.S. Congress. 1950. *Extending the Act of June 6, 1933 (48 State. 113), as Amended, to Puerto Rico and the Virgin Islands*. Report to accompany S. 3546. 81st Congress. 2d session, August 14. Washington, DC: Senate Committee on Labor and Public Welfare.

USDOL. 1937a. Dates of Legislative Acceptance of Wagner-Peyser Act and Dates of Affiliation with the United States Employment Service, April 1. Washington, DC: U.S. Department of Labor.

———. 1937b. Recommendation of the Social Security Board to the Secretary of Labor, February 20. Washington, DC: U.S. Department of Labor.

———. 1937c. Agreement between the Secretary of Labor and the Social Security Board, March 30. Washington, DC: U.S. Department of Labor.

———. 1937d. Resolution No. 1 under the Agreement of March 30, 1937, between the Secretary of Labor and the Social Security Board, May 18–19. Washington, DC: U.S. Department of Labor.

———. 1937e. Letter Sent by the Executive Director of the Social Security Board to Each of the State Unemployment Compensation Commissions, February 27. Washington, DC: U.S. Department of Labor.

———. 1953. The Public Employment Service System 1933–53. *Employment Security Review* 20(6): 1–70. Washington, DC: U.S. Department of Labor, Bureau of Employment Security.

———. 1955. "Twenty Years of Unemployment Insurance in the USA, 1935–1955." *Employment Security Review* 32(8): 1–66. Washington, DC: U.S. Department of Labor, Bureau of Employment Security.

———. 1957. The Scope and Complexity of the Employment Security Budgets. *Employment Security Review* 24(11): 1–32. Washington, DC: U.S. Department of Labor, Bureau of Employment Security.

———. 1982. *Employment and Training Report to the President.* Washington, DC: U.S. Department of Labor, Employment and Training Administration.

———. 1985. "Beginning the Unemployment Insurance Program—An Oral History." UI Occasional Paper No. 85-5. Washington, DC: U.S. Department of Labor, Employment and Training Administration.

———. 1986. "Fifty Years of Unemployment Insurance—A Legislative History: 1935–1985." UI Occasional Paper No. 86-5. Washington, DC: U.S. Department of Labor, Employment and Training Administration.

———. 1994. "Implementation of a System of Profiling Unemployment Insurance (UI) Claimants and Providing Them with Reemployment Services." Field Memorandum No. 35–94, March 22. Washington, DC: U.S. Department of Labor, Employment and Training Administration.

———. 2009. "Wagner-Peyser Act Employment Services, State-by-State PY 2009 Performance." Washington, DC: U.S. Department of Labor, Employment and Training Administration. www.doleta.gov/performance/results/Wagner-Peyser_act.cfm (accessed July 12, 2016).

———. 2014. "Wagner-Peyser Act Employment Services, State-by-State PY 2014 Performance." Washington, DC: U.S. Department of Labor, Employment and Training Administration. https://www.doleta.gov/performance/results/Wagner-Peyser_act.cfm (accessed June 8, 2016).

———. 2015a. "Fiscal Year (FY) 2015 Unemployment Insurance (UI) Reemployment Services and Eligibility Assessments (RESEA) Grants." Unemployment Insurance Program Letter No. 13-15, March 27. Washington, DC: U.S. Department of Labor, Employment and Training Administration.

————. 2015b. "Workforce Innovation and Opportunity Act and Wagner-Peyser Allotments for Program Year 2015." Training and Employment Guidance Letter No. 29-14, Advisory System, April 27, 2015 (data for 2015). Washington, DC: U.S. Department of Labor, Employment and Training Administration.

————. 2016a. *Comparison of State UI Laws.* Employment and Training Administration. Washington, DC: U.S. Department of Labor. https://workforcesecurity.doleta.gov/unemploy/statelaws.asp (accessed August 16, 2016).

————. 2016b. "FY 2017 Congressional Budget Justification, Employment and Training Administration, State Unemployment Insurance and Employment Service Operations." Washington, DC: U.S. Department of Labor. https://dol.gov/sites/default/files/documents/general/budget/CBJ-2017-V1-08.pdf (accessed February 13, 2017).

————. 2017. *ET Financial Data Handbook 394: General Notes.* U.S. Department of Labor, Employment and Training Administration. https://oui.doleta.gov/unemploy/hb394/notes.asp (accessed May 18, 2017).

Waiwood, Patricia. 2013. *The Recession of 1937.* Cleveland, OH: Federal Reserve Bank of Cleveland. http://www.federalreservehistory.org/Events/DetailView/27 (accessed June 28, 2016).

Wandner, Stephen A. 2010. *Solving the Reemployment Puzzle from Research to Policy.* Kalamazoo, MI: W.E. Upjohn Institute for Employment Research.

————. 2015. "The Future of the Public Workforce System in a Time of Dwindling Resources." In *Transforming Workforce Development Policies for the 21st Century,* Carl Van Horn, Tammy Edwards, and Todd Greene, eds. Kalamazoo, MI: W.E. Upjohn Institute for Employment Research, pp. 129–166.

Wandner, Stephen A., David E. Balducchi, and Christopher J. O'Leary. 2015. *Selected Public Workforce Development Programs in the United States: Lessons Learned for Older Workers,* Washington, DC: AARP.

West, Rachel, Indihar Dutta-Gupta, Kali Grant, Melissa Boteach, Claire McKenna, and Judy Cont. 2016. *Strengthening Unemployment Protections.* Washington, DC: Center for American Progress.

The White House. 2016. "Fact Sheet: Improving Economic Security by Strengthening and Modernizing the Unemployment Insurance System." Washington, DC: Office of the Press Secretary. https://obamawhitehouse.archives.gov/the-press-office/2016/01/16/fact-sheet-improving-economic-security-strengthening-and-modernizing (accessed August 15, 2016).

Chapter 4

State UI Financing Response to the Great Recession

Wayne Vroman
The Urban Institute

$\mathbf{T}$he Great Recession of 2007–2009 placed a heavy strain on state unemployment insurance (UI) programs and their method of financing. This short chapter introduces and discusses several aspects of the state UI responses during and after the downturn. Individual programs within the state UI system are highly varied. Whereas many states still have low net balances in their UI trust fund accounts at the Treasury, many other states have restored their trust funds to pre-recession or even higher levels. This chapter documents the varied financing responses of the state programs to the recession with special attention to a number of specific elements in their responses. The chapter also assesses the health of the state trust funds as of mid-2016.

PROGRAM FINANCING RESPONSES

Two factors that contributed to the financing difficulties experienced by state UI programs during and after the Great Recession were the low level of reserves prior to the recession and the severity (both depth and duration) of the downturn. At the end of March 2011, the states had trust fund debts that exceeded $40 billion. At the end of June 2016, net reserves totaled roughly $36 billion. While the states still owed approximately $8 billion, this $76 billion turnaround was achieved by taking several distinct types of state-level actions.

Trust fund restoration was achieved both by actions that increased tax revenue and those that reduced UI benefit payments. Table 4.1

summarizes six different actions that states took affecting revenues. For each type of financing response, the states are sorted according to their prerecession reserve ratio multiple (RRM, also termed the average high-cost multiple [AHCM]) measured at the end of 2007.[1] The RRM is an index of trust fund adequacy that incorporates information on three factors: past payouts, the current trust fund balance, and

Table 4.1 State Actions to Improve UI Program Financing (Number of States), 2007 to 2016

Reserve ratio multiples (RRM)	State programs (1)	Let UI tax law work (2)[a]	Early active changes (3)[b]	Tax base indexation (4)[c]	Large tax base increases (5)[d]	Issued muni bonds (6)[e]	FUTA credit offsets (7)[f]
Below 0.25	13	0	1	0	1	1	7
0.25–0.499	17	1	4	1	5	5	2
0.50–0.749	8	3	0	2	3	2	0
0.75–0.999	6	6	0	0	0	0	0
1.0–1.249	3	3	0	0	0	0	0
1.25 and above	4	2	0	0	2	0	0
Total number	51	15	5	3	11	8	9
Mean RRM	0.54	0.92	0.30	0.52	0.61	0.37	0.17
Median RRM	0.43	0.83	0.30	0.59	0.44	0.40	0.16

[a] Alabama, Alaska, District of Columbia, Iowa, Louisiana, Montana, Maine, Maryland, New Mexico, North Dakota, Oklahoma, Oregon, Utah, Washington, and Wyoming.
[b] Legislation to improve solvency in 2008 and 2009: Arkansas, New Hampshire, South Dakota, Tennessee, and West Virginia.
[c] Tax base indexation adopted after 2009: Colorado, Rhode Island, and Vermont.
[d] Tax base in 2015 at least 50 percent higher than in 2007: Delaware, Kansas, Mississippi, New Hampshire, North Dakota, Rhode Island, South Carolina, South Dakota, Vermont, West Virginia, and Oklahoma (2013).
[e] Municipal bonds issued during 2010–2013 to repay Treasury UI loans: Arizona, Colorado, Idaho, Illinois, Michigan, Nevada, Pennsylvania, and Texas.
[f] FUTA tax credit offsets during 2012–2015 equal to at least 10% of total tax revenue: California, Connecticut, Georgia, Indiana, Kentucky, Missouri, New York, North Carolina, and Ohio.
SOURCE: Table developed by the author with data from the Office of Unemployment Insurance, U.S. Department of Labor.

the size of a state's economy. The latter is approximated by the total payroll of employers covered by the UI program in each state. Higher RRM levels signal more adequate trust fund balances. An RRM equal to 1.0 means there are 12 months of benefits in the trust fund, and many view an RRM of 1.0 as signaling an adequate UI trust fund balance.

Column (1) in Table 4.1 summarizes the distribution of RRMs for the 51 UI programs[2] at the end of 2007 or just prior to the Great Recession. The mean and median RRMs for the 51 programs of 0.54 and 0.43 indicate that the average prerecession trust fund balances were about half of the balances needed to meet the suggested actuarial standard of 1.0. Only seven states had an RRM of 1.0 or higher and 30 had RRMs below 0.50, so many states entered the Great Recession with low trust fund reserve balances.

Columns (2) to (7) identify the number of states undertaking specific revenue-enhancing actions. The identification of specific actions in individual states is somewhat arbitrary, reflecting my own judgments. The 15 states in column (2) allowed their UI tax laws to operate as written in their tax statutes. These states moved to higher tax rate schedules and made other adjustments automatically without legislative changes. Note that these states had trust funds with mean and median RRMs of 0.92 and 0.83, respectively, much larger than the group as a whole. This group also included 11 of the 13 states with a prerecession RRM of 0.75 or higher. Having large trust funds meant that these states had limited need for loans from the Treasury, and only two (Alabama and Maryland) borrowed from the Treasury from 2009 to 2012.

Column (3) summarizes five states that took early policy actions to avoid or reduce the volume of borrowing. All five of these states had low prerecession reserves, with RRMs below 0.50. Three of the five (New Hampshire, South Dakota, and Tennessee) instituted temporary quarterly taxes to enhance revenue. These taxes were to sunset when the trust fund's recovery was deemed adequate by program administrators.

Prior to the Great Recession, 16 states plus the Virgin Islands had indexed taxable wage bases with increases tied automatically to changes in statewide average wages. Following the recession, three states adopted indexation. In two, the tax base started to increase automatically in 2013 (Colorado and Rhode Island). In the third, Vermont, the base increased from $8,000 in 2009 to $16,000 in 2012, with indexed increases commencing in 2015.

During and after the recession, 11 states increased their tax bases by at least 50 percent (column [5]). The largest increases occurred in Delaware, Mississippi, South Carolina, and Vermont, where the tax base at least doubled between 2007 and 2015. Note that the states making these large increases had a prerecession average RRM that about matched the national average.

Six of the eight states that issued municipal bonds (column [6]) had prerecession RRMs below 0.50. Four of these states (Illinois, Michigan, Pennsylvania, and Texas) issued municipal bonds with long maturities (final maturities of 2020 or later). Each of the four used the proceeds from the bonds to repay Treasury loans that carried higher interest rates than the bonds. The issuances could be described as arbitrage (or debt-restructuring) transactions that delayed repayment dates as well as secured lower interest rates. It is quite likely some of these bonds will still be outstanding when the U.S. economy enters the next recession.

If a state's debt to the Treasury is outstanding on January 1 of two consecutive years and not fully repaid by November 10 of the second year, it may be subject to Federal Unemployment Tax Act (FUTA) credit offsets payable in January of the following year. Roughly half the state UI programs were subject to FUTA credit offsets in at least one year between 2009 and 2015. From 2012 to 2015, these added federal taxes accounted for 10 percent or more of state UI tax revenue in nine states. These nine states had very low prerecession reserves, with seven of nine RRMs falling below 0.25 in 2007 (column [7]). These states exhausted their trust funds early in the recession and became subject to FUTA credit offsets in 2012.

Several of the nine states experienced prolonged indebtedness to the Treasury, hence multiple years of reduced FUTA credit offsets. The mean and median RRMs for these states in 2007 are the lowest of any group in Table 4.1, both below 0.20.

FUTA CREDIT REDUCTIONS

As just noted, one feature of the Great Recession was the widespread and prolonged indebtedness of most state UI trust funds. From 2009 to 2011, 35 state programs (36 including the Virgin Islands) borrowed from the Treasury. Many states had debts for multiyear periods, and 11 programs were still making debt repayments in April 2016.[3] Because these debts were outstanding for multiyear periods, 26 programs were subject to the automatic debt repayment through reductions in their FUTA tax credits. Typically 5.4 percent of the 6.0 percent FUTA tax levied on the first $7,000 of taxable payroll is waived in states with acceptable experience-rating systems. However, if Treasury loans are outstanding on January 1 of two consecutive years and not fully repaid by November 10 of the second year, the 5.4 percent FUTA tax waiver usually starts to be reduced, with the reduction payable in January of the following year. The initial reduction is 0.3 percent of federal taxable payroll ($21), but the reduction then grows with each successive year of continued indebtedness.

From 2009 to 2015, 24 states and the Virgin Islands were subject to FUTA credit reductions. Eighteen states plus the Virgin Islands experienced credit reductions for three or more years during this period. The aggregate revenue from the credit reductions totaled $10.7 billion, with $10.4 billion paid from 2012 to 2015.[4] Total state UI taxes (including FUTA credit reductions) paid during this period were $128.3 billion. Thus, over these four years, the credit reductions accounted for 8.3 percent of total state UI tax revenue.

The FUTA credit reductions were of varying importance in individual states. Table 4.2 focuses on the experiences of 18 states

Table 4.2 FUTA Credit Reductions as a Share of Total UI Tax Revenue, 2012 to 2015

Share of total tax revenue	Number of state programs	States
0.20 and above	2	IN, OH
0.15–0.199	1	KY
0.10–0.149	6	CA, CT, GA, MO, NY, NC
0.05–0.099	3	AR, FL, WI
0.00–0.049	4	IL, NJ, PA, VA
0	2	MA, TX
Total	18	

SOURCE: Estimates of FUTA credit reduction shares made by the author.

from 2012 to 2015, the 13 largest states (in terms of taxable covered employment in 2013) and five other states where FUTA credit reductions accounted for at least 5.0 percent of total UI tax revenue during the period. The 13 largest states were singled out for two reasons: 1) they dominate in aggregate UI program performance, accounting for about two-thirds of tax revenue and benefit payments; and 2) their debt repayment behavior differs from that of smaller states, as documented in Vroman (2016). Only 2 of the 13 largest states (Texas and Massachusetts) were not subject to FUTA credit reductions from 2012 to 2015. Texas issued municipal bonds in late 2010, while Massachusetts incurred debts for just a few months during 2011. The other 11 states paid $8.0 billion in credit offsets, about 77 percent of the national total in that four-year period.

With widespread trust fund restoration now underway, 2017 and 2018 may be the final years when FUTA credit offsets will make a measurable contribution to state UI tax revenue. Estimates made at the Urban Institute indicate that the credit reductions will total $2.0 billion in 2017 (California) and $2.4 billion in 2018 (again California). Although the payments could extend into 2019, it seems more likely that California's trust fund balance on November 10, 2018, will be positive, obviating the need for a credit offset in 2019. If this is the case, FUTA credit offsets will have been active for nine consecutive years from 2010 to 2018, with total offsets exceeding $18.0 billion.

Although FUTA credit offsets have helped many states to repay their debts, their positive effect on tax revenue occurs only in years when a state's net trust fund balance is negative. Once the net balance starts to consistently exceed zero, these added UI taxes automatically stop. Thus, only California, Connecticut, Ohio, and the Virgin Islands paid FUTA credit offsets in 2016. FUTA credit offsets, in other words, help states eliminate negative trust fund balances, but they do not continue to help in fund building after a positive balance has been achieved.

To summarize the responses of the state UI tax systems following the Great Recession, four points should be emphasized. 1) The individual states responded in a wide variety of ways, and Table 4.1 summarizes the responses. 2) About one-third of the states, mostly those with adequate prerecession reserves, allowed their experience-rating systems to operate as specified in their state statutes. These states had limited need for Treasury loans, and their trust funds have been restored to generally high levels. 3) Eleven states made large increases in their taxable wage bases, and each of them had a tax base in 2015 that was at least 50 percent higher than it had been in 2007. 4) One-third of the states either issued municipal bonds (eight) or allowed FUTA credit reductions to account for at least 10 percent of their postrecession tax revenue responses (nine). Neither strategy promoted robust trust fund recoveries. The states that issued bonds deferred part of their debt repayment until much later time periods. The FUTA credit offsets stopped contributing to trust fund recoveries after net trust fund balances became positive. Both strategies retarded the restoration of adequate trust fund balances in the states that followed these policies.

POSTRECESSION RESPONSES OF STATE UI BENEFITS

Improvements in fund solvency also can be achieved through benefit reductions. Over the long run, of course, benefit reductions also weaken the performance of UI as an automatic stabilizer of the macro economy. Documenting the recent changes in program benefits can provide a basis for estimating how much UI's stabilizing performance has been weakened.

Among various benefit adjustments made by states following the Great Recession, three were particularly prevalent, one passive and two active. The passive adjustment was not increasing the maximum weekly benefit for several consecutive years. One active adjustment was reducing the maximum number of potential weeks of regular UI benefits starting in 2011. The other active adjustment was increasing the amount of administrative activity to monitor payment accuracy, which, coupled with ongoing problems of program administration, could adversely affect receipt of benefits.

Changes in the Replacement Rate

About half the state programs operate with an indexed maximum weekly benefit that increases automatically as statewide wages increase. Other states raise the maximum periodically by state legislation. Several of these latter states have not increased their maximum benefits for many years.

To document the prevalence of this nonadjustment pattern, each state's maximum weekly benefit amount (WBA) was noted for January 2016 and for previous Januarys, and the number of consecutive Januarys with the same maximum was counted. Of the 24 states without an indexed maximum, the number of consecutive years with an unchanged maximum ranged from 4 to 19. In all but one state, the maximum WBA was unchanged for at least 5 consecutive years, and in five states, it ranged from 13 to 19 (Florida). The mean for the 24 states was 9.75 years, and the average 2016 maximum WBA had been unchanged for a decade.

From 2004 to 2015, the annual earnings in taxable covered employment nationwide increased from $39,141 to $52,066 or by 33.0 percent. For a state with average wage inflation and whose maximum was stable during 12 consecutive years, the maximum benefit would be 33.0 percent lower relative to annual wages at the end of the period. This decrease would exert a downward pressure on the replacement rate (the ratio of weekly benefits to the average weekly wage).[5] Because so many states have operated with unchanged maximum benefits for several consecutive years, many replacement rates have also been adversely affected. From 2005 to 2015, the replacement rate decreased in 35 of 51 programs. Although changes in monetary eligibility requirements and some actual reductions in weekly maxima also contributed to these decreases,[6] the average replacement rate decreased by 0.03 or more in 10 states from 2010 to 2015. Seven of the 10 experienced reductions of between 0.03 and 0.049,[7] while even larger reductions occurred in Indiana (−0.086), Rhode Island (−0.091), and North Carolina (−0.116). Thus, the generosity of weekly benefits decreased in the majority of states from 2010 to 2015, with particularly large reductions occurring in Indiana, North Carolina, and Rhode Island.

Figure 4.1 provides a visual summary of the national replacement rate for the 31 years from 1985 to 2015. The figure identifies three multiyear periods when the national replacement rate was noticeably lower than in adjacent years: 1997 to 2000, 2005 to 2008, and 2011 to 2015. The 2011 to 2015 period has the lowest average replacement rate of all five-year periods covered by Figure 4.1. A large part of the explanation for these low replacement rates has been the failure of many nonindexed states to increase their maximum WBAs in the years following the Great Recession. Compared to the earliest five years in Figure 4.1, the national average replacement rate from 2011 to 2015 was 2.6 percentage points lower (32.8 versus 35.4).

112   Vroman

Figure 4.1 UI Replacement Rate, 1985 to 2015

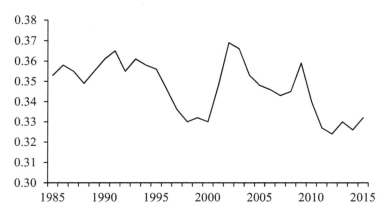

SOURCE: Replacement rates from column (33) of ET Handbook 394, Unemployment Insurance Financial Data.

Potential Benefit Duration

An important recent change in several state UI programs has been to reduce maximum potential benefit duration. Since 2011, eight states have reduced maximum potential duration to fewer than 26 weeks, and at least one additional state (Idaho) planned to implement a reduction in 2017. The reductions follow four decades when all state programs offered at least 26 weeks of potential benefits in every year.[8] During the first half of 2016, maximum duration was between 12 and 20 weeks in these eight states, and three of them have reduced potential benefit duration twice since 2011.[9] In the rest of this section, I examine the effects of the benefit reductions on benefit recipiency as well as the overall benefit recipiency rates in individual states.

Figure 4.2 shows maximum potential benefit duration in the eight states that paid fewer than 26 weeks of potential benefits during the first half of 2016. The maximum durations ranged from 12 weeks (Florida) to 20 weeks (Arkansas, Michigan, Missouri, and South Carolina). Shorter potential benefit durations would be expected to

Figure 4.2 Maximum Potential Benefit Duration, Eight States, 2000 to 2016 (weeks)

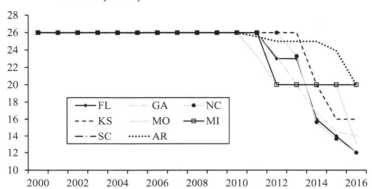

SOURCE: Data from "Significant Provisions of State Unemployment Insurance Laws," various issues through July 2016. The maxima can change in January and June of each year. Figure 4.1 shows annual duration with weights of 0.55 and 0.45 for the two periods.

reduce the recipiency rate (the ratio of weekly beneficiaries to weekly unemployment) through shorter periods of potential eligibility and more rapid exhaustion of benefits. Another potential determinant of the recipiency rate is the unemployment rate, because average unemployment duration increases during recessions when unemployment increases.

The approach followed here is to fit recipiency rate regressions for a period prior to the reduction in potential benefit duration, project the recipiency rate for later periods, and examine projection errors with particular attention to periods of shorter potential duration. A recipiency rate regression using annual data was fitted for each state for the years 1967 to 2007. Each regression used two explanatory variables: the state's current total unemployment rate (TUR) and TUR lagged one year. Table 4A.1 presents the regressions.

Table 4A.1 shows that state-level recipiency rates display considerable short-run noise. Although the table has regressions for 51 UI programs, the eight highlighted in bold in the table are shown in

Figure 4.2. Seven of the eight have adjusted R^2s of less than 0.50, and all eight standard errors of the estimates are between 0.034 and 0.049. The coefficient patterns for the TUR variables are consistent. All current TURs have positive coefficients, and six have t ratios of at least 2.0, a common threshold for statistical significance. All eight lagged TURs have negative coefficients, and all eight have t ratios of least 2.0. The recipiency rate increases in years with high unemployment rates but then decreases when the lagged unemployment rate is high.

The regressions in Table 4A.1 were used to project recipiency rates through 2015. Two sets of average projection errors are shown in Table 4.3: 2008 to 2011 and 2012 to 2015. Note that all projections are for years beyond the regressions' estimation periods, which ended in 2007, and that nearly all of the reductions in average potential duration below 26 weeks occurred during 2012 to 2015, the latter of the two four-year projection periods.[10]

The reduced maximum durations would be expected to cause larger projection errors during 2012 to 2015 as compared to 2008 to 2011, and the average projection errors for the two periods generally support this expectation. Six of eight averages are negative (i.e., they are overprojections) in the first period, but all eight are negative in the second. Six of eight equations were overprojecting by larger amounts during the first period relative to the second one; that is, the changes in these four-year averages are negative in all states but Georgia and Kansas. When the changes are examined for individual states (bottom row of Table 4.3), note that five changes are more negative than –0.045 (Florida, North Carolina, Michigan, South Carolina, and Arkansas).

Table 4.3 Average Projection Errors by State, 2008 to 2015

Period	FL	GA	NC	KS	MO	MI	SC	AR
2008–11	0.025	–0.125	–0.054	–0.034	–0.034	–0.021	–0.066	0.034
2012–15	–0.051	–0.108	–0.112	–0.033	–0.070	–0.083	–0.113	–0.038
Change	–0.076	0.017	–0.058	0.001	–0.036	–0.062	–0.047	–0.072

SOURCE: Average projection errors based on the regressions displayed in Table 4A.1.

The projection analysis indicates that recipiency declined in the period of 2012 to 2015, the period when potential duration decreased in these states. The explanation for the decline may include factors besides changes in potential duration. For example, changes in UI program administration could be linked to the decreases. On the other hand, the 2012 to 2015 period was characterized by much lower unemployment than that of 2008 to 2011. Thus, the analysis yielded results consistent with the expectation that a shorter potential duration reduced recipiency rates in these eight states.

UI Program Administration

State UI administrative activities are financed mainly by grants allocated by the Office of UI, which is part of the Employment and Training Administration of the U.S. Department of Labor. These administrative grants are based mainly on workloads related to UI claims. About one-fifth of the states supplement their federal grants with state resources.

Over the past 20 years, program administration has evolved away from face-to-face contact between claimants and administrators to electronic contacts, either by telephone or over the Internet. Nearly all decisions affecting initial eligibility and continuing eligibility are now made through electronic media, with Internet claims accounting for more than half of all administrative decisions related to UI eligibility.

Several ongoing challenges have been faced in the transition to electronic program administration, particularly in providing timely and accurate eligibility decisions. The computer IT systems in many states use old programming languages, and updating them has proven challenging. Also, since administrative allocations are closely linked to claims volume, financial support has decreased as the economic recovery has progressed.

A recent analysis by the U.S. Government Accountability Office (GAO) documented these challenges with results from a recent survey of all states and intensive interviews with claimant focus groups in three states (GAO 2016). Frequent problems with telephone claims identified by the GAO were long wait times, frequent dropped calls, difficulty in reaching program representatives, and frequent abandoned calls. Inadequate staffing was identified as a major cause of these problems. Inadequate administrative funding and outmoded IT systems also were frequently identified as underlying causes of administrative problems.

In recent years, the national office of the UI program has placed greater emphasis on payment accuracy. Increased emphasis is being paid to the states' Benefit Accuracy Measurement reports, which summarize payment accuracy and identify the source(s) of payment errors by the party (claimant, employer, or agency) and individual administrative process, and also include estimates of claimant fraud. While no research has thoroughly documented the effects of the administrative problems and increased emphasis on payment accuracy, these factors could be contributing to a decrease in UI recipiency. These administrative issues are present in all states to some degree, and they may have macro consequences in reducing the recipiency rate.

RECIPIENCY RATES IN INDIVIDUAL STATES

To develop a more nuanced understanding of the recent decline in UI recipiency, a state-level regression analysis was conducted. For each state, a background time series regression was fitted using annual data. The estimation period was from 1967 to 2007, the 41 years prior to the onset of the Great Recession. For each state, the recipiency rate was regressed on TUR and TUR lagged one year. The recipiency rate measure was the ratio of weekly regular UI beneficiaries to weekly total unemployment (the WKTU ratio), the latter measured by the Bureau of Labor Statistics (BLS).

It is well known that the recipiency rate increases at the start of a recession when unemployment increases but then declines in later periods because of UI benefit exhaustion and other factors. Hence, the regressions included the current and lagged TURs as explanatory variables. In the highly varied labor markets of individual states, local factors besides unemployment undoubtedly also influence the recipiency rate, but this analysis used only the two unemployment rate variables as arguments to explain variation in state-level WKTU ratios.

After fitting the regressions, the equations were then used to project the recipiency rate for the eight years following the end of the estimation period, that is, from 2008 to 2015. The patterns in the projection errors were then examined. Table 4A.1 displays the underlying regressions for the period from 1967 to 2007. There are 51 equations, one for each state plus the District of Columbia. Generally, TUR had the expected positive coefficient while lagged TUR generally had a negative coefficient. The regressions had relatively low explanatory power, with a simple average of only 0.245 for the adjusted R^2s.

Table 4.4 displays the average equation residuals for the final eight years of the estimation period (2000 to 2007) and for the eight years after the estimation period (2008 to 2015). Because the underlying regressions had generally low explanatory power, the errors were averaged for four-year periods at the end of the estimation period and in the postestimation years: 2000 to 2003, 2004 to 2007, 2008 to 2011, and 2012 to 2015. The average residuals are shown for three groups: the whole group (51), the 8 that have shortened maximum potential durations of less than 26 weeks, and the 43 that have not shortened the maximum potential duration.

For the groups of 8 and 43 states, the averages during 2000 to 2003 and 2004 to 2007 are quite similar, positive, and greater than 0.030 for 2000 to 2003, and negative but only –0.0009 and –0.0046, respectively, for 2004 to 2007. During 2008 to 2011, the average residuals are noticeably more negative (i.e., larger overpredictions) for the 8 states compared to the other 43 (–0.0339 versus –0.0101). The average residuals for both groups of states become even more negative during 2012 to 2015, but the average overpredictions are much larger for the eight reduced-duration states (–0.0752 versus –0.0425). Measured relative to their respective averages during 1967

Table 4.4 Average Residuals for Selected Four-Year Periods

	2000–03	2004–07	2008–11	2012–15
Average residuals by four-year period				
All states (51)	0.0320	−0.0040	−0.0138	−0.0476
Reduced duration states (8)	0.0327	−0.0009	−0.0339	−0.0752
Others (43)	0.0319	−0.0046	−0.0101	−0.0425
Number of negative average residuals				
All states (51)	9	29	33	43
Reduced duration states (8)	2	4	6	8
Others (43)	7	25	27	35

SOURCE: Residuals based on the regressions in Table 4A.1. The averages weight each state equally.

to 2007, the overprediction averages are 27.3 percent for the reduced duration states and 13.2 percent for the other 43 states. Not surprisingly, recipiency decreased by a larger percentage in the states that have reduced maximum potential durations.

Table 4.4 also shows the number of state-level four-year average residuals that were negative during each of the four periods. Overall, 33 of 51 were negative during 2008 to 2011, and 43 were negative during 2012 to 2015. For the most recent four years, the averages were negative for all 8 reduced-duration states and for 35 of the 43 remaining states. Underlying the negative averages in Table 4.4's top panel were widespread negative averages for all 8 of the reduced maximum duration states and 35 of the 43 other states in the 2012 to 2015 period.

An important finding of this analysis is that on average recipiency in the most recent years has decreased in most state UI programs. Actual recipiency rates during 2012 to 2015 fell below projected recipiency rates in 43 of 51 programs. The decrease in recipiency apparent in national data (shown below) has occurred in most of the individual state programs that make up the system of regular UI programs.

What underlies the decrease in UI recipiency? Since recipiency rates in the eight reduced-duration states decreased more than in the other states, one part of the explanation is the reductions in maximum potential duration. However, there must be other factors, as evidenced by the widespread negative error averages in the 43 other states during 2012 to 2015. The exact cause (or causes) for the decrease in recipiency cannot be determined from the regression analysis presented here. What the regressions in Table 4A.1 do show, however, is that the recent decrease in the recipiency rate has been widespread throughout the system of state UI programs.

THE UI PROGRAM NATIONWIDE

The final section of this chapter examines the regular state UI program at the national level, with attention to benefit recipiency and the aggregate trust fund. The analysis concentrates on the years from 2006 to 2015, that is, from just before the Great Recession to five years after it ended.

Figure 4.3 displays the ratio of weekly regular UI claims to unemployment (IUTU ratio), as measured in the monthly labor force survey from 2006 to 2015. A salient feature of the figure is the contrast in the recipiency rate prior to the Great Recession and the recipiency rate since 2012. The average monthly IUTU ratio between January 2006 and December 2007 was 0.356, whereas between January 2012 and December 2015, the average IUTU ratio was 0.268, or 24.7 percent below the average for 2006 and 2007. Note also that the IUTU ratio does not display a pronounced upward trend during 2012 to 2015 (at most an increase of 0.030) as the economy was moving closer to full employment. The UI recipiency rate is now substantially lower than it was prior to the Great Recession. This decline will have adverse

Figure 4.3 IUTU Ratio, 2006 to 2015

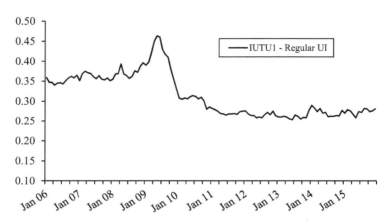

SOURCE: IUTU ratios calculated at the Urban Institute.

effects on the performance of state UI as an automatic stabilizer when the U.S. economy experiences the next recession.

Figure 4.4 traces the overall net trust fund balance of the state UI programs from the end of 2005 to mid-2016. The quarterly patterns clearly show how reserves are lowest at the end of the first calendar quarter and then recover sharply during April and May when first quarter tax accruals are received.

Figure 4.4 also shows the continuing presence of outstanding municipal bond principal (i.e., the vertical distance between total net reserves and the net reserves at the Treasury). At the end of June 2016, the states owed approximately $4.5 billion in the municipal bond market as well as approximately $3.5 billion to the U.S. Treasury. These debts were owed by UI programs in eight states plus the Virgin Islands, despite the fact that seven full years have elapsed since the end of the Great Recession.

Finally, note that net reserves at the end of June 2016 totaled $36.0 billion, which was nearly back to the prerecession level of approximately $40.0 billion. However, since the covered payroll

Figure 4.4 Net UI Trust Fund Reserves, 2005Q4 to 2016Q2

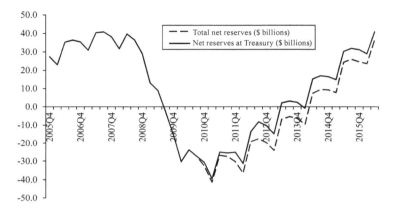

SOURCE: Net reserve estimates made at the Urban Institute.

in 2016 was more than 20 percent greater than it was in 2007, net reserves should be roughly $48 billion to just match the reserve ratio at the end of 2007. Thus, while substantial trust fund building has occurred since the trough of the recession, the net balance would have to have been 24 percent higher than it was just to be equivalent to the balance at the end of 2007.

Although the aggregate net trust fund was about three-fourths of the way to matching the balance at the end of 2007, the situation in individual state programs remains highly varied. In 19 states, the reserve ratio (net reserves as a percent of total payroll) at the end of June 2016 matched or exceeded its level at the end of 2007. However, net reserves were still negative in 2 states (California and Pennsylvania) plus the Virgin Islands, and another 11 had reserve ratios of less than half of their 2007 reserve ratios. In short, reserves in individual states were highly varied at the end of June 2016, and many states still had very low or negative net reserves.

Even though substantial progress has been made in trust fund restoration, more fund building is needed to return to the reserve position held just prior to the Great Recession. Given the inadequacy of reserves at the start of the Great Recession and the subsequent amount of state borrowing, prudent fund management requires continued trust fund building in the immediate future.

Compared to the years prior to the Great Recession, the benefit side of the state system of UI programs is now measurably smaller. The orders of magnitude presented here suggest that the recipiency rate is approximately 25 percent lower (0.268 compared to 0.356) than prior to the Great Recession, while the benefit replacement rate is about 7 percent lower (0.328 compared to 0.354). Combined, these two changes suggest the benefit side of the UI system is now only about 70 percent as generous as it was prior to the Great Recession. While benefit reductions have contributed to the recovery of state UI trust funds, they have also significantly reduced the generosity of the system of state UI programs. These reductions in benefit generosity will permanently weaken the performance of UI as an automatic stabilizer in future recessions.

Notes

Financial support was provided by the Urban Institute. The opinions expressed in the paper are those of the author and do not necessarily represent the views of the Urban Institute or its sponsors. Thoughtful comments were provided by Richard Hobbie.

1. The RRM is the ratio of two ratios. The numerator is the reserve ratio, which is the end-of-year trust fund balance (net of UI debts) as a percentage of total covered payroll. The denominator is the highest past annual payout rate (benefits as a percentage of payroll for the high-payout period).
2. There are 53 UI programs, but the table does not include the programs in Puerto Rico and the Virgin Islands.
3. The five programs with debts to the Treasury in mid-April 2016 were California, Indiana, Kentucky, Ohio, and the Virgin Islands. The six states with debts in the municipal bond market were Colorado, Illinois, Michigan, Nevada, Pennsylvania, and Texas. Total indebtedness at the end of March 2016 was approximately $12.0 billion.

4. Annual data on FUTA credit reductions from 2010 to 2015 were provided by the actuarial staff of the Unemployment Insurance Service of the U.S. Department of Labor. Estimates for 2016 and later years were made by the author.
5. The change in the replacement rate would depend upon several factors, but the unchanged maximum and the share of beneficiaries at the maximum WBA are very important.
6. Most notably, North Carolina reduced its weekly maximum from $535 to $350 in July 2013.
7. The seven states are California, Georgia, Michigan, Missouri, New York, Tennessee, and Washington. All but Washington experienced prolonged periods with a constant maximum WBA.
8. The last state to offer fewer than 26 weeks prior to 2011 was South Carolina, with a 22-week maximum in 1969.
9. Missouri enacted a 20-week maximum in 2011 and a sliding scale of between 13 and 20 weeks in January 2016. The sliding scale was overturned by a court ruling in mid-2016, restoring the 20-week maximum. Arkansas enacted a 25-week maximum in 2011 and a 20-week maximum in October 2015. Florida enacted a 23-week maximum in 2012 and a sliding scale of between 12 and 20 weeks in 2014.
10. The only reductions before 2012 were to 25 weeks in Arkansas and 20 weeks in Missouri, both in July 2011.

References

Government Accounting Office. 2016. *Unemployment Insurance: States' Customer Service Challenges and DOL's Related Assistance.* Report No. GAO-16-430. Washington, DC: Government Accountability Office. https://www.gao.gov/assets/680/677082.pdf (accessed November 17, 2017).

Vroman, Wayne. 2016. "The Big States and Unemployment Insurance Financing." Urban Institute Issue Brief. Washington, DC: Urban Institute. https://www.urban.org/sites/default/files/publication/78776/2000661The -Big-States-and-Unemployment-Insurance-Financing.pdf (accessed November 17, 2017).

Appendix 4A
State-Level Recipiency Rate Regressions

Table 4A.1 displays state-level regressions that explain regular UI recipiency rates for the period from 1967 to 2007. The dependent variable is measured as the ratio of average number of weekly regular UI beneficiaries to average weekly unemployment (the WKTU ratio). The data period includes the years for which the BLS has published unemployment rate estimates for individual states.[1]

Each regression has two explanatory variables: TUR and TUR lagged one year. The two TUR variables reflect the common observation that the recipiency rate increases in the early stages of a recession as overall unemployment is increasing but then decreases in later periods due to increased benefit exhaustions by recipients. The expectation for these two variables is that TUR will have a positive regression coefficient and that lagged TUR will have a negative coefficient.

Table 4A.1 shows these expectations are generally met. For TUR, 48 of the 51 slope coefficients are positive, and 29 have t ratios of at least 2.0 (a common indicator of significance). For lagged TUR, 48 coefficients are negative, and 38 have t ratios of 2.0 or larger. Although the slope coefficients generally have the expected signs, the regression fits are modest. The average adjusted R^2 is only 0.245, and only 16 exceed 0.30.

Two factors undoubtedly account for the low R^2 values. First, there is considerable noise in state-level estimates of annual unemployment (the denominator of the recipiency rate variables) due to the limited size of Current Population Survey samples in individual states. Second, several other factors influence unemployment and UI recipiency at the state level, and those factors are not controlled for in the regressions.

After the regressions were fitted, the regression errors were noted for each year. Each equation then was used to project the recipiency rate in the postsample years 2008 to 2015. The residuals for the years 2000 to 2007 and the projection errors for the years 2008 to 2015 were then averaged by four-year period (see Table 4.4 in the text). The underlying projections for the individual years were saved and are available, but the text presents four-year average residuals for simplicity.

Table 4A.1 State-Level Regressions of the Regular UI Recipiency Rate, 1967 to 2007

State	Constant	t	TUR	T	TURlag	T	Adj. R^2	Std. Err.	D.W.	Mean
Alabama	0.287	13.6	−0.496	1.7	0.002	0.2	0.025	0.046	0.98	0.255
Alaska	0.684	5.6	1.133	0.5	−2.541	1.2	−0.008	0.143	0.42	0.564
Arizona	0.208	9.0	1.915	4.1	−1.954	4.1	0.312	0.036	1.45	0.205
Arkansas	**0.371**	**10.6**	**1.547**	**1.8**	**−2.816**	**3.2**	**0.210**	**0.049**	**0.49**	**0.289**
California	0.435	25.8	1.092	3.3	−2.085	6.2	0.507	0.021	1.05	0.365
Colorado	0.104	5.1	1.679	2.8	−0.105	0.2	0.288	0.032	0.67	0.182
Connecticut	0.574	12.4	2.233	1.7	−4.311	3.4	0.230	0.092	0.52	0.468
Delaware	0.488	14.3	0.534	0.5	−2.391	2.1	0.180	0.069	0.86	0.390
Dist. of Col.	0.352	8.1	1.658	1.6	−1.405	1.3	0.010	0.069	1.38	0.370
Florida	**0.183**	**8.7**	**1.008**	**1.9**	**−1.140**	**2.1**	**0.063**	**0.036**	**0.33**	**0.176**
Georgia	**0.138**	**4.6**	**4.230**	**5.1**	**−2.621**	**3.2**	**0.386**	**0.044**	**1.72**	**0.224**
Hawaii	0.377	17.7	3.299	3.8	−3.553	4.1	0.271	0.043	1.42	0.364
Idaho	0.349	9.6	0.480	0.5	−0.960	0.9	−0.024	0.050	0.35	0.320
Illinois	0.380	14.5	2.314	3.0	−3.021	4.0	0.267	0.051	0.63	0.338
Indiana	0.274	12.9	2.201	3.4	−2.828	4.5	0.317	0.047	0.67	0.240
Iowa	0.383	18.7	2.554	2.3	−3.787	3.6	0.281	0.048	0.67	0.334
Kansas	**0.269**	**9.1**	**5.758**	**5.5**	**−4.878**	**4.9**	**0.420**	**0.041**	**0.83**	**0.309**
Kentucky	0.328	11.7	1.862	2.4	−2.644	3.4	0.212	0.050	0.88	0.280
Louisiana	0.210	5.2	2.382	2.3	−1.900	1.8	0.081	0.065	1.02	0.245
Maine	0.394	12.3	2.302	2.4	−2.722	2.9	0.143	0.056	0.79	0.371

127

Maryland	0.304	14.3	2.993	4.1	-3.518	4.8	0.343	0.033	1.00	0.278
Massachusetts	0.676	28.3	0.764	1.1	-4.567	6.8	0.716	0.049	0.64	0.470
Michigan	**0.428**	**27.8**	**1.992**	**5.8**	**-3.270**	**9.8**	**0.738**	**0.034**	**1.30**	**0.335**
Minnesota	0.362	14.5	1.880	2.1	-2.306	2.6	0.111	0.041	1.14	0.344
Mississippi	0.199	10.5	2.473	4.5	-2.296	4.2	0.314	0.035	1.04	0.212
Missouri	**0.417**	**16.3**	**2.195**	**2.7**	**-4.208**	**5.3**	**0.479**	**0.044**	**1.47**	**0.311**
Montana	0.354	10.2	-1.305	1.2	0.292	0.3	0.045	0.045	0.55	0.294
Nebraska	0.241	11.5	1.525	1.7	-0.267	0.3	0.078	0.035	1.15	0.284
Nevada	0.410	10.7	1.729	1.8	-2.334	2.4	0.091	0.058	0.58	0.373
New Hampshire	0.257	6.3	4.984	3.2	-5.136	3.4	0.202	0.089	0.92	0.254
New Jersey	0.640	18.6	0.641	0.7	-3.397	3.6	0.405	0.062	0.44	0.477
New Mexico	0.275	10.7	1.076	1.7	-2.010	3.0	0.188	0.033	1.06	0.213
New York	0.534	13.8	1.432	1.4	-3.633	3.6	0.321	0.061	0.43	0.396
North Carolina	**0.222**	**8.4**	**3.278**	**5.2**	**-2.326**	**3.7**	**0.386**	**0.044**	**0.93**	**0.271**
North Dakota	0.213	4.4	1.732	0.9	0.586	0.3	0.050	0.060	0.35	0.308
Ohio	0.244	13.2	2.778	5.9	-2.580	5.6	0.463	0.037	0.92	0.258
Oklahoma	0.267	8.8	1.289	1.5	-2.333	2.8	0.138	0.049	0.92	0.215
Oregon	0.459	15.0	1.058	1.5	-2.369	3.5	0.266	0.046	0.77	0.369
Pennsylvania	0.480	16.5	2.645	3.0	-3.306	3.8	0.245	0.053	0.34	0.441
Rhode Island	0.665	16.2	-0.902	1.0	-1.755	1.9	0.261	0.081	0.48	0.510
South Carolina	**0.213**	**6.6**	**3.309**	**4.7**	**-2.745**	**3.9**	**0.338**	**0.048**	**1.51**	**0.247**
South Dakota	0.191	6.1	2.342	1.5	-2.874	1.9	0.036	0.043	0.40	0.173

(continued)

128

Table 4A.1 (continued)

State	Constant	t	TUR	T	TURlag	T	Adj. R^2	Std. Err.	D.W.	Mean
Tennessee	0.367	15.9	2.169	3.3	−3.414	5.3	0.427	0.045	1.20	0.296
Texas	0.105	5.0	2.287	3.6	−1.046	1.6	0.295	0.031	0.64	0.175
Utah	0.164	5.4	2.367	2.7	−0.719	0.8	0.204	0.047	0.47	0.247
Vermont	0.484	22.6	1.320	1.8	−2.226	3.0	0.184	0.040	0.86	0.441
Virginia	0.152	5.1	2.875	2.6	−2.275	2.0	0.103	0.048	0.53	0.178
Washington	0.440	11.7	1.768	2.2	−2.655	3.2	0.186	0.058	0.57	0.377
West Virginia	0.336	12.5	1.495	2.3	−2.240	3.4	0.229	0.055	0.35	0.273
Wisconsin	0.482	14.2	1.509	1.4	−3.035	2.8	0.179	0.067	0.42	0.405
Wyoming	0.180	5.2	4.940	4.1	−3.445	2.8	0.285	0.060	0.53	0.250
U.S. average	0.344	12.1	1.967	2.6	−2.452	3.1	0.245	0.051	0.80	0.313

The regressions generally have low Durbin Watson statistics, indicating a high degree of positive serial correlation in the residuals. The final column shows the mean WKTU ratio for each state. The average recipiency rate was 0.313, but it varied widely across the 51 programs. Eight means exceed 0.400, and five fall below 0.200.

Appendix Note

1. State level estimates of unemployment rates are incomplete from 1967 to 1975, particularly for 1967 to 1969. Estimates have more complete geographic coverage starting in 1970. For years prior to 1976, there are divisional estimates of unemployment, and these have been used to construct state-level estimates for states where there are no BLS estimates.

Chapter 5

Unemployment Insurance Reform

Evidence-Based Policy Recommendations

Christopher J. O'Leary
W.E. Upjohn Institute for Employment Research

Stephen A. Wandner
*W.E. Upjohn Institute for Employment Research
and The Urban Institute*

The federal-state unemployment insurance (UI) system was established under provisions in the Social Security Act of 1935. The last set of comprehensive system reforms addressing both benefits and financing was enacted in 1976. The labor market has undergone dramatic changes in the intervening 40 years, and the UI system has not kept pace. There have been major declines in the shares of total employment in manufacturing, union members in the labor force, and full-time work as a share of all work, while there have been large increases in employment in the services, occupational licensing, and part-time and temporary work. Some federal UI statutory provisions that worked in an earlier time have not aged well. This chapter reviews UI policy reforms suggested by research evidence in the context of current labor market conditions. We examine the adequacy of benefit amounts, durations, and access for experienced workers who become unemployed through no fault of their own. We also consider the sufficiency of funding rules to support adequate income replacement. In this context, it must be noted that the federal UI taxable wage base has not been increased from $7,000 since 1983, and tax rates have eroded with the declining effectiveness of the experience-rated tax rate system. This chapter takes a fresh look at the UI research and policy issues covered in our earlier work, *Unemployment Insurance in the United States: Analysis of Policy Issues* (O'Leary and Wandner 1997).

The chapter starts with a research-informed review of policy issues, followed by a presentation of a comprehensive package of suggested UI reforms. Our core proposals aim to renew the social insurance principles upon which the UI system was based, programmatic incentives, and the financing structure underpinning UI so that it can serve workers and employers over the long term. We also recommend updating the program to accommodate the realities facing American workers in twenty-first century labor markets. An essential element of assuring long-term stability of the system involves balancing UI benefits and taxes over time, while also establishing a countercyclical financing structure based on forward funding. Our recommendations reflect the principle of shared responsibilities of all partners in the system. In particular, we address benefit eligibility, regular and extended benefits, benefit financing, administrative financing, reemployment services, and employment incentives.

On the benefit payment side, adequate benefits should be paid to eligible workers who are unemployed through no fault of their own. Eligibility should be offered to bona fide labor force members involuntarily separated from work, who are engaged in an active search for reemployment. Benefits levels should provide socially adequate income replacement that does not introduce excessive disincentives for reemployment. Benefit durations should accommodate an energetic and exhaustive search for new work with sufficient reemployment supports.

Sufficient benefit standards will increase costs for regular UI benefits in some states. As a balance, we propose that the federal government should partially offset increased state costs by taking full responsibility for financing an improved permanent Extended Benefit (EB) program. Reflecting the increased risk of long-term unemployment in the U.S. economy today, experience-rated employer financing should be limited to the regular benefit program, with the Federal

Unemployment Tax Act (FUTA) levy covering the full cost of EB during high unemployment periods. It is appropriate that any future temporary emergency unemployment compensation continue to be funded from federal general revenues. We also discuss effective mechanisms for improved experience rating and forward funding of benefits together with a strengthened emphasis on reemployment of beneficiaries. We restrict the scope of our recommendations to the UI program and its extensions and do not consider any means-tested unemployment assistance programs of the type recently proposed (e.g., West et al. 2016).

BENEFIT PAYMENTS

Federal UI law leaves it to the states to make their own statutory determination about eligibility, benefit levels, and duration of the basic "regular UI" program. Federal law is mostly silent about benefit provisions. The federal government occasionally has responded, however, to perceived misuse of state UI programs, placing restrictions on benefit receipt by groups, such as professional athletes, school employees, and individuals collecting pensions.

Eligibility

Monetary eligibility requirements are relatively modest in most states for experienced workers who work full time and full year. UI claimants generally have to have had minimum earnings in their "base period"—the first four of the last five completed calendar quarters—before they became unemployed and have had earnings in more than one quarter. Prior earnings by UI applicants are considered evidence of labor force attachment, as well as an indication that tax contributions have been made to the system by prior employers to finance the benefit system. Most states consider only prior earnings for eligibility, but some states also consider prior hours worked. An eligibility rule based on earnings is easiest to apply. Most states have a high quarter earnings requirement and an earnings dispersion requirement. That is, at least one quarter in the base period must have earnings above a minimum level, and a sufficient amount of earnings must be outside the high earnings calendar quarter. Some states require no more than about $1,000 in the high quarter of the base period and at least $500 in the second highest quarter.

Monetary eligibility is harder to achieve by workers who are recent entrants to the labor force or who are low-wage or part-time workers. Recent entrants to the labor force may not have sufficient wages to qualify for UI because their base period lags, and they would qualify only if their most recent earnings were used to determine if they are monetarily eligible. A number of individual states dealt with this issue by introducing an alternate base period (ABP), which uses all earnings in the four most recently completed calendar quarters.

As participation in the labor force has changed over time, more people work part time. States have generally required unemployed workers to search for full-time work to qualify for UI. This restriction particularly affects older workers.

In February 2009, Congress enacted the American Recovery and Reemployment Act (ARRA) that included UI Modernization provisions that provided states with financial incentives to change provisions of their state UI laws in ways that would increase participation in the UI program. A $7 billion incentive fund was established, with each state's grant amount set in proportion to the state share of national unemployment. States were paid one-third of their allocation for having an ABP for monetary determination of UI eligibility that includes the most recently completed calendar quarter. States were paid the remaining two-thirds of their allocation for having two of the following four additional program features: 1) UI eligibility while seeking only part-time work, 2) UI eligibility after job separations due to harassment or compelling family reasons, 3) continuation of UI benefits for at least 26 additional weeks after exhaustion of regular benefits while in approved training, and 4) dependents' allowances of at least $15 per dependent up to $50 (O'Leary 2011).

The UI Modernization effort was successful at more than doubling the number of states with ABPs from 19 to 41 and increasing the number of states adopting part-time work provisions from 6 to 28. Because states did not commit to permanently maintaining their UI Modernization provisions, one state later rescinded its ABP provision, and two states removed their part-time work provisions (Table 5.1).

Nonmonetary eligibility conditions cover both job separation and continuing eligibility. Rules require that the job separation must be involuntary, that is, not resulting from a voluntary quit, discharge for misconduct, or other causes justifiable by an employer. A notable exception has been earlier state legislation and a federal option for states in the UI Modernization incentives section of the ARRA of 2009. That exception resulted in a total of 21 states permitting initial nonmonetary eligibility when leaving a job for compelling family reasons.[1] For benefit eligibility to continue for each weekly claim, the UI claimant must be able, available, and actively seeking fulltime work. Furthermore, to satisfy both the initial and continuing non-monetary eligibility rules, beneficiaries may not refuse an offer of suitable work, including any bona fide job offer resulting from an Employment Service (ES) job referral.

Table 5.1 Unemployment Insurance Modernization: States with Provisions before and after ARRA

UI Modernization provisions	Number of states with provisions before ARRA	Number of states with provisions as of 7/1/2016
Alternative base period	19	40
Part-time work	6	26
Compelling family reasons	0	20
Dependents allowance	4	6
Training extension	0	13

SOURCE: www.workforcesecurity.doleta.gov/unemploy/laws.asp#modern and updates from Suzanne Simonetta, USDOL, September 2016.

High levels of state UI borrowing during the double-dip recession in the early 1980s led to tightening of eligibility requirements, and a falling share of unemployed persons who were insured receiving UI benefits (Burtless 1983).[2] A common measure of UI recipiency is the ratio of the insured unemployment rate (IUR) to the total unemployment rate (TUR). Figure 5.1 shows that this ratio declined from around 60 percent prior to 1980 to about 40 percent through the most recent recession. Since then, the recipiency rate has fallen to about 30 percent nationwide, and several states now have recipiency rates far below 30 percent. A new dimension of the recent drop in recipiency results from reductions from the normal maximum potential duration of 26 weeks of regular UI benefits to shorter potential durations in eight states (see Chapter 4). Reasonable duration provisions are discussed below, but state eligibility rules and the fairness of their enforcement also are relevant.

State policy and procedures have a substantial effect on UI receipt. It is possible that new automated systems for accepting UI applications and for qualifying continued claims are depressing recipiency rates. In fact, the U.S. Department of Labor (USDOL), Civil Rights Center, filed an initial determination supporting Florida complainants suing the Department of Economic Opportunity for discrimination because of the imposition of access and language barriers to the successful filing of initial and continuing UI claims for benefits (USDOL 2013). The 2015 IUR/TUR ratio in Florida was 0.148, one of the lowest in the United States. Florida law requires Internet-only applications for benefits, its UI application call centers have been closed, and UI is no longer a required partner in local One-Stop employment centers.

In 1976, the federal government enacted retirement income offset provisions, two decades before the surge in labor force participation by older workers in the mid-1990s. The legislation reflected the expectation that older workers were likely to retire and would not really be looking for new employment. Today, however, older workers are the only U.S. demographic group with a continued increasing labor force participation rate, and public policymakers are looking for

Figure 5.1   Ratio of IUR to TUR (Recipiency Rate) in the United States and among Normal and Shorter Potential UI Duration States, 1947 to 2016

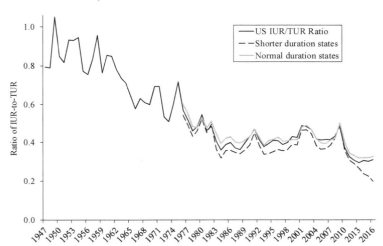

ways to continue this upward trend. Although states have discretion in applying the federal retirement offset provisions, they continue to work at cross purposes to the policy of encouraging older workers to stay in the labor force (Agbayani et al. 2016).

Suitable work provisions in state laws generally allow UI claimants to search for work in their customary occupation at their customary wage. With the increasing severity of worker dislocation and the upward trend in the duration of unemployment, however, the likelihood of returning to a customary occupation at the prior wage has been decreasing.

Recommendations

Eligibility provisions should encourage unemployed workers to remain in the labor force and increase future employment and earnings in the economy. Six recommendations are discussed below.

Initial eligibility. Initial eligibility requirements should require moderate earnings in more than one-quarter of UI claimants' benefit year. For example, some states require that earnings in the high quarter of the base period should be at least $1,000, and earnings in the second highest earning base period quarter must be at least $500.

Alternative base period. Applicants for UI must demonstrate attachment to the labor force by demonstrating monetary eligibility, that is, evidence of sufficient recent earnings. The standard base period (SBP) for determining UI monetary eligibility is the first four of the previous five calendar quarters completed before application for benefits. For UI applicants who are not eligible based on the SBP, all states should apply a more recent ABP, which should be the four most recently completed calendar quarters. The ABP broadens eligibility to include a group of UI applicants who have earned sufficient UI earnings but are excluded simply by the timing of their application. The UI Modernization provisions of the 2009 federal economic stimulus bill, the ARRA, provided financial incentives for states to adopt an ABP (Table 5.1; GAO 2007). The ABP has been estimated to have a relatively low cost, at about 1.2 percent of regular benefit payments (O'Leary 2011).

Part-time work provisions. All states should allow workers to collect UI while seeking part-time work if their base period earnings were from part-time work. Similar to the ABP, adoption of a part-time job search rule would broaden eligibility to a significant group of American workers who have earned entitlement through labor force participation and earnings. This provision is estimated to have a cost on par with that of the ABP, at about 1.2 percent of regular benefits (O'Leary 2011). It also should be noted that part-time workers often hold multiple jobs for which UI taxes may be payable on their full wage base for each job. As a result, it is possible that the tax contributions for these workers actually exceed those for full-time job holders with much higher wages and salaries. Without this reform, many part-time workers will continue to shoulder a disproportionate share of

UI benefit financing without enjoying the benefits of income security available through the program.

Retirement income offset. The UI benefit offset for retirement income should be repealed, given the great increase in the labor force participation rate of older workers. There should be no benefit reduction for receipt of payments from defined benefit pensions or for withdrawals from defined contribution pension accounts (e.g., 401k, 403b, IRA, Roth, and Keogh plans) for beneficiaries age 59.5 years or older, regardless of who made the original deposits to the defined contribution plan. UI applicants who have been involuntarily separated from their jobs through no fault of their own and are actively seeking return to work should not be denied benefits or have their benefit levels reduced because they are entitled to draw benefits from another source. Benefits from UI are an earned entitlement to be paid with regard to job separations, not a means-tested income transfer.

Suitable work. Refusal of suitable work requirements in state UI statutes should specify a schedule for the acceptable wage by which the adequate replacement rate of prior earnings declines as the duration of unemployment rises. Unemployment caused by involuntary separations from employers is beyond the control of the worker. Under UI benefit provisions, jobless workers are expected to seek return to alternate comparable employment as soon as possible. The wage rate on a particular job is normally determined by market forces in the occupation and individual factors associated with unique features associated with the employer, the job, and the workers. It is not unreasonable to expect full wage replacement at the start of job search, but it is important to recognize that unique skills associated with a particular employer or job may be worth less in new employment settings. It is reasonable to lower wage demands below prior earning levels after an initial period of search that yields no offers at the old wage rate, because of the loss in value of firm-specific skills. Prolonged unemployment could indicate a decline in job demand for the prior occupation. Naturally, vigorous in-person reemployment and job placement services should be available to all UI beneficiaries from the time they first apply for benefits. The possibility of job training, particularly in incremental job skills that are in demand, also should be available.

Nine states currently have nonmonetary eligibility rules that change the definition of suitable work during the benefit year.[3] For example, in Montana, suitable work after 13 weeks of benefit receipt is a job that pays 75 percent of the prior wage. Of course, no unreasonably low wage levels are acceptable under any circumstances, but the realities of the job market should inform reemployment efforts.

Employment service staffing levels. An active work search is expected of all UI beneficiaries, and efforts should be undertaken by the state agency to ensure this is the case. These include conducting the UI work test, the Worker Profiling and Reemployment Services (WPRS) system procedures, and eligibility review procedures (ERPs) or reemployment and eligibility assessments (REAs). Based on past experimental evaluations, there are a combination of eligibility review procedures and reemployment services that should be used, for example, as under the recently implemented Reemployment Services and Eligibility Assessment (RESEA) program. Key to undertaking these efforts is a vital and active public ES funded through the Wagner-Peyser Act by the FUTA tax.

Improved job search technologies are available through the Internet, but economies gained through these systems have not replaced the professional human resources lost by ES since the 1980s. A fully competent and professionally staffed ES is essential to providing effective reemployment services for all UI recipients, yet total staffing levels in ES service delivery has declined steadily over the past 30 years. One reflection of the decline in the availability of ES services is the decline in the number of local offices in which reemployment services are provided. As of May 2018, there were 1,478 full service One-Stop centers and 973 affiliate offices.[4] ES should be a full partner in every One-Stop center with staffing of at least four full-time persons.

Funding for ES staffing should be restored to the real 1984 level. Funding was $740 million in 1984 and has fallen to only $644 million in 2016—or about 45 percent of the 1984 level in real terms. To reach full ES funding, the budget should have been $1.5 billion in 2017 or $856 million above the 2016 level (see Chapter 3 by Balducchi and O'Leary). Since ES is funded through Wagner-Peyser by the FUTA tax, reform of the FUTA wage base would support improved ES funding. The UI program should be restored as an on-site partner in One-Stop centers, with ES administering an active UI work test and UI eligibility assessments. Furthermore, every state should have a central office administrative unit with at least 10 full-time staff for program administration, including program management and program evaluation. This central office unit would support a number of functions, including monitoring work-test enforcement, supporting reemployment services, and WPRS development and management. To support these and other uses of FUTA tax revenue, the FUTA wage base and tax rate should be sufficient to accommodate ongoing financing of both 15,000 ES staff and UI administration.

Regular Benefits: Levels and Durations

The setting of both levels and durations of UI benefits has been affected by the fact that UI beneficiaries respond in their labor supply behavior to the availability, level, and duration of UI benefits. Economists have made several efforts to measure the size of these "disincentive effects."

Public policy to change the UI program benefit structure should take disincentive effects into consideration. Decker notes, however, that even though researchers have found UI work disincentive effects, they have not reached consensus on the size and importance of these effects (Decker 1997, pp. 295–298). Woodbury and Rubin (1997, pp. 272–273) have a more definitive assessment in their review of the literature. They note that research on benefit adequacy and consumption smoothing suggests that UI recipients are overcompensated in the short run and undercompensated in the long run, pointing toward variable replacement rates as a possible improvement in the system. They also report on evidence that shows increasing the potential duration of UI benefits by one-week results in an increase in unemployment benefit duration of one day or less, and that this small response suggests that the average UI recipient is not abusing the system.

Benefit levels

The U.S. UI system is based on a consensus that the program should replace approximately one-half of lost wages. This level was not determined empirically. Rather, it was set low enough to encourage workers to search for work quickly and by taking into consideration that unemployed workers would not have expenses that they would incur when they were working. Nonetheless, USDOL sponsored a number of benefit adequacy studies in the 1950s. Early analysis of benefit adequacy revealed that benefits would be adequate if they equaled half or more of wages, prevented "too much" hardship, kept beneficiaries from collecting welfare benefits, and would cover "non-deferrable expenditures" (Haber and Murray 1966).

More recently, economists have tried to determine how benefit rules for the UI program should be structured. One line of inquiry has aimed to determine the optimal level of benefits to balance program goals for income replacement against work disincentives. Economists have agreed that UI benefits should replace considerably less than all lost income, because of work disincentives and the fact that added leisure time is valuable. However, there still is no agreement on the optimum wage replacement rate. Estimates have ranged from 20 to 65 percent, with rates depending on assumptions about adequate levels of precautionary savings and forced borrowing by workers (Nicholson and Needels 2006, pp. 55–58).

Practical considerations require that there be a maximum benefit level governed by social adequacy considerations. High wage workers (e.g., earning $5,000 a week) are not going to get weekly benefit amounts of $2,500. States set the maximum benefit amount either as a fixed amount that must be adjusted periodically by the state legislature or an amount that automatically increases over time, generally tied to the state average weekly wage (AWW) in UI-covered employment. The federal Advisory Council on Unemployment Compensation recommended a benefit standard such that the maximum benefit level would be indexed to two-thirds of a state's average weekly wage in UI-covered employment (ACUC 1996, p. 242). No such standard has been enacted, and most states would not meet the proposed standard.

Duration of benefits

When states first paid UI benefits under the Social Security Act in 1938, weekly benefit amounts were small, and durations were short because the program was new and actuarial estimates were uncertain as the Great Depression continued.

Fortunately, the actuarial estimates of the mid-1930s were overly pessimistic. The potential entitled duration of UI increased steadily among states from the program origins in the 1930s through the late 1950s (O'Leary 2013). After World War II, states found that they could afford to pay more benefits, and by the mid-1970s, an "American consensus" had emerged (O'Leary and Wandner 1997). All states paid at least 26 weeks of regular UI benefits to experienced workers who were unemployed through no fault of their own. Eligibility conditions varied by state, but states paid UI in the amount of approximately half of a worker's prior wage up to a maximum benefit amount to workers who were actively seeking reemployment. Benefit payment provision generosity varied by state and by region.

By 2010, all states had provided potential UI durations of at least 26 weeks for more than 50 years.[5] In response to the Great Recession, starting in December 2010, however, the American consensus broke down. A substantial minority of states have raised eligibility standards and lowered potential durations to less than 26 weeks. The eight states that cut maximum potential durations were primarily motivated by the heavy levels of UI debt that they had incurred during the Great Recession.[6] The new state legislation was designed to cut future UI costs, not because there was agreement that paying benefits for a shorter duration would be sufficient for workers to search for and find employment.

During normal economic conditions, most transitions to new jobs, after involuntary job loss, occur within 13 weeks, and almost all transitions happen within 26 weeks. The high exhaustion rates of UI benefit entitlements during and after the long and deep Great Recession led to historically high average durations of benefit receipt and caused massive state borrowing to pay regular UI benefits. Thirty-six of 53 state UI programs needed loans to pay regular UI benefits during the Great Recession. At the end of 2010, the system was $29 billion in debt. The federal unemployment trust fund reached a modest $2 billion net surplus at the end of 2013, but as of January 2016, 10 states still had outstanding private market loans or bond debts, declining to 5 states by January 2018.[7] The eight states that cut potential durations improved their reserve positions faster than they otherwise would have, but the reductions in potential durations in these states have eroded the fundamental intent of UI to provide temporary partial wage replacement to involuntarily unemployed workers. The shorter limits on potential durations could curtail productive job search and result in inferior job matches, resulting in lower productivity and states failing to fully benefit from the talents of their citizens.

Recommendations

Benefit levels. Consistent with earlier proposals for benefit level standards, states should pay benefits that replace 50 percent of lost wages up to a maximum set at two-thirds of the state AWW in UI-covered employment. Having a maximum of two-thirds of the AWW will ensure that approximately 80 percent of beneficiaries will receive at least one-half wage replacement while receiving regular UI benefits. This standard was most recently endorsed by the Advisory Council on Unemployment Compensation (1996). However, no standard for the weekly benefit amount has ever been set in federal statute as a state conformity requirement (Blaustein 1993, pp. 211–212, p. 241).

Several strands of research support the 50 percent wage replacement standard as the proper balance of adequate wage replacement while avoiding excessive work disincentives. For example, literature on household expenditures, consumption smoothing, optimal UI, compensating wage differentials, and consumer choice theory all support 50 percent wage replacement (O'Leary 1998, pp. 65–75).[8]

Duration. States should provide adequate regular weekly UI benefit payments for at least 26 weeks through employer financing. Eligibility provisions should accommodate modern workforce patterns including increased part-time work and sharply increased rates of labor force participation by older workers. Benefit provisions also should accommodate labor market realities, particularly for persons in part-time, low wage, and low skill jobs.

Permanent Extended Benefits and Temporary Emergency Compensation

The basic 26-week regular UI program can be considered adequate in periods of low unemployment. Starting in the 1950s, however, Congress found regular UI to be inadequate when unemployment rises and more workers exhaust their entitlement benefits. Congress reacted in 1958 and 1961 by enacting emergency EB programs to fill a temporary need for additional UI benefits during a recession. In 1970, Congress enacted a permanent EB program designed to eliminate the need for temporary extensions. The EB program set triggers for payments based on the level of unemployment, and the benefits were equally financed by the state and federal governments. Unfortunately, the EB program has not actively functioned as originally intended for the past 40 years.

Originally, the EB program was a good example of federal-state cooperation.[9] However, for many years, because of low UI recipiency rates, the triggers based on insured unemployment rarely activated EB as total unemployment rose (Nicholson and Needels 2006). Under the original 1970 law, EB could be activated by a national trigger affecting all states or a state-level trigger affecting EB only in that particular state. In the early 1980s, cost-cutting federal legislation eliminated the national trigger, and the state trigger threshold was raised from 4.0 to 5.0 percent insured unemployment rate (Woodbury and Rubin 1997). Additionally, increasing eligibility requirements in some states resulted in low UI recipiency rates and low IURs that failed to trigger EB even when the TUR had risen quite high (Blank and Card 1991). In response to this failure in more than a few states during the early 1990s recession, Congress enacted legislation in July 1992 allowing states to adopt an alternative trigger based on TUR as estimated by the Current Population Survey.

In the 1990s and 2000s, emergency federal UI extensions were structured to be paid before any EB that might be available. The ARRA of 2009 provided temporary 100 percent federal reimbursement of EB payments for states that adopted alternative EB triggers based on the TUR. The 100 percent EB payment was continued through December 31, 2013, in states with conforming TUR triggers. During the Great Recession, EB became effective in all states that adopted TUR triggers, but a survey of states revealed that almost all TUR adopters said they would return to IUR triggers after the 100 percent federal funding ended (Mastri et al. 2016).

Despite the fact that EB is a permanent program with a statutory basis, Congress has enacted additional emergency programs in response to all six economic recessions since 1971. These discretionary emergency extensions were similar to Congressional actions in 1958 and 1961 and were preferred by states over EB, because all were fully federally funded. Both the EB and the emergency extensions lengthened the potential duration of benefits, but until 2009 the total was never greater than 72 weeks and was frequently not greater than 52 weeks.

Just as the Great Recession was unprecedented in it severity, the extension durations also were unprecedented. During the Great Recession, the combination of the three UI programs yielded a maximum potential duration of benefits that reached 99 weeks in some states from early 2009 through late 2012 (USDOL n. d.).

Research

Research evidence suggests that the EB system should be revised. IUR triggers operated effectively for a brief period in the early 1970s, but given the low UI recipiency rates nationwide, IUR triggers are no longer responsive to surges in unemployment. Even though Congress enacted an optional TUR trigger, not all states have adopted or retained it because states pay for half the EB costs, thus increasing state UI expenditures.

Because maximum potential UI durations were raised to as high as 99 weeks during and after the Great Recession, some policy analysts and politicians have raised old concerns about the moral hazard effect of UI benefits unnecessarily prolonging unemployment (Decker 1997). That is, UI benefits act as a disincentive to return to work. Although good estimates of the magnitude of this effect have been known for many years, concern about it was magnified by the unprecedented increase in the potential duration of UI benefits during the Great Recession.

Estimates of the labor supply disincentive effects suggest that reduced job search efforts by UI recipients may have contributed to an increase in the unemployment rate.[10] The estimated effects of the UI expansions on the unemployment rate, however, are somewhat modest, ranging from 0.3 percentage point of the 5.5 percentage-point recessionary increase in the unemployment rate (Rothstein 2012) to approximately 1 percentage point (Mazumder 2011). Another study (Elsby, Hobijn, and Sahin 2010) essentially split the difference, suggesting that the 2008 emergency unemployment benefits program increased the unemployment rate by approximately 0.7 percentage point.

It is important to distinguish between UI's effect on the unemployment rate and its effects on unemployment and economic activity.

For example, part of the rise in the unemployment rate is caused by the increased labor force participation of UI recipients. Without UI benefits, some jobless workers would have stopped looking for work and thus would not have been counted as unemployed. Katz (2010) cites a number of positive offsetting impacts of the UI program, including consumption smoothing effects for unemployed workers, spillover effects of shorter spells of unemployment for workers not receiving UI benefits, the macroeconomic stimulation of the economy from expenditures made with UI benefits, and long-term positive impacts of UI by keeping workers in the labor force rather than encouraging them to leave.

The UI program had a significant macroeconomic effect on the U.S. economy during the Great Recession. The increase in UI benefit payments during the recession represented a significant portion of the economic stimulus provided by the ARRA and other UI extensions. The Congressional Budget Office (2012) estimated that each dollar spent on extended UI benefits generated $1.90 in increased economic activity. Burtless and Gordon (2011) state that UI is a particularly effective form of targeting economic stimulus funds for both equity and practical reasons. The equity argument is that unemployed workers suffer the biggest income loss, while the practical argument relates to effectiveness, since these individuals are more likely to spend and spend quickly. Burtless and Gordon also point out that even though potential UI benefit durations reached unprecedented levels during the recession, the United States normally is at the bottom of the list of industrial nations with respect to UI duration. Even at 99 weeks, the U.S. potential duration was approximately equal to that of Spain, Portugal, Norway, Finland, and France, and below Australia, New Zealand, and Belgium.

Recommendations

During the Great Recession, the federal government agreed to pay the full cost of EB initiated and ended by a TUR trigger. This practice should be a permanent feature of the federal-state UI system, but it should be conditional upon states providing adequate amounts and durations of regular UI benefits. Making the federal partner permanently responsible for the cost of EB should establish a quid pro quo with the states responsible for paying the full cost of up to 26 weeks of regular UI benefits, that is, enacting federal UI benefit standards.[11] The EB program would then be fully funded by the federal share of revenues from the FUTA tax. The EB program is currently 50 percent financed by states, with the federal partner paying the other half with revenues from the federal share of FUTA taxes. The result of changing the EB program in this manner would be the provision of more adequate UI benefits in good and bad economic times, without unduly burdening state financial resources.

Permanent EB, with federal financing from FUTA, should provide benefits of up to an additional 52 weeks to provide adequate benefits during periods of high unemployment. The maximum available duration should vary, depending on the severity of unemployment in a state. Under the current formula for a state to be EB eligible, there is both an IUR trigger level and a duration stipulation requiring unemployment to be at least 120 percent of the level 12 months earlier, with an optional TUR trigger that has not been adopted by many states. Future state triggers should be based on a state's TUR because the IUR triggers have proven ineffective. Under the 2009 ARRA, states had the option to switch from an IUR to a TUR trigger. We propose a simple TUR trigger with the following schedule of EB durations:

- 7 weeks EB are available when TUR reaches 6.5 percent,
- 13 weeks EB are available when TUR reaches 7 percent,
- 26 weeks EB are available when TUR reaches 8 percent,
- 39 weeks EB are available when TUR reaches 9 percent, and
- 52 weeks EB are available when TUR reaches 10 percent.

States that have objected to a TUR trigger in the past when they have paid part of EB costs should have no objections to such a trigger mechanism once the costs are fully federally financed.

Naturally, the creation of an improved EB program would not inhibit the right of Congress and the President to provide emergency extended unemployment compensation in times of severe labor market surplus. However, in times of normal labor markets, 26 weeks of regular UI benefits, when accompanied by vigorous provision of ES reemployment services, will accommodate successful job search by the majority of UI beneficiaries. In times of high unemployment, the EB program will support extended job search, with the length of support increasing with the severity of labor market conditions. Finally, when economic conditions are extremely severe and widespread, Congress and the President may act on an emergency basis to supplement the regular and EB programs. This approach would provide more timely provision of adequate durations of UI benefits when recessions occur, since the current system depends on Congressional action that often lags behind the deterioration of economic conditions.

BENEFIT FINANCING

Most economic research on UI financing has concerned the effect of experience-rated UI tax rates on employment stability. Woodbury (2014) summarized research results that suggest experience rating encourages employment stability when tax rates are responsive to benefit charges. However, the evidence indicates that employers at tax rate maximums are not induced to avoid layoffs and instead have their benefit costs subsidized by employers with stable employment. Experience rating in setting UI tax rates is a feature unique to the American UI system; it was essential in establishing the system and is unlikely to be eliminated, but it can be improved. A more pressing issue in UI finance is the failure of the system to adequately forward fund benefit reserves in anticipation of recessions. This failure has compromised the fundamental mission of the system to provide adequate income replacement to the involuntarily unemployed.

The original intent of the UI financing provisions in the Social Security Act and FUTA was that state UI programs should be self-financing in good times and bad. States were to forward fund benefits by generating positive net system revenues in times of economic expansion to provide sufficient reserves for paying benefits in years of high unemployment. Forward funding is countercyclical, while the alternative of raising taxes to pay for benefits in the depth of a recession is pro-cyclical, driving the economy into a lower level of economic activity.

Each state was expected to have a range of tax schedules from which they could select each year, depending on the reserve balance in the state unemployment trust fund account. A higher tax schedule would be selected in years when system reserves were low relative to expected future needs. By experience rating, the tax rates in each schedule were to vary directly with each employer's UI benefit charge experience—usually measured by either a reserve history ratio to payrolls or a benefit charge ratio to payrolls. The UI taxable wage bases (TWBs) in states and for the FUTA were to be sufficient to raise adequate resources for the states and federal UI accounts. Many of these expectations are currently not being met by existing state UI tax systems because of policy decisions at both the state and federal levels that affect both the TWB and the structure and application of tax rate schedule alternatives.

Reserves generated by the FUTA tax are kept in federal Unemployment Trust Fund (UTF) accounts at the U.S. Treasury to pay for state and federal UI program administration, loans to states that become insolvent paying regular benefits, extended benefits, and employment services through the Wagner-Peyser program. The FUTA tax rate is applied to the federal UI TWB to fund the federal unemployment accounts. The FUTA tax base is also the minimum TWB that states can set to pay for regular state UI benefits. The UI TWB was originally set at the same level as that for the Social Security TWB for public pensions. The Social Security TWB became indexed in 1972 and has increased steadily to $128,400 in 2018, or about 18 times the size of the FUTA TWB, which is not indexed and has only increased three times, with the last increase effective in 1983. At only $7,000, the FUTA TWB is less than half the annualized federal minimum wage, essentially making it a flat tax per employee. It is inadequate to generate sufficient revenues for federal and state use. States can set their TWB at any level at or above $7,000. Most states keep their tax bases relatively low—more than half have TWBs of less than double the FUTA level. Those with tax bases of more than double the FUTA level are much more likely to avoid debt problems in periods of high unemployment (Vroman 2016).

Low TWBs also might depress hiring in the low wage labor markets. In many states, employers face the same UI tax bill for one worker paid $10,000 in a year and another paid $90,000 in that same year. Whereas the latter might provide a living wage, the former worker might be a multiple job holder earning $10,000 at each of two jobs. Each employer pays UI taxes on the full TWB every year, and that amount is paid multiple times on behalf of multiple job holders.[12] This discourages adding low-wage workers against the alternative of expanding hours for higher wage workers.

Having adequate levels of UI reserves to weather recessions depends upon raising enough revenue over the business cycle. States have multiple tax schedules, and state laws usually specify movement to a higher tax schedule that raises more revenue when state reserve balances are low. However, state legislatures often override their UI statutes and do not allow higher schedules to go into effect because of employer resistance to higher UI taxes. In addition, some states have tax schedules with an insufficient range in rates to sufficiently translate employer unemployment experience into tax rates that adequately distinguish experience. There are no federal requirements on the range of rates other than the residual statutory FUTA range from 0.0 to 5.4 percent. Since the FUTA maximum is 6.0 percent with a 90 percent reduction to employers in states with conforming UI systems, the FUTA tax is 0.6 percent and the lowest allowable state maximum rate is the difference, or 5.4 percent applied to a state tax base of at least $7,000. Furthermore, some states have a small number of tax rates in their schedules and often include a zero rate, with many employers assigned the zero rate. The most extreme case is for states to have only two rates—a zero rate and a 5.4 percent rate, with large numbers of employers assessed the zero rate. In practice, such a system is not truly experience-rated because the tax rate is unresponsive to benefit charges over large ranges.

To achieve adequate forward funding, the Advisory Council on Unemployment Compensation found that state accounts in the federal UTF should maintain balances "sufficient to pay at least one year of unemployment insurance benefits at levels comparable to its previous high cost" (ACUC 1996, p. 11). In 2010, this rule was established as a federal requirement for interest-free loans from the loan account in FUTA. The rule requires states to hold one year of reserves in the UTF based on the average of the three highest-cost rates experienced in the prior 20 years. This rate is known as the average high-cost rate (AHCR). The rule becomes fully effective in 2019; in 2014, it started to be phased in at a target rate of 50 percent of the AHCR, and it increases 10 percentage points each year until it will reach the AHCR in 2019.[13]

Recommendations

- State UI tax rate schedules should be sufficient to provide forward funding of reserves so that ongoing benefit charges can be paid while building reserves for future periods of high unemployment. Regular UI benefits must be financed by a tax system with rates that vary directly with an employer's layoff experience. The degree of experience rating must be more than nominal, such that each tax schedule has a substantial number of rates—we recommend at least 10 rates in each schedule that vary from the maximum to the minimum by uniform amounts. The minimum should be a small positive value to maintain employer involvement in the system (such as 0.1 percent). Avoiding a zero minimum will help maintain a broad tax base for funding UI benefit payments. The maximum can remain at 5.4 percent, provided that the TWB levels are sufficient.

- As average weekly earnings or average annual wages (AAW) increase over time, UI benefits and taxes should increase in tandem to maintain long-term balance between system inflows and outflows. A key to financing is the definition of the TWB. With the weekly benefit amount (WBA) and maximum WBA definitions based on average wages in UI-covered employment, the TWB must be linked to the AAW in UI-covered employment to create a balanced system. A formula that has proven reliable is for the TWB to be two-thirds of the AAW in the prior year.[14] Vroman (2016) reports that 19 states currently index the TWB, and he finds that an indexed TWB is essential for balance in financing if the maximum WBA is also indexed to the AAW.

- An adequate FUTA TWB should be set at 26 times the national AWW in UI-covered employment. Alternatively, the TWB could be pegged at 33 percent of the Social Security TWB. This would index the UI wage base to change in step with the Social Security base and ensure that FUTA revenues increase in step with aggregate earnings, while setting the UI TWB at a modest but adequate level.

A TWB that is too low sets up a tax that is essentially a flat per-capita amount that creates all the inequities associated with a regressive tax system. The current excessively low TWB (the first $7,000 of each worker's annual earnings) falls more heavily on employers of low wage workers for whom the UI tax is often a significantly larger proportion of the wage bill. FUTA revenues must be sufficient to support UI administration, the permanent EB program, necessary loans to states, and administration of a well-staffed and effective ES to enforce the work test and promote reemployment of UI beneficiaries and other ES-registered job seekers.

- Financial incentives should be created to encourage forward funding of benefits. This goal can be encouraged by paying graduated interest rates on trust fund balances. That is, higher rates of interest would be paid to state accounts with higher reserve balances. At the same time, the rates of interest charges to states that must borrow to pay benefits should be closer to the private sector alternatives many states have used recently. Under no circumstances should the federal interest charges exceed market rates for short-term U.S. Treasury debt.

- To address the exemption of government and nonprofit employers from FUTA taxation, a 3 percent premium should be assessed on reimbursements of benefit charges to state and local government employers and nonprofit firms that choose to operate as reimbursing employers. This FUTA payment would contribute to financing UI administrative costs and ES reemployment services available to job seekers formerly employed by those employers.

- Maintaining a UI system that pays adequate benefits to experienced workers who become unemployed through no fault of their own has met resistance both at the state and federal levels from employers who directly pay the full cost of UI taxes. This resistance is not likely to fade in the future. However, economic studies show that the UI tax burden also falls indirectly on workers, and public finance studies have shown that employees directly pay a considerable amount for UI coverage (Anderson and Meyer 2006).

We suggest that half or more of the UI payroll taxes to finance benefits be directly paid by employees. Workers paying tax contributions would be in a much stronger position to advocate for UI benefits with adequate amounts and durations. Employee contributions would improve benefit financing by broadening the tax base. Furthermore, benefit recipiency would most likely be higher with employee UI taxes, as has been the experience in other countries (Card and Riddell

1993). Even a low tax rate for workers would increase tax revenues because average UI tax rates on employers are also low—less than two-thirds of one percent (USDOL 2016).

ADMINISTRATIVE FINANCING

The administration of the UI, ES, and other federal-state labor market programs is funded by the FUTA tax. Administrative funding is divided among three accounts: Employment Security Administrative Account (ESAA), Extended Unemployment Compensation Account (EUCA), and Federal Unemployment Account (FUA). ESSA funds UI and ES administrative costs and the cost of some labor market information programs. USDOL provides these funds to the states based on Congressional approval of a formula involving state employment and unemployment data. In recent years, the ESAA has received 80 percent of FUTA funds. Of the other accounts, EUCA normally pays for half of the costs of the permanent EB program. FUA is the loan account from which states can borrow if their state UI trust fund accounts are insufficient to pay regular state UI benefits.

States have had severe problems in the administration of their UI, ES, and related labor market programs. Funding has been inadequate for UI computer systems automation and staffing of ES service delivery, and this problem has become more severe over time. The balances in the accounts have been inadequate. Moreover, Congress has appropriated a declining percentage of the tax revenues that are deposited into the ESAA. These low appropriations from the federal unemployment accounts to the states have been a long-term phenomenon.

At the beginning of the UI program, employer FUTA tax payments were recorded as general revenues of the U.S. government, and UI administrative expenses were paid for out of general revenues.[15] By the early 1950s, it was estimated that FUTA revenues exceeded appropriated UI administrative grants to states by between $500 million and $1 billion annually. The Employment Security Administrative Financing Act of 1954 requires that any excess amount of FUTA revenues over UI administrative grants to states be deposited into the UTF in FUA to make loans to states when their reserves were insufficient to pay UI benefits. This act, commonly known as the Reed Act, set a limit on the level of reserves in the loan account and provided that reserves above that ceiling level be distributed to states for payment of regular benefits, program administration, or ES delivery. Motivated by the desire to control annual deficits in the unified federal budget, Congress raised the Reed Act ceiling from 0.33 percent of total payrolls in UI-covered employment in 1982 to 1.02 percent of covered payrolls today. Consequently, the incentive supplied by the Reed Act for Congress to adequately appropriate money from the UTF for UI administration has diminished. Increased revenues from the FUTA tax and new rules for Congressional appropriation of funds to the states could improve UI administration and funding of ES reemployment services.

Recommendations

Although payment of UI benefits is an entitlement and does not require appropriations from Congress, payment of administrative funds to the state agencies for UI and Wagner-Peyser Act programs is discretionary and must be appropriated. UI administrative funding includes a formula for additional (contingency) funding when unemployment increases above anticipated levels, but the Wagner-Peyser Act program has been underfunded for decades, and reemployment services are no longer directly funded, including for mandated reemployment services provided under the WPRS initiative.

Unemployment Insurance administration

Congress should annually appropriate adequate funds for UI administration from the ESAA in the UTF. Beyond funding for benefit payment administration and tax collection, separate funding should be appropriated for integrity efforts, including benefit payment control and reemployment services and eligibility assessments. Although benefit payment control can pay for itself by collecting overpayments, the formal eligibility review and reemployment process—recently renamed Reemployment Services and Eligibility Assessments (RESEA)—can also pay for itself by helping to reduce the duration of UI compensated unemployment.

It is important that administrative funding be sufficient to support the UI administrative process, especially during periods of high unemployment. Consideration should be given to making UI administration funding an entitlement, so that it can rise and fall to support the UI program in periods of high and low unemployment. An automatic funding formula could be developed and distributed based on each state's share of FUTA contributions.

Employment Service administration

FUTA/ESAA should fully pay for the following Wagner-Peyser Act functions: 1) UI work test enforcement, 2) provision of labor exchange services to all ES applicants, and 3) provision of reemployment services for permanently separated UI claimants. Each of these functions is statutorily assigned to ES by the Wagner-Peyser Act. In addition, these functions have been evaluated and found to be cost effective (Jacobson et al. 2004).

Wagner-Peyser Act program funding under ESAA should be restored to a more robust level (e.g., the 1984 level in real terms) and then indexed to grow at the rate of the Social Security TWB (O'Leary and Eberts 2009).

Alternatively, given that the UI work test and the provision of reemployment services require mediated/in-person services, ESAA should provide funding for an adequate number of Wagner-Peyser positions, and then index funding to the Social Security TWB.

EMPLOYMENT AND REEMPLOYMENT SERVICES

Background

In its early history, the UI program focused heavily on temporary, cyclical unemployment. It mainly paid unemployment benefits until demand for workers picked up in the firms for which they had previously worked, and they were called back to their prior jobs. However, during the 1970s the incidence of permanent worker layoffs greatly increased, and that trend has continued and expanded. Permanent layoffs spread from blue collar jobs to white collar jobs and became a larger share of total unemployment. Temporary layoff rates have declined and become less sensitive to the business cycle (Groshen and Potter 2003). During the Great Recession, permanent layoffs reached an all-time high at more than 55 percent of the unemployed (O'Leary 2010). Current Population Survey data reveal an upward trend in unemployment duration, with more workers unemployed for 27 weeks or longer. The UI program burden increased as compensated durations and exhaustion rates increased, and UI beneficiaries correspondingly needed increased assistance in finding new jobs.

USDOL responded to the growing worker dislocation problem by conducting demonstration projects in the 1970s, 1980s, and early 1990s to test methods of assisting dislocated workers to return to work. Federal UI legislation responded to the growing worker dislocation problem in the early 1990s. Permanent work-sharing legislation was enacted in 1992, permitting states to establish work-sharing programs as part of their state UI laws. In 1993, similar permissive legislation was enacted allowing states to pay self-employment allowances in lieu of UI benefits for workers who work full time to establish a small business (Wandner 2010).

Worker Profiling and Reemployment Services

Most significantly, WPRS was enacted in 1993, requiring that all states establish early job search assistance referral programs for UI beneficiaries most likely to exhaust benefits as part of their state UI programs. States developed methods to target services to dislocated workers using WPRS models. They then began referring selected UI claimants to employment services that often included orientation to the job seeker resource room, job referral, assessment and counseling, job search workshops, and occasionally referral to job training or Self-Employment Assistance (SEA) programs. The WPRS system represents the formal recognition of the adverse effect of worker dislocation on UI claimants and the need to supplement referrals to jobs with a major initiative to train workers to search for their own jobs.

The UI, ES, and the public job training system adapted to these 1990s employment and reemployment provisions in federal and state UI laws.[16] At the national level, the Employment and Training Administration of USDOL provided extensive guidance to states about WPRS, developing a systems approach for state UI, ES, and Workforce Investment Act (WIA; now called the Workforce Innovation and Opportunities Act [WIOA]) programs to work together to provide reemployment and training services. The national UI program has provided model state legislation and continuing technical assistance regarding WPRS methods (Wandner 2010). Ongoing technical assistance and guidance was provided throughout the 1990s and has been renewed recently as part of the RESEA initiative. The ES and WIA provided early guidance for these innovations, but funding was not stable or sufficient to support increased reemployment rates.

Work sharing

The national UI program provided model state legislation and guidance for the 1982 temporary work-sharing program, but not for the 1992 permanent work-sharing program because of concerns about possible technical flaws in that legislation. A new round of technical assistance followed clarification of the rules and incentives for work sharing in the Middle Class Tax Relief and Job Creation Act of 2012. In a boost to labor demand similar to that of work sharing, model legislation and guidance were provided to states in 1994 to support establishment of state SEA programs (Wandner 2010).

UI, ES, and reemployment services

In the mid-1990s, the UI program updated its mission and function statement to take responsibility for supporting workers' efforts to return to work, as well as for properly paying UI benefits and collecting UI taxes. Similarly, the national ES program responded to the WPRS system's referral of UI claimants to Wagner-Peyser Act programs for the provision of reemployment services. Starting in the mid-1990s, state ES programs provided a substantial increase in the number of "reportable services" to UI recipients, assisting them to search for and find work (Wandner 2010).

As a result, both the UI and ES programs have become responsible for helping workers return to work, and both programs should continue to speed the return to work and raise reemployment rates. The WIA/WIOA Adult and Dislocated Worker programs participate in WPRS by receiving about one-third of their training referrals from workers receiving reemployment services in the WPRS system. Since UI claims taking has increasingly occurred outside the One-Stop career centers, state UI programs have little ability to directly provide UI eligibility reviews or referral to job openings or reemployment services. In response, ES has been providing most of these services.

Research and Recommendations

Reemployment Services and Eligibility Assessments (RESEA)

Research. Since the 1970s, many studies have shown the effectiveness of UI eligibility reviews, including the Charleston Claimant Placement and Work Experiment, the Washington State Alternative

Work Experiment, and the Maryland UI Work Search Demonstration (Corson, Long, and Nicholson 1985; Johnson and Klepinger 1991, 1994; Klepinger et al. 1998). The Charleston Experiment also found that providing reemployment services as well as eligibility reviews can further shorten durations of UI compensated unemployment.

The original UI eligibility review program (ERP) of the 1970s was allowed to wither until the early 2000s with the establishment of Reemployment and Eligibility Assessments (REAs). The REA initiative combines one-on-one in-person UI eligibility reviews, labor market information, and referral to reemployment services. A series of REA evaluations in four states found evidence that the REA programs were effective in reducing UI duration and generating savings for the UI Trust Fund (Benus et al. 2008; Poe-Yamagata et al. 2011). Because the Nevada program generated substantially larger impacts than the other study states' programs, the Nevada REA program study was extended to confirm those findings. The results confirmed the earlier results—the Nevada REA program was very effective in assisting claimants to exit the UI program sooner than they would have in the absence of the program (Michaelides et al. 2012). Based on these results, the study concluded that the combination of REA and reemployment services is a highly effective model for reducing UI duration and assisting UI claimants to return to productive employment.

In 2015, USDOL changed the name of the REA program to RESEA to make clear that reemployment services were expected to be provided as well as UI eligibility reviews. Based on positive results from the Nevada evaluation of REA, the Obama administration proposed significant increases in program funding as part of its FY 2017 budget request. An additional increase in RESEA funding was placed in the President's FY 2018 budget proposal (White House 2017). However, the proposed increase was at the expense of ES funding, which is a counterproductive plan because RESEA requires adequate ES staffing to be effective.

Recommendations. REAs should be established and monitored in all states. The eligibility review process is an essential component of the UI work test process, so it is critical to assure that the UI program operates as an insurance program, reducing concern about moral hazard that can occur in the absence of incentives to encourage UI claimants to actively search for work. ERPs also speed the return to work.

Eligibility reviews also should be conducted in conjunction with the provision of reemployment services for unemployed workers in need of these services. As a result, ERPs should be fully funded so they can be provided in person whenever possible, rather than through a voice response or computer claims process.

The RESEA program emphasizes the equal importance of reemployment services and eligibility assessments. Funding for RESEA, however, was to be through the UI program. The provision of reemployment services has been done by ES, and funding should be provided directly to ES for the WPRS initiative, which remains a part of federal law.

Worker Profiling and Reemployment Services (WPRS)

Research. While there have been a number of studies of the effectiveness of reemployment services since the 1970s, the WPRS initiative was enacted based on evaluation findings regarding job search assistance treatment in the final report of the New Jersey UI Reemployment Demonstration Project (Corson et al. 1989). The findings were strengthened by a five-year follow-up study (Corson and Haimson 1996) that found positive second year effects from the job search assistance treatment. A Job Search Assistance Demonstration supported the New Jersey results (Decker et al. 2000), and random trials in Kentucky provided further evidence in support of targeting attention to those most likely to exhaust their UI entitlements (Black et al. 2003). Early implementation of WPRS was rigorously evaluated (Dickinson et al. 1999).

Recommendations. WPRS should be fully funded through FUTA, including regular financial support to states for updating WPRS statistical selection models. Specifically, sufficient funding should be provided to maintain timely systems for selection and referral of claimants most likely to exhaust UI, and have ES conduct in-person/mediated reemployment services to at least a substantial percentage of workers who would benefit from these services.

Under the WPRS system, nearly all UI beneficiaries without a definite employer recall date are profiled, and 10 to 15 percent of these workers are referred to services. This referral rate appears to reasonably reflect the capacity of the workforce system to provide reemployment services. However, the reemployment services currently provided to participants are limited in quantity and quality. WPRS funding should be increased by about $300 million per year, which should be provided through Wagner-Peyser Act ES programs (Wandner 2010).

In addition, ES is underfunded throughout the country. Its funding level has remained almost constant in nominal terms, but declined dramatically in real terms, over the past 25 years. For example, Minnesota received $14 million per year in Wagner-Peyser grants in 1984 and employed 485 workers. In 2017, its annual grant was still $14 million, but that amount only funded 120 workers. The overall funding for ES should be increased to about $1.5 billion per year to restore its funding in real terms to its early 1980s levels.[17] Without improved funding, the states will continue to reduce mediated/in-person services and replace them with automated services (Wandner 2013a).

The above recommendations are consistent with a 1999 report by a WPRS work group composed of national, regional, and state experts that reviewed the system based on early operational experience. The work group made seven recommendations to improve the WPRS system, including that state agencies should provide more extensive reemployment services to participating UI claimants and that USDOL should separately fund these reemployment services (Wandner and Messenger 1999).

Work sharing/short-time compensation

Research. California enacted the first work-sharing program in the United States. The federal government enacted temporary work-sharing legislation in 1982 and then permanent legislation in 1992 and 2012. As a result, California conducted an early evaluation of its program (Employment Development Department 1982), and USDOL followed, conducting two national evaluations of the work-sharing program, one in the 1980s and another in the 1990s (Kerachsky et al. 1986; Walsh et al. 1997). Other industrialized countries have evaluated their work-sharing programs, analyzing program operation as well as effectiveness and efficiency. For example, Canada has conducted several evaluations (Ekos Research Associates 1993; HRSDC 2005), as has Germany (Crimmann, Wiessner, and Bell 2010) and other European countries (Vroman and Brusentsev 2009). Although none of these studies has been as rigorous as the experimental evaluations of other reemployment services, a consensus has developed among researchers and policy analysts that work sharing helps prevent unemployment and does so at a modest cost, because in the absence of the program, an equivalent expenditure would be made to pay UI benefits to workers who become totally unemployed.

The Middle Class Tax Relief and Job Creation Act of 2012 (MCTRJCA) was enacted into law on February 22, 2012. The act's work-sharing subtitle D describes the Short-Time Compensation (STC) program and required the Secretary of Labor to report to Congress and the president on the implementation of the STC provisions by February 2016. It expanded and clarified the definition of STC, and that definition has been adopted by all states with a conforming STC program. MCTRJCA provided the Secretary of Labor with sufficient flexibility to guide states through the interpretation of their laws and assist them in bringing their state laws into conformity with the new federal definition.

To implement the provisions of the act, USDOL initiated two work-sharing studies, a survey of employers and a study of the implementation of the 2012 act. The employer survey was conducted in four states for both participating and nonparticipating employers: Kansas, Minnesota, Rhode Island, and Washington (Balducchi et al. 2015). The survey findings include:

- Work-sharing employers overwhelmingly were very satisfied with their state's program, with many employers believing it was instrumental in allowing them to retain highly skilled workers.

- Awareness of the work-sharing program is limited.

- Usage was greatest among manufacturing employers, larger employers, employers who had been in business for longer periods than nonparticipating employers, and employers with more skilled workers.

- From 43 to 65 percent of the work-sharing employers were repeat users.

- From 16 to 21 percent of the work-sharing employers eventually laid off some participating employees because of lack of work.

- From 60 to 70 percent of participating employers found that work sharing imposed an increased administrative burden compared to the regular UI program. The burden was primarily associated with the continued claim process, because the great majority of employers found it easy to apply for the program.

The second MCTRJCA study (Bennicci and Wandner 2015) reported that states found enacting conforming work-sharing legislation to be easy because most of the changes were minor. In addition, USDOL facilitated the process by reviewing each state's law and communicated directly with the states about the necessary changes to their state laws to achieve conformity. For states enacting legislation to implement a new or revised work-sharing program, USDOL provided model legislation and guidance, including reviewing drafts of legislation. In enacting new STC legislation, most study states faced little public opposition to the legislation, although the effort to achieve enactment was lengthy and contentious in some states. For study states with existing STC laws, implementing changes to their programs for conformity to the MCTRJCA was not a significant challenge. The changes were primarily focused on revisions to the STC application, state STC policies and procedures, and educating employers about the changes. One major administrative challenge for state agencies was getting ready to scale up the program during the next recession. A few states were better prepared than others because they had automated systems for applications and claims filing.

In February 2016, Secretary of Labor Perez transmitted a report to Congress based on the findings of Bennicci and Wandner (2015) and Balducchi et al. (2015). USDOL also supported a field experiment to evaluate ways to inform employers about the availability of the work-sharing program as an alternative to layoffs.

Recommendations. A number of changes to the work-sharing program should be considered:

- Work sharing should be extended to all states, and program use should be expanded within states during recession periods. USDOL should encourage states to adopt work-sharing legislation and make use of the program.

- States enacting new work-sharing legislation should be provided with funding to implement and initially market the program.

- USDOL should increase administrative funding for work-sharing program administration because the program requires more staff time than the regular UI program.

- Congress should consider legislation to relieve employers from paying for the costs of work sharing, instead paying for the program from FUTA or federal general revenue—not state trust fund accounts. Congress should also consider having STC benefits not reduce participants' future potential duration for regular UI benefits. These reforms would greatly encourage employers, workers, and states to participate in the STC program.

Self-Employment Assistance (SEA)

Research. SEA is a small but effective program in several states. It has been actively used in Maine, New Jersey, New York, and Oregon. SEA is also a statutory option in Delaware, Maryland, and Pennsylvania. Although similar programs serve considerably more workers in other major industrial nations, it is not clear that the SEA in its present form will expand to other states in the United States. The program is not likely to be adopted by other states unless sufficient funding for entrepreneurial counseling and training is provided to unemployed workers participating in the program. States with SEA programs frequently have no steady source of funding for training in the basic management, accounting, and marketing skills needed to run a successful business.

Before enacting a federal SEA statute, USDOL conducted two self-employment allowance experiments in Washington and Massachusetts (Benus et al. 1995). The Washington experiment involved a one-time lump-sum payment, while the Massachusetts experiment involved weekly payments like regular UI. The Massachusetts demonstration project was found to be cost effective, whereas the Washington program was not. The Massachusetts experiment estimated that the program reduced participants' spells of unemployment and increased their total time in employment. Participation also had a positive impact on participants' earnings. When placed in a benefit-cost framework, the Massachusetts experiment provided net benefits to participants, society, and the government sector. This meant that the cost of the program was exceeded by the benefits to the government, especially in the form of increased tax payments, since participants were found to earn a great deal more than nonparticipants.

The Massachusetts experimental program with weekly payments was chosen as the design for the federal SEA program. On the basis of an interim evaluation report (Benus et al. 1991), Congress enacted a temporary program in late 1993 with a five-year sunset provision as part of the North American Free Trade Act (NAFTA). The final evaluation (Benus et al. 1995) provided strong findings of cost effectiveness and was the basis for making the federal SEA program permanent in 1998.

Because of dissatisfaction with the small size of the SEA program, proposals were developed to make administrative and legislative changes to it, including the provision of administrative funds and federal technical assistance. Under the MCTRJCA, new SEA provisions were adopted to encourage state adoption and expansion of SEA. However, no new states adopted the program, even though USDOL provided guidance and model legislation to the state workforce agencies in 2012 (Employment and Training Administration 2012). Even states that were interested in adopting the SEA program did not do so because they were overburdened with operating their own UI programs during a period of continued high unemployment after the Great Recession.

Although the SEA program has been open to adoption to all states since it was included as a displaced worker alternative in NAFTA, few states have chosen to establish and use SEA programs. Even in the seven states with SEA programs, participation is limited because only a small percentage of the UI claimants want to set up their own businesses. Moreover, few of the workers who are ready to participate are actually given a chance, largely because of difficulty in securing funds for entrepreneurial training. Participation was low before the Great Recession, and program use increased somewhat after its onset in Maine, New Jersey, New York, and Oregon.

Recommendations. SEA should be made available to unemployed workers in all states. The program should become a part of all state UI laws. Eligibility for SEA should continue to be limited to UI claimants who are permanently separated from their jobs and have a high probability of exhausting their UI benefits as indicated by their WPRS profiling score.

The principal impediment to offering SEA participation in states with SEA programs has been a lack of funding for entrepreneurial training that prepares unemployed workers to establish their own businesses. The state SEA programs should partner with state WIOA and Small Business Development Centers to have them fund and/or provide such entrepreneurial training. The federal government also should encourage and fund these partnering arrangements.

Reemployment bonuses

Research. Between 1984 and 1989, four reemployment bonus experiments were conducted in the states of Illinois, New Jersey, Pennsylvania, and Washington. All four experiments involved providing lump-sum payments to permanently separated workers who took new, full-time jobs within 6 to 12 weeks after becoming unemployed and held those jobs for at least three to four months. These experiments were conducted to find a strategy to overcome the work disincentive effect of cash UI payments to unemployed workers. The reemployment bonus design was intended to speed the return to work of dislocated workers in a way that would benefit employees and be cost effective. The concept behind these experiments was that UI claimants would be better off if they went back to work sooner and took jobs similar to the jobs they would have taken in the absence of their bonus offers. Bonus offers were tested to see if they would be cost effective to the government sector, that is, if the cost of offering bonuses was offset by a decrease in UI payments to unemployed workers and an increase in tax receipts during their longer period of employment.

An analysis simulating profiling reemployment bonuses was conducted with data from the Pennsylvania and Washington state experiments, the two experiments that appeared to have the greatest policy relevance (O'Leary, Decker, and Wandner 2005). This analysis was conducted for two reasons. First, reemployment bonuses seemed to be policy appropriate only for permanently separated dislocated workers, a conclusion that had already been recognized by a 1994

Clinton administration proposal to implement targeted reemployment bonuses.[18] Second, the Pennsylvania and Washington state results were rather small across the 10 treatments tested, with five of the treatments in those two states found to be cost effective to society and to the government sector, but only two treatments were cost effective for the UI system (Corson et al. 1992; O'Leary, Spiegelman, and Kline 1995). In the absence of profiling, no optimum reemployment bonus design emerged from the experimental results.

Analysis of the profiled reemployment bonus data suggested that profiling improved the cost effectiveness from the perspective of the UI program. In all treatments in both states, impact estimates with profiling generally were stronger than those without it. Offering bonuses to the top 50 percent of the profiled distribution—that is, the half identified as most likely to exhaust UI benefits—was more cost effective than setting the threshold at either 25 percent or 75 percent. The results comparing bonus amounts (high and low in Pennsylvania and high, medium, and low in Washington) and eligibility periods (short and long in both states) suggested that a low bonus amount combined with a long eligibility period was most cost effective. These estimates "suggest that such a targeted bonus offer would yield appreciable net benefits to the UI trust funds if implemented as a permanent program" (O'Leary, Decker, and Wandner 2005, p. 279). Their recommendation was for a bonus amount of about three times the weekly benefit and a qualification period of about 12 weeks offered to the 50 percent of profiled UI beneficiaries most likely to exhaust their UI entitlements. Using the national average weekly benefit amount for the 12 months ending in February 2018, the bonus would average $1,057. Even though the reemployment bonus experiments were completed in the early 1990s, reemployment bonuses have not yet been implemented as part of U.S. labor market policy.

Recommendations. Reemployment bonuses speed the return to work of dislocated workers by increasing their work search efforts. Bonuses do not have an adverse economic effect on workers because, as research shows, workers do not take jobs that pay less than those that they would have taken (later) in the absence of a reemployment bonus offer. Reemployment bonuses tend to be cost effective if they are offered to dislocated workers with a high probability of exhausting their UI benefit entitlements as measured by their WPRS profiling score. Reemployment bonuses should be enacted into federal law using the language of the proposed Reemployment Act of 1994. The result would be a permissive program that states could adopt, offering modest reemployment bonuses to targeted UI beneficiaries who have been permanently separated from their prior jobs.

Education and training

The UI program has declined in its ability to provide benefits to experienced, covered workers who become unemployed through no fault of their own. Declining benefit adequacy has resulted from insufficient forward funding of the system. Nonetheless, there have been numerous proposals to fund education and training programs from state and federal UI funds. Despite prohibitions on the use of UI funds for anything other than the payment of UI benefits and the administration of UI and related programs, the substantial size of the program makes it a target for attempts to use UI funds for non-UI purposes. Specifically, the existence of the large (but dedicated) UI Trust Fund makes the UI program a target for funding other programs. The public finance literature shows that dedicated trust funds frequently have been targets of budgetary raiders.

Recommendations. The integrity of the UI system must be maintained. To that end, FUTA reserves should be limited to supporting UI and ES administration and services. While FUTA funding should support the provision of more and better reemployment services, FUTA funds should continue to be limited to funding UI and ES administration. Specifically, education and training for the long-term unemployed should not be funded from either FUTA reserves or state accounts in the UTF. Congress should consider funding training from U.S. Department of Education grants and loans because WIOA grants to states are not adequate to provide even the amount of job training currently needed.

CONCLUSION

The recommendations presented in this chapter are part of our attempt to develop a comprehensive UI reform proposal that would create a program that would be adequately funded and would help speed the return to work for all UI recipients.

In Appendix 5A, our recommendations are compared to three other sets of recommendations: the recommendations in the 2017 budget request by President Obama (WHO); a proposal by the authors from the Center for Law and Social Policy, Georgetown University, and the National Employment Law Project (CGN); and recommendations from the 2018 budget request by President Trump (WHT). A detailed summary of the elements of the proposals is given in Appendix 5B. Our recommendations are the most comprehensive with respect to the reform of UI as a social insurance program across the full range of issues that relate to the UI program. By contrast, although the WHO proposals try to enhance the basic role of UI as a social insurance program, they are incomplete and would not create an adequate, balanced, and effective UI system. Similarly, the CGN is not comprehensive and fails to respect social insurance principles and financing challenges. The WHT proposal is the most limited approach to UI reform of the three programs compared.

Comprehensive UI reform is urgently needed. The UI program is out of balance today, and it is not prepared or preparing for the next recession. Despite the urgent need for reform, it is difficult to believe that comprehensive reform is likely to occur at the state or national level, given widespread employer opposition to expanding the unemployment benefit system and raising taxes to fund these benefits. We suggest that the most likely route to comprehensive UI reform involves reducing or eliminating employer taxes by instead having employees directly fund much or all of the UI program.

Notes

We thank David Balducchi and Wayne Vroman for constructive comments on an earlier version of this chapter.

1. The three main separation reasons covered by the ARRA concern: 1) domestic violence, 2) illness or disability of an immediate family member, and 3) moving to accompany a spouse who relocates to a distance impractical for commuting to the job.
2. Gary Burtless (1983) also described how the lower recipiency ratio weakened the countercyclical strength of the UI system to dampen economic downturns.
3. The states are Florida, Iowa, Idaho, Georgia, Maine, Mississippi, Missouri, Montana, and North Dakota.
4. There has been a sharp downward trend in the number of local offices from nearly 3,600 in 2003 and 2004 to 2,451 in May 2018. (A temporary increase in the number of offices occurred in 2009 and 2010 with funding from the ARRA.) Most of the decline has occurred in the affiliate offices, which has disproportionately affected ES (compared to the WIA) and reduced public workforce services in less densely populated parts of the United States.
5. Two states offer slightly longer potential durations; Massachusetts provides up to 30 weeks while Montana offers up to 28 (USDOL 2016).
6. The states are Arkansas, Florida, Georgia, Kansas, Michigan, Missouri, North Carolina, and South Carolina. In Kansas, the potential duration is 26 weeks if state unemployment is 6 percent or higher, but 20 weeks when the unemployment rate averaged over the prior 3 months is below 6 percent at the time of UI benefit application.
7. In 2013, four UI programs (California, Connecticut, Ohio, and the U.S. Virgin Islands) were still paying on loans from the U.S. Treasury, while six other states (Colorado, Illinois, Michigan, Nevada, Pennsylvania, and Texas) were still repaying other loans or bond debts from UI benefit payments (O'Leary and Kline 2016, p. 1).
8. Note, however, that applicants qualifying for the minimum weekly benefit amount usually receive higher than 50 percent wage replacement per week.
9. This discussion is drawn from O'Leary and Barnow (2016). In January 2018, California and the Virgin Islands were still repaying loans to the

Treasury, and Michigan, Nevada and Pennsylvania were still repaying other loans or bond debts (USDOL 2018).

10. The rest of this section draws on Wandner (2012).
11. Suggestions for federal benefit standards are fully described below.
12. Despite having multiple employers make tax payments on their behalf, multiple job holders have difficulty accessing UI in many states when they lose one of their jobs because work search rules require availability for full-time work. As we assert above, eligibility rules should permit seeking part-time work if employment has customarily been part time.
13. This paragraph draws on O'Leary and Barnow (2016, pp. 21–22).
14. Among the 19 states with indexed TWBs, the average rate is 72 percent of the average annual wage in UI-covered employment.
15. This paragraph is drawn from O'Leary and Barnow (2016).
16. When WPRS started operations in 1994, job training was delivered under the Job Training Partnership Act (1982), which later was reorganized as the Workforce Investment Act (1998), and now is the Workforce Innovation and Opportunity Act (2014). In areas where funding was sufficient, ES provided WPRS services; elsewhere the training partners helped starting with JTPA. The WIA program established one-stop centers where all services were available under one roof, and WIOA continued the one-stop model.
17. This is discussed in greater detail in Chapter 3 by Balducchi and O'Leary.
18. The proposed Reemployment Act of 1994 was never enacted into law.

Appendix 5A
Comparison of UI Reform Proposals

This Appendix considers UI system reforms that should be addressed before the next recession. Three comprehensive UI system reform proposals are reviewed. We start with our own (O'Leary and Wandner or OW), based on the principles and research reviewed in this chapter. We then describe the main elements of two other proposals from governmental and nongovernmental sources: the Obama Administration FY 2017 Presidential Budget Request (White House-Obama or WHO) and a consortium led by the Center for American Progress and including Georgetown University and the National Employment Law Project (CGN).[1] Table 5A.1 provides an overview of the areas where each of the groups proposes reforms. An expanded version of this summary is given in Appendix 5B, which includes details of each proposal.

We also discuss a list of proposals for reforming four UI features made by the Trump administration.

COMPARATIVE SUMMARIES OF PROPOSALS

The three recent UI reform proposals differ in many of their details, but they all propose reasonably comprehensive system-wide reform—with the WHO proposal being the least comprehensive of the three—while placing a different emphasis on some issues, including the commitment to maintaining the social insurance character of the UI program and the use of federal standards versus financial incentives for state action. In this section, the programs are compared with a focus on the topic areas listed in Table 5A.1.

O'Leary-Wandner (OW) Proposal

The following is a summary of the UI reform proposals we believe should be set as federal conformity requirements for state UI programs.

Initial eligibility: Requires states to have an alternate base period (ABP). Permits suitable work to be limited to part-time work if that was customary, and lets the minimum acceptable wage for suitable work decline with the duration of benefit receipt. Sets a low minimum monetary eligibility requirement such as having one base period quarter with earnings of at least $1,000 and a second base period quarter with at least $500.

Table 5A.1 Comparison of Unemployment Insurance (UI) Reforms Proposed by O'Leary and Wandner (OW), the Obama White House (WHO), and the Center for American Progress/Georgetown University/National Employment Law Project (CGN)

Proposals by UI feature	OW	WHO	CGN
Initial eligibility (number of states)	Dollars and HQ	Dollars and HQ	Weeks and HQ
Alternate base period (40)	Yes	Yes	Yes
Seeking part-time work (26)	Yes	Yes	Yes
Good cause quits—family (20)		Yes	Yes
Definition of suitable work	Declining wage		
Extended base period			Yes
Continuing eligibility			
Work search and employment services	Yes		RESEA
High quality reemployment services	Yes		
Benefit standards	50%, max 2/3 AWW	50%, max 2/3 AWW	50%, max 2/3 AWW
Duration of regular benefits	26 earnings related	26 uniform	26 uniform
Partial UI benefits			Yes
Retirement income offset	Eliminate		
Training allowance (13)			Yes
Dependents allowance (6)			
Disaster unemployment assistance			
Stipends in OJT and apprenticeships			Expand
Extended benefits—reform EB system	TUR triggers fed-state	TUR triggers fed-state	Add
Emergency extended compensation	Federal discretion		TUR triggers fed-state

Financing features	O'Leary and Wandner (this paper)	White House (2017)	West et al. (2016)
Minimum tax rates	Yes	Yes	Yes
Number of rates	Yes		
Range of rates	Yes		
Taxable wage base (FUTA) reforms	Yes	Yes	Yes
Forward funding standards	Yes	Yes	Yes
Payroll tax year end rebates	Yes		Yes
Funding EB and EUC	Yes		Yes
Fund ES and UI administration	Yes		Yes
Special programs			
Work sharing/STC	All states	All states	All states
Self-employment assistance	All states	All states	All states
Reemployment bonuses	Proposed-targeted		
Wage insurance	Research	Proposed	Proposed
Relocation allowances			Proposed
Supportive services			Proposed
Direct job creation			Proposed
Unemployment assistance			Proposed
UI program policy research	Proposed		Proposed

NOTES: A more detailed comparison is given in Appendix 5B. OJT: on-the-job training; HQ: high-quarter earnings; AWW: average weekly wage; TUR: total unemployment rate; EB: Extended Benefits; FUTA: Federal Unemployment Tax Act; STC: Short-Time Compensation.
SOURCE: O'Leary and Wandner (this paper), the White House (2017), and West et al. (2016).

Continuing eligibility: Requires continuous active work search monitoring and federally fund quality reemployment services for all UI beneficiaries.

Benefit standards: Sets a maximum potential duration of at least 26 weeks, with actual duration increasing with base period earnings. Makes the wage replacement rate at least 50 percent of the maximum weekly benefit amount (WBA), and sets the state maximum WBA at two-thirds of the state average weekly wage (AWW) in UI covered employment.

Extended benefits: Each state should have a schedule of benefit durations for state extended benefits (EB) based on total unemployment rate (TUR) triggers, paid from federal funds. Emergency Unemployment Compensation (EUC) would be provided during high unemployment periods by the federal government at the discretion of Congress, paid from general revenue.

Financing features: The taxable wage base (TWB) should be equal to one-third of the Social Security base and be indexed to increase in proportion to the Social Security TWB. State tax schedules would not include a zero tax rate and must have at least 10 different rates in each tax schedule, resulting in all employers supporting UI system costs. Both employers and employees should pay UI taxes, with employees paying at least half of the total tax contributions to increase political support and assure full engagement with the UI program. Annual UI tax schedule waivers may not be granted; that is, states should adhere to the appropriate tax schedule under state law, without any legislative deferral for movement to higher schedules. States with insufficient forward funding would be subject to loss of UI offset credits. The tax schedule would be selected annually based on the adequacy of system reserves. USDOL would set required standards for reserve adequacy.

Special programs: All states would have programs for work-sharing and self-employment assistance. USDOL would permit states to establish targeted reemployment bonus programs and sponsor several different state random trials to evaluate wage insurance.

Administrative financing: Provides adequate federal funding for administration and Reemployment Services and Eligibility Assessment (RESEA).

White House Obama (WHO) Proposal: Differences from the OW Proposal

Initial eligibility: Requires all ARRA UI modernization features, including family reasons for good-cause quit, does not specify base period earnings requirements, and recommends a high quarter earnings rule, but does not reduce the value of suitable wage with duration of unemployment.

Continuing eligibility: Requires RESEA during EB receipt.

Benefit standards: Sets a uniform potential duration of 26 weeks with the same wage replacement rate and same maximum weekly benefit amount formula as OW. Calls for TUR triggers for state EB and offers an EB program that makes use of a TUR schedule. EB is funded from EUCA or general federal revenues, and there is no mention of a discretionary EUC program.

Financing features: TWB is raised to $40,000 and indexed, and the FUTA tax rate is reduced to be revenue neutral. State tax schedules are not addressed. The forward funding criterion is a 0.5 Average High Cost Multiple (AHCM) subject to a reduction in UI offset credits. The tax schedule would be selected annually based on the adequacy of system reserves. USDOL should set required standards for reserve adequacy.

Special programs: Requires that work sharing be available and provides wage insurance.

Administrative financing: Not addressed.

CGN: Differences from the OW Proposal

Initial eligibility: Permits compelling family reasons for good-cause quits. Specifies base period earnings as 300 times state minimum hourly wage and requires hours worked in at least two calendar quarters. Recommends a move toward hours-based eligibility. State UI agency notifies potentially eligible unemployed workers. Sets standards for automated monetary eligibility procedures. Does not reduce the value of suitable wage with duration of unemployment.

Continuing eligibility: Requires providing RESEA to UI recipients during EB receipt.

Benefit standards: Requires a uniform potential duration of 26 weeks. Federal government pays 25 percent of the cost for benefits between 27 and

39 weeks. Calls for TUR triggers for state EB, similar to the OW EB-TUR schedule. EB is funded from FUTA or general federal revenues. Provides a 26-week job stipend during classroom job training, on-the-job training, or apprenticeship. Does not mention discretionary EUC.

Financing features: TWB raised to one-half the Social Security TWB and then indexed. Require a minimum UI tax rate greater than zero for states. Standardize experience rating across states. Year-end rebates for multiple job holders.

Special programs: Requires that work sharing be available and provides wage insurance.

Administrative financing: Proposes adequate federal funding for administration and RESEA.

MAJOR DIFFERENCES BETWEEN PROPOSALS

The U.S. labor market has changed dramatically since the inception of the UI program in 1935. Nonetheless, there has been no systematic updating of coverage and eligibility provisions at the state level. Some needed changes have been made by individual state initiatives and others were encouraged by the 2009 UI Modernization program. However, the weakness of UI Modernization is revealed by the fact that five of the states that received incentive payments for introducing elements of UI Modernization have already repealed the new features. The following contrasts the three main reform proposals on the important policy areas.

The OW proposals are based on the assertion that the current UI program is broken. The regular UI benefit system and the benefit financing system does not support a self-sustaining program that pays adequate benefits for sufficient durations to support reemployment. Similarly, the aim of the WHO proposal is to introduce balance between the basic benefit and financing provisions of the regular UI program, such that the regular program provides adequate UI benefits that are fully funded over the business cycle. The CGN program contains several elements in the OW and WHO proposals, but the CGN presses many dimensions of proposed UI reforms beyond social insurance principles and toward social welfare aims.

Eligibility and Benefits

In contrast to WHO and CGN, the OW proposal recommends fewer changes to be mandated by federal law, with states free to choose among reform options. The OW proposed changes would:

- require states to provide for an Alternative Benefit Period,
- permit part-time workers to search for part-time work,
- remove retirement income offset, and
- permit states to reduce suitable reemployment wage rates as the duration of unemployment increases.

The WHO and CGN proposals require states to allow voluntary quits for compelling family reasons. CGN includes all the above plus some changes that would go beyond social insurance principles to add elements of social welfare to UI, with benefits based on means or household composition. For example, it proposes means-tested benefits for very long-term unemployed persons no longer eligible for regular UI.

Extended Benefits

The OW proposal would introduce a schedule for EB potential durations tied to the state or federal TUR level and would require 100 percent federal financing of EB. The WHO and CGN proposals are similar to those of OW, and all three require EB to be fully paid by the federal government from the UTF, with any necessary supplements from general revenues.

All three EB proposals presume that states provide potential durations of at least 26 weeks of regular UI benefits regardless of the TUR level. The OW proposal also recognizes that Congress, in times of deep recessions, may exercise discretion to provide emergency EB to supplement state regular UI and EB programs.

Benefit Financing

The OW proposal aims to restore the UI program as an automatic stabilizer for the macro-economy—injecting spending during high unemployment and withdrawing tax contributions during economic recoveries. The financing system is countercyclical if benefits are paid through a forward funding mechanism, that is, by having adequate state trust fund reserves at the beginning of recessions. Spending is injected immediately, but tax rates rise only after experience-rating systems factor in increased benefit charges. The OW proposal incentivizes forward funding of benefits by paying increasingly higher rates of interest on reserves as balances increase, and by increasing the credit offset penalties as negative balances increase.

The main WHO incentive to accomplish forward funding is paying states higher interest rates when their trust fund accounts reach higher AHCM levels. This goes beyond the existing USDOL policy of offering zero-interest short-term loans when AHCMs reach specified levels. The WHO proposal would apply a FUTA credit reduction to states with an AHCM of less than 0.5. A FUTA credit reduction is the way states currently pay back borrowed funds when they prefer not to adjust state tax rates or TWBs or to issue bonds.

The CGN proposal requires states to achieve a 1.0 AHCM within 5 years and also requires USDOL to establish minimum rates below which states' tax revenues cannot fall. The plan would pay differentially high interest rates to states with balances greater than the target AHCM.

The CGN and WHO proposals would probably achieve sound counter-cyclical financing. However, the outcome of the CGN's setting of the AHCM target is uncertain because it depends on annual discretionary administrative action.

Reemployment

The OW proposals argue that a strong ES is necessary to implement the UI work test to ensure that UI recipients are able, available, and actively searching for work. ES needs to refer UI recipients to jobs and provide labor market information. Additionally, OW proposals cite evidence that job search assistance and other reemployment services (RES) have been shown to be highly cost effective in promoting return to work and shortening durations of UI benefit receipt. Nonetheless, UI claimants currently receive inadequate reemployment services both because of general underfunding of ES and because of inadequate funding of UI reemployment services (Wandner 2015). The OW proposal is to fund both from FUTA. This could be accomplished by increasing and indexing the FUTA TWB. At a minimum, ES funding should be returned to the 1984 level in real terms.

WHO also recommends expansion of other complementary reemployment and unemployment prevention services, including STC, SEA, and targeted reemployment bonuses. A new federal law would be required to make reemployment bonuses a legally permissible use of UTF reserves.

WHO and CGN also recognize the need for enhanced ES and reemployment services funding, but they deal with this issue in different ways. The WHO proposal leaves this entire issue to a new UI Modernization program with no additional federal funding, which would most likely result in inadequate implementation. WHO proposes a financial incentive to states for adopting and implementing STC. It also proposes a new wage insurance program outside the UI program and recommends a field experiment to evaluate the possible cost effectiveness and take-up rate under this type of program. Wage insurance has been a little-used feature of the Alternative Trade Adjustment Assistance program for older displaced workers (age 50 or more) (Wandner 2013b).

CGN recommends increased funding for ES and RES. They would require state implementation of STC and SEA programs. They also propose providing relocation allowances, apprenticeship stipends, referral to national service jobs, and SEA services, all funded from a portion (up to 10 percent) of an enhanced ES budget.

The WHO proposal recognizes statutory funding for ES through the Wagner-Peyser Act. The proposal would 1) not yield adequate funding for ES or for UI RES, 2) add potentially expensive and unproven wage insurance, and 3) not address SEA or reemployment bonuses. The CGN proposal for ES/RES is sound, but the proposed use of enhanced ES funding (up to 10 percent of a new fund) is an unprecedented funding source for these initiatives. CGN does not propose reemployment bonuses.

Special Programs

All three proposals recommend that all states have statutory authorization to permit employers to provide work-sharing payments through the UI system and that self-employment assistance be available for targeted UI beneficiaries.

The CGN proposal for a Job Seekers' Allowance, which would programmatically be a form of unemployment assistance, is not social insurance but rather a means-tested benefit. Indeed, several CGN proposals for expanding the UI system go beyond the social insurance approach and, in some cases, look more like public assistance than social insurance.

TRUMP WHITE HOUSE PROPOSALS

The following set of four UI reform legislative recommendations were presented in the Trump administration's FY 2018 Budget (USDOL 2017b, p. 4):

1) A proposal to establish a federal-state paid parental leave benefit program within the UI program that provides six weeks of benefits for mothers, fathers, and adoptive parents to help families recover from childbirth and to bond with their new children.

2) A proposal to reduce improper payments in the UI program with a package of reforms that would allow states to target more tools and resources toward the problem.

3) An expansion of RESEA. This proposal would provide mandatory funding for states to provide RESEA to one-half of eligible UI claimants, as well as all ex-military service members.

4) A minimum solvency standard that would apply the FUTA credit reduction rules to states that have an AHCM of less than 0.5 on January 1 of two consecutive years (rather than the current zero trust fund balance). This proposal would strengthen states' ability to adequately fund their UI systems.

Because these proposals were briefly described in a budget document, have not been fleshed out, and were presented without analysis by the Trump administration, we have considered them separately from the other more developed recent UI reform proposals.

Parental Leave Proposal

Most OECD countries offer parental leave benefits, and they have been found to be an effective policy to increase fertility (Lalive and Zweimuller 2009). The proposal for parental leave therefore might be very good social policy, but paying benefits from the UTF for parental leave is currently not an allowable use of UI program funds. To protect the integrity of the UTF, state trust fund account reserves are paid by employer taxes on payrolls and may only be used to pay UI benefits. During periods of recession, state reserves are often not even sufficient to pay regular benefits to eligible UI applicants. Parental leave benefits would be a new entitlement with simple eligibility conditions, but for a parental benefit to be sustainable, a new tax would be required. Furthermore, either the UTF withdrawal rules would have to be statutorily revised, or a separate fund would have to be established with a new tax and a dedicated revenue stream. Actuarial computations of revenue adequacy for such a fund would require new behavioral analysis. Rough estimates suggest that parental leave payments would have increased fund payments by at least 25 percent, or about $8 billion dollars, if it had been in place in 2017.[2]

Improper Payment Proposal

Improper UI payments are a serious problem, but they are inherent in any social insurance system and impossible to eliminate entirely. In a recent 12-month period, 11.2 percent of all regular UI payments involved errors, and 10.6 percent of payments were incorrectly high (Gilbert 2011). However, even if all overpayments were eliminated, the savings would not be enough to pay for the proposed parental leave program.[3] Overpayment errors have become a structural component of the UI system because of the federal rules relating to the initial eligibility of applicants. These rules are based on a 1970 California state Supreme Court decision that ordered payment of benefits during appeal periods. USDOL has complied with this decision by applying it nationwide, such that administrative performance targets for timeliness require UI benefit payments to be made when due and not delayed (O'Leary and Barnow 2016).

The biggest cause of overpayment errors on continuing claims is the failure to fully comply with the UI work test (Burgess and Kingston 1987; Clarkwest et al. 2012). Expanded ES funding by USDOL to provide one-on-one eligibility reviews to UI beneficiaries should reduce work test overpayments through the RESEA program, but since the Trump proposal would only provide RESEA to half of the WPRS group, RESEA still would not entirely eliminate overpayments.

RESEA Proposal

USDOL increased funding for the RESEA program in 2017 and provided grants to all states starting that year. The White House 2018 proposal aims to provide RESEA to the top 50 percent of WPRS-eligible UI beneficiaries—that is, those neither awaiting employer recall nor union hiring hall members. Earlier research suggested that shorter UI durations from WPRS result from the unwelcome prospect of having to participate in services rather than the actual content of those services (Black et al. 2003), but a more recent evaluation of the RESEA predecessor, REA, estimated significantly shorter UI durations resulting from the RES component of REA (Michaelides et al. 2012). RESEA offers the prospect of reducing, but not eliminating, overpayments on continuing UI claims. About half of UI recipients are subject to referral to WPRS services, and only about half of these will get RESEA. Furthermore, most state WPRS profiling systems have not been updated in many years, so the top half of the profiling distribution does not necessarily include those most likely to exhaust UI.

Minimum Solvency Standard

The Trump proposal would institute a federal rule that would reduce a state's FUTA credit if the state's AHCM for its reserves in the UTF is lower than 0.5 on two consecutive January firsts, which would nudge states toward forward funding of regular UI benefits. However, this would be only a partial and probably an inadequate solution. The accepted standard for forward funding is an AHCM of 1.0. Relying on the FUTA credit reduction would be a slow mechanism to restore reserves. For example, after borrowing to pay benefits during the recent recession, 25 states experienced FUTA credit reductions in one or more year since 2009. In fact, 13 states had credit reductions in three or more consecutive years, with negative reserve balances on January first.[4] It is reasonable to conclude that these states consciously chose to let the FUTA credit reduction mechanism improve reserves instead of reforming their state benefit financing mechanisms. Credit reduction is a slow way to improve reserves because the FUTA TWB is only $7,000, and the statewide annual increment in the federal tax rate is only 0.3 percentage point. In fact, since 2011, two states have had FUTA credit reductions in place for seven consecutive years. The proposed USDOL solvency mechanism would be more effective if the FUTA TWB were increased. This also would improve benefit financing in states with TWBs below any new higher required federal level. A 0.5 AHCM is an inadequate forward funding standard and could prolong reliance on the federal credit reduction mechanism by some states.

Appendix 5B
Detailed Comparison of Unemployment Insurance Reform Proposals by O'Leary and Wandner (OW), the White House-Obama (WHO), and the Center for American Progress–Georgetown University–National Employment Law (CGN)

Proposals by UI feature	OW	WHO	CGN
Initial eligibility (number of states with this provision, if applicable)			
Monetary criteria	Dollars and high-quarter earnings (HQ)	Dollars and HQ	Weeks and HQ Federal requirement that workers are eligible if they earn at least 300 times the state's hourly minimum wage during base period and worked in at least 2 quarters. In the long run, require state to adopt an alternative federal standard of hours-based eligibility.
Alternate base period (ABP) (40)	Require states to have an ABP	Require states to have an ABP	Require states to have an ABP

(continued)

Proposals by UI feature	OW	WHO	CGN
Seeking part-time work (26)	Encourage adoption by all states for part-time workers seeking part-time work	Require adoption by all states for part-time workers seeking part-time work	Require adoption by all states for previously part-time workers seeking part-time work; also require adoption for previously full-time workers seeking part-time work due to "major life change."
			Part-time benefit formula: allow claimants working part time to collect benefits as long as they are earning less than 150% of their weekly benefit amount (WBA), disregarding from this calculation part-time wages equal to 50% of the WBA (p. 63).

Proposals by UI feature	OW	WHO	CGN
Good cause quits– family (20)		Require adoption by all states for workers leaving jobs for compelling family reasons	Require states to adopt for workers leaving jobs for compelling personal and family reasons, including domestic violence, caring for themselves or family member during illness or injury, providing child care when no alternative arrangement is available, and following spouse, partner, or co-parent. Federal government pays for these benefits and employers are not charged (pp. 52, 77).

Require states to expand definition of good cause separations to include employer introduction of erratic job schedules or cut in hours and pay.

Require all states to eliminate eligibility restrictions for both temporary and seasonal workers. |

(continued)

Proposals by UI feature	OW	WHO	CGN
Good cause quits–family *(cont.)*			Require state UI programs to provide methods for employer-filed initial and continued claims for short-term layoffs and business shutdowns, as well as work sharing (pp. 67, 70).
			Require states to notify all employees of potential UI eligibility following separation from an employer (p. 70).
			Require states' automated claims filing systems to comply with federal standards (p. 71).
Definition of suitable work	Encourage states to gradually reduce suitable wage level during regular UI benefit period as duration of benefit receipt increases.		
Extended base period			Require states to adopt an extended base period for workers with qualifying conditions, e.g., illness or injury. Also require an 18-month base period for workers with an erratic work schedule.

Proposals by UI feature	OW	WHO	CGN
Continuing eligibility			
Work search requirements and Employment Services (ES)	Worker Profiling and Reemployment Services (WPRS)-selected UI beneficiaries who are likely UI exhaustees are required to participate in Reemployment Services and Eligibility Assessment (RESEA)	All EB recipients required to participate in RESEA	Provide RESEA to every EB recipient
Quality of reemployment services and sufficiency of ES staffing	FUTA should fund ES at 1984 levels in real terms. Supplementary funding for RESEA and other initiatives should be provided to all states.		
Benefit standards			
Benefit standards	Require all states to replace 50% of lost wages, with maximum WBA of 2/3 of average weekly wage (AWW).	Encourage states to adopt federal benefit standard using a new UI Modernization program. $5 billion in grants for 1) benefit expansion and 2) "pro-work reforms." Benefit expansions: 1) UI payments while in training and 2) maximum WBA of at least 2/3 AWW; improve eligibility for temporary workers.	Encourage states to adopt a 50% wage replacement standard, with an indexed WBA equal to two-thirds of the state's AWW (pp. 61–62). Additional duration: federal government pays 25% of regular duration greater than 26 weeks up to 39 weeks (p. 61).

(continued)

Proposals by UI feature	OW	WHO	CGN
Benefit standards *(cont.)*			Require elimination of waiting week (p. 61).
			Require lump-sum payments of UI benefits for "qualifying reasons" (p. 61).
			Disaster Unemployment Assistance: improve and extend (p. 63).
Duration of regular benefits	Encourage adoption of at least 26 weeks of benefits	Require states to have a maximum duration of at least 26 weeks	Require all states to have uniform maximum duration (p. 60)
Partial UI benefits			Allow claimants working part time to collect benefits as long as they are earning less than 150% of their WBA, disregarding from this calculation part-time wages equal to 50% of the WBA (p. 63)
Retirement income offset	Eliminate pension income as a federally required benefit reduction		
Training allowance (13)			Fund up to 26 weeks of additional UI benefits for workers in training

Proposals by UI feature	OW	WHO	CGN
Stipends for on-the-job training (OJT) and apprenticeships			If otherwise eligible, continue to receive UI benefits while in OJT, other job training, or apprenticeship
Extended benefits (EB)—reform EB system	Federal TUR triggers variable EB: 7 weeks when 6.5% TUR 13 weeks when 7% TUR 26 weeks when 8% TUR 39 weeks when 9% TUR 52 weeks when 10% TUR	Federal TUR triggers variable EB: 13 weeks when 6.5% TUR 26 weeks when 7.5% TUR 39 weeks when 8.5% TUR 52 weeks when 9.5% TUR	Federal TUR triggers variable EB: 13 weeks when 6.5% TUR 26 weeks when 7.5% TUR 39 weeks when 8.5% TUR 52 weeks when 9.5% TUR Additional 6 weeks of EB would be payable in states for each added one percentage point of TUR after 9.5. Also a national TUR EB trigger should be enacted: 13 weeks when 7% TUR 26 weeks when 8% TUR 39 weeks when 9% TUR 52 weeks when 10% TUR
Emergency extended compensation	Discretionary and effective upon Congressional action		

(continued)

Proposals by UI feature	OW	WHO	CGN
Financing features			
Minimum tax rates	Encourage states to have a non-zero minimum rate	Impose a minimum tax per employee of 0.175%	Require a minimum tax rate for all states (p. 78)
Number of rates	Encourage states to have at least 10 steps in every UI tax rate schedule		Standardize experience- rating practices across states (p. 78)
Range of rates	Encourage states not to override triggers moving to higher schedules in response to higher costs, e.g., use responsible countercyclical financing		
Taxable wage base (TWB) Federal Unemployment Tax Act (FUTA) reforms	Congress should enact a FUTA TWB equal to 33% of the Social Security TWB and then tie it to the Social Security index	Effective 2018, the TWB would be $40K and thereafter indexed to inflation; federal tax reduced to 0.167% to be cost neutral in 2018	Over 6 years, raise UI TWB to one-half the SS TWB and thereafter growing at the rate of the SS TWB; federal tax reduced, while raising sufficient revenue to support an expanded role for ES (pp. 75–76, 78)
Forward-funding standards	Vary interest payment rates depending on state reserve balance in their trust fund accounts, increasing the rate above the 10-year T-bill rate as the state high cost multiple (HCM) increases	FUTA credit reduction: apply FUTA credit reduction rules to states with average HCM < 0.5 in two consecutive years	HCM of 1.0 required of all states within 5 years. Federal policymakers establish minimum rate below which states' tax revenue cannot fall (p. 76). Pay differentially higher interest rate payments to states that exceed the target average HCM (p. 78).

Proposals by UI feature	OW	WHO	CGN
Year-end payroll tax rebates	Year-end rebates proportionate to calendar year wages to employers of multiple job holders		At end of year, reconcile tax payments for workers who have held more than one job during the tax year (p. 61)
Funding EB and extended unemployment compensation	FUTA payment of EB costs	Funding from Extended Unemployment Compensation Act when sufficient, otherwise from General Fund	Full funding of EB by federal government
Funding ES and UI administration	Congress should provide adequate funding for UI administration, including all components of the program, including funding for eligibility reviews/ reemployment eligibility assessments in all states. FUTA funds ES in real terms at the 1984 level, then indexed at the rate of increase of the Social Security TWB.	Require adoption of UI Modernization features in American Recovery and Reemployment Act (ARRA)	Fully fund UI administrative funding by increasing by $600 million over the next 3 years. After 3 years, implement updated administrative formula reflecting the cost of administration (pp. 69, 71). Improve UI administrative technology by appropriating and providing one-time grants of $300 million for IT upgrades and updating worker profiling models. Increase federal oversight of UI IT systems and institute federal UI IT audits (pp. 69–71).

(continued)

Proposals by UI feature	OW	WHO	CGN
Funding ES and UI administration *(cont.)*	Reemployment Services (RES) funding should be about $400–500 million, then indexed at the rate of increase of the Social Security TWB. Funding as part of WPRS from FUTA provided to ES.		Appropriate a total of $1.68 billion (an additional $1 billion) for ES for FY 2017 (p. 21). Appropriate $650 million (an additional $535 million) for RE-SEA for FY 2017 (p. 21)
Special programs			
Work sharing/ short-time compensation (STC)	All states should be encouraged to adopt and make use of STC programs. New states should be provided with implementation and marketing funds. Congress should increase administrative funding for STC and consider relieving employers of the cost of STC.	Incentives to adopt or expand for 2 years, similar to provisions under ARRA. Reimbursement of benefits, $100 million in implementation grants. While on EB, 50–50 split of costs between federal and state and non-charge of the federal share	Require all states to create an STC program. Provide federal grants for implementation and marketing for new states. 100% federal funding for at least 1 year when states are on EB. Federal STC automation grants. States encouraged not to have STC benefits reduce maximum potential duration. State encouraged to adopt best practices. Full funding of STC by federal government whenever EB trigger is on, whether state or nationally triggered. States should not experience rate STC benefits during federal reimbursement period.

Proposals by UI feature	OW	WHO	CGN
Self-employment assistance (SEA)	All states should be encouraged to adopt and use SEA programs. Workforce Innovation and Opportunities Act and Small Business Administration should be required to provide entrepreneurial training to SEA participants.	All states should establish SEA programs.	All states should be required to maintain SEA programs and connect participants to Small Business Development Centers. SEA participants could claim up to half of their remaining UI entitlement up-front (p. 23, 25).
Reemployment bonuses	Congressional legislation similar to the Reemployment Act of 1994 should permit states to adopt targeted reemployment bonus programs using WPRS models.		
Wage insurance	USDOL should conduct a wage insurance demonstration project for this untested initiative.	For workers with 3 years of tenure, earning less than $50,000. Pay half of wage reduction up to $10,000 over 2 years.	
Relocation allowances			Use ES funding to fund relocation allowances, as a lump sum up to 3 times the average WBA, capped at a maximum of $2,000 per year.

(continued)

Proposals by UI feature	OW	WHO	CGN
Supportive services and direct job creation			Connect UI recipients to apprenticeships, national service jobs (funding source not specified), and traditional employment opportunities and SEA. Relocation allowances and supportive services could be funded with up to 10% of ES funds.
Unemployment assistance			Available to new entrants, re-entrants, UI exhaustees, self-employed workers, and intermittent workers with limited resources.
UI program policy research			
	USDOL should support field tests of policy innovations, establish a repository for state administrative data to support program policy research, and establish 6 regional research hubs for research including biennial revisions of state WPRS models.		

SOURCE: Authors' compilation; White House (2017); West et al. (2016).

Appendix Notes

1. The White House-Obama (WHO) proposal was published in White House (2017), and the Center for American Progress (CAP) proposal was published in West et al. (2016).
2. There were just under 4 million live births in the United States in 2015, the average UI weekly benefit amount was $347 in the 12 months preceding April 1, 2017, and assuming every child had one parent collect 6 weeks of parental leave benefits, the payments would total $8.3 billion per year. Total UI payments in the year prior to April 1, 2017, were $31.2 billion. Parental leave payments would be higher if more than one parent draws benefits, and payments would be lower if the duration of parental leave were less than six weeks or if the take-up rate were less than 100 percent (as it is for regular UI payments). Our computations are based on figures from cdc.gov/nchs/fastats/births.htm and ows.doleta.gov/unemploy/content/data.asp (accessed April 26, 2018).
3. For 2016, overpayments were estimated to total $3.4 billion (USDOL 2017a).
4. See the Table of States with FUTA Reductions, 2009–2017 at: https://oui.doleta.gov/unemploy/futa_credit.asp (accessed April 26, 2018).

References

Advisory Council on Unemployment Compensation (ACUC). 1996. *Collected Findings and Recommendations*. Washington, DC: U.S. Department of Labor.

Agbayani, Cassandra, Bruno Gasperini, James Moore, Neha Nanda, Luke Patterson, and Stephen Wandner. 2016. *Labor Market and DOL-Funded Employment Assistance for Older Workers: Literature Review Report*. Columbia, MD: IMPAQ International, LLC. https://www.dol.gov/asp/evaluation/completed-studies/Lit_Review_Older_Workers_Labor_force .pdf (accessed September 29, 2017).

Anderson, Patricia M., and Bruce D. Meyer. 2006. "Unemployment Insurance Tax Burdens and Benefits: Funding Family Leave and Reforming the Payroll Tax." *National Tax Journal* 59(1): 77–95.

Balducchi, David, Stephen A. Wandner, Annalies Goger, Zachary Miller, Cassandra Agbayani, Jasmine Eucogco, and Sandeep Shetty. 2015. *Employer Views about the Short-Time Compensation Program: A Survey and Analysis in Four States*. Report prepared for the Employment and Training Administration. Washington, DC: U.S. Department of Labor.

Bennicci, Frank, and Stephen A. Wandner. 2015. *Short-Time Compensation after Enactment of the Middle Class Tax Relief and Job Creation Act of 2012: A Qualitative Assessment of the Short-Time Compensation Program*. Report from the Secretary of Labor to Congress. Washington, DC: U.S. Department of Labor.

Benus, Jacob M., Terry R. Johnson, Michelle Wood, Neelima Grover, and Theodore Shen. 1995. "Self-Employment Programs: A New Reemployment Strategy, Final Report on the UI Self-Employment Demonstration." Unemployment Insurance Occasional Paper 95-4. Washington, DC: U.S. Department of Labor, Employment and Training Administration, Unemployment Insurance Service.

Benus, Jacob, Eileen Poe-Yamagata, Ying Wang, and Etan Blass. 2008. *Reemployment Eligibility Assessment (REA) Study: FY2005 Initiative*. ETA Occasional Paper 2008-02. Washington, DC: U.S. Department of Labor, Employment and Training Administration.

Benus, Jacob M., Michelle L. Wood, Chris J. Napierala, and Terry R. Johnson. 1991. "Massachusetts Unemployment Insurance

Self-Employment Demonstration: Interim Report to Congress." In *Self-Employment Programs for Unemployed Workers*, Stephen A. Wandner, ed. Washington, DC: U.S. Department of Labor, Employment and Training Administration, Unemployment Insurance Service, pp. 167–236.

Black, Dan, Jeffrey Smith, Mark Berger, and Brett Noel. 2003. "Is the Threat of Reemployment Services More Effective than the Services Themselves? Experimental Evidence from Random Assignment in the UI System." *American Economic Review* 93(4): 1313–1327.

Blank, Rebecca M., and David E. Card. 1991. "Recent Trends in Insured and Uninsured Unemployment: Is There an Explanation?" *Quarterly Journal of Economics* 106(4): 1157–1189.

Blaustein, Saul J. 1993. *Unemployment Insurance in the United States: The First Half Century*. Kalamazoo, MI: W.E. Upjohn Institute for Employment Research.

Burgess, Paul L., and Jerry L. Kingston. 1987. *An Incentives Approach to Improving the Unemployment Compensation System*. Kalamazoo, MI: W.E. Upjohn Institute for Employment Research.

Burtless, Gary. 1983. "Why Is Insured Unemployment So Low?" *Brookings Papers on Economic Activity* 1983(1): 225–253.

Burtless, Gary, and Tracy Gordon. 2011. "The Federal Stimulus Programs and Their Effects." In *The Great Recession*, David B. Grusky, Bruce Western, Christopher Wimer, eds. New York: Russell Sage Foundation, pp. 249–293.

Card, David, and Craig Riddell. 1993. "A Comparative Analysis of Unemployment in Canada and the United States." In *Small Differences That Matter: Labor Markets and Income Maintenance in Canada and the United States*, David Card and Richard B. Freeman, eds. Chicago: University of Chicago Press, pp. 149–190.

Clarkwest, Andrew, Andrea Mraz Esposito, Nathan Wozny, Ji-Hyeun Kwon-Min, and Chelsea Swete. 2012. *Analysis of State UI Policies in Support of Efforts to Reduce Work Search Improper Payments: Final Report*. Submitted to the Office of Unemployment Insurance, U.S. Department of Labor. Washington, DC: Mathematica Policy Research.

Congressional Budget Office. 2012. *Understanding and Responding to Persistently High Unemployment*. Washington, DC: Congress of the United States, Congres-

sional   Budget   Office   (February).   http://www.cbo
.gov/sites/default/files/cbofiles/attachments/02-16-Unemploy-
ment.pdf (accessed September 29, 2017).

Corson, Walter, Paul T. Decker, Shari Miller Dunstan, and Anne R.
Gordon. 1989. *The New Jersey Unemployment Insurance Reemployment Demonstration Project: Final Report.* Unemployment
Insurance Occasional Paper 89-3. Washington, DC: U.S. Department of Labor, Employment and Training Administration.

Corson, Walter, Paul Decker, Shari Dunstan, and Stuart Kerachsky.
1992. Pennsylvania Reemployment Bonus Demonstration Final
Report. Unemployment Insurance Occasional Paper 92-1. Washington, DC: U.S. Department of Labor.

Corson, Walter, and Joshua Haimson. 1996. "The New Jersey Unemployment Insurance Reemployment Demonstration Project: Six-
Year Follow-Up and Summary Report." 2nd ed. Unemployment
Insurance Occasional Paper 96-2. Washington, DC: U.S. Department of Labor, Employment and Training Administration.

Corson, Walter, David Long, and Walter Nicholson. 1985. "Evaluation of the Charleston Claimant Placement and Work Test Demonstration." Unemployment Insurance Occasional Paper 85-2. Washington, DC: U.S. Department of Labor, Employment and Training
Administration.

Crimmann, Andreas, Frank Wiessner, and Lutz Bell. 2010. "The Ger-
man Work-Sharing Scheme: An Instrument for Crisis." Conditions
of Work and Employment Series No. 25. Geneva: International
Labour Organization.

Decker, Paul T. 1997. "Work Incentives and Disincentives." In *Unemployment Insurance in the United States: Analysis of Policy Issues*,
Christopher J. O'Leary and Stephen A. Wandner, eds. Kalamazoo,
MI: W.E. Upjohn Institute for Employment Research, pp. 285–
320.

Decker, Paul T., Robert B. Olsen, Lance Freeman, and Daniel
Klepinger. 2000. "Assisting Unemployment Insurance Claimants:
The Long-Term Impacts of the Job Search Assistance Demonstra-
tion." Office of Workforce Security Occasional Paper 2000-02.
Washington, DC: U.S. Department of Labor, Employment and
Training Administration.

Dickinson, Katherine P., Paul T. Decker, Suzanne D. Kreutzer, and

Richard W. West. 1999. *Evaluation of Worker Profiling and Reemployment Services: Final Report*, Research and Evaluation Report Series 99–D. Washington, DC: U.S. Department of Labor, Employment and Training Administration, Office of Policy and Research.

Ekos Research Associates. 1993. *Work Sharing Evaluation: Technical Report*. Ottawa: Employment and Immigration Canada.

Elsby, Michael W. L., Bart Hobijn, and Aysegul Sahin. 2010. "The Labor Market in the Great Recession." *Brookings Papers on Economic Activity* 2010(1): 1–70.

Employment and Training Administration. 2012. "The Middle Class Tax Relief and Job Creation Act of 2012 (Public Law (P.L.) 112-96 – Provisions on Self-Employment Assistance Program. https://wdr.doleta.gov/directives/attach/UIPL/UIPL_20_12_acc.pdf (accessed May 22, 2018).

Employment Development Department. 1982. *California Shared Work Unemployment Insurance Evaluation*. Sacramento: State of California, Employment Development Department.

Gilbert, Gay. 2011. "Testimony on Unemployment Insurance," before the Committee on Appropriations, Subcommittee for Labor, Health and Human Services, Education, and Related Agencies, U.S. House of Representatives, March 17. Washington, DC: U.S. Department of Labor, Employment and Training Administration, Office of Unemployment Insurance.

Government Accountability Office (GAO). 2007. *Unemployment Insurance: Low-Wage and Part-Time Workers Continue to Experience Low Rates of Receipt*. GAO-07-1147. Washington, DC: Government Accountability Office.

Groshen, Erica L., and Simon Potter. 2003. "Has Structural Change Contributed to the Jobless Recovery?" *Current Issues in Economics and Finance* 9(8): 1–7.

Haber, William, and Merrill G. Murray. 1966. *Unemployment Insurance in the American Economy*. Homewood, IL: Richard D. Irwin.

Human Resources and Skills Development Canada (HRSDC). 2005. Summative Evaluation of Work Sharing while Learning and Increased Referral to Training. Ottawa: HRSDC, Strategic Policy and Planning Branch.

Jacobson, Louis, Ian Petta, Amy Shimshak, and Regina Yudd. 2004. "Evaluation of Labor Exchange Services in a One-Stop Delivery System Environment." ETA Occasional Paper 2004-09. Washington, DC: U.S. Department of Labor, Employment and Training Administration.

Johnson, Terry R., and Daniel H. Klepinger. 1991. "Evaluation of the Impacts of the Washington Alternative Work Search Experiment." Unemployment Insurance Occasional Paper 91-4. Washington, DC: U.S. Department of Labor, Employment and Training Administration.

————. 1994. "Experimental Evidence on Unemployment Insurance Work-Search Policies." *Journal of Human Resources* 29(3): 695–717.

Katz, Lawrence F. 2010. "Comments" in Elsby, Michael W. L., Bart Hobijn, and Aysegul Sahin. 2010. "The Labor Market in the Great Recession." *Brookings Papers on Economic Activity* (Spring): 1–70.

Kerachsky, Stuart, Walter Nicholson, Edward Cavin, and Alan Hershey. 1986. "An Evaluation of Short-Time Compensation Programs." Unemployment Insurance Occasional Paper 86-4. Washington, DC: U.S. Department of Labor, Employment and Training Administration.

Klepinger, Daniel H., Terry R. Johnson, Jutta M. Joesch, and Jacob M. Benus. 1998. "Evaluation of the Maryland Unemployment Insurance Work Search Demonstration." Unemployment Insurance Occasional Paper 98-02. Washington, DC: U.S. Department of Labor, Employment and Training Administration.

Lalive, Rafael, and Josef Zweimuller. 2009. "How Does Parental Leave Affect Fertility and Return to Work? Evidence from Two Natural Experiments." *Quarterly Journal of Economics* 124(3): 1363–1402.

Mastri, Annalisa, Wayne Vroman, Karen Needels, and Walter Nicholson. 2016. *States' Decisions to Adopt Unemployment Compensation Provisions of the American Recovery and Reinvestment Act: Final Report.* Princeton, NJ: Mathematica Policy Research.

Mazumder, Bashkar. 2011. "How Did Unemployment Insurance Extensions Affect the Unemployment Rate in 2008–2010?" *Chicago Fed Letter* 285(April). Chicago, IL: Federal Reserve Bank of Chicago.

Michaelides, Marios, Eileen Poe-Yamagata, Jacob Benus, and Dharmendraa Tirumasatta. 2012. "Impact of the Reemployment and

Eligibility Assessment (REA) Initiative in Nevada." Employment and Training Administration Occasional Paper 2012-08. Washington, DC: U.S. Department of Labor.

Nicholson, Walter, and Karen Needels. 2006. "Unemployment Insurance: Strengthening the Relationship between Theory and Policy." *Journal of Economic Perspectives* 20(3): 47–70.

O'Leary, Christopher J. 1998. "The Adequacy of Unemployment Insurance Benefits." In *Research in Employment Policy*. Vol. 1, Laurie J. Bassi and Stephen A. Woodbury, eds. Stamford, CT: JAI, pp. 63–110.

———. 2010. "Policies for Displaced Workers: An American Perspective." Upjohn Institute Working Paper No. 10-70. Kalamazoo, MI: W.E. Upjohn Institute for Employment Research.

———. 2011. "Benefit Payment Costs of Unemployment Insurance Modernization: Estimates Based on Kentucky Administrative Data." Upjohn Institute Working Paper No. 11-12. Kalamazoo, MI: W.E. Upjohn Institute for Employment Research.

———. 2013. "A Changing Federal-State Balance in Unemployment Insurance?" *Employment Research* 20(1): 1–4.

O'Leary, Christopher J., and Burt S. Barnow. 2016. "Lessons from the American Federal-State Unemployment Insurance System for a European Unemployment Benefits System." Upjohn Institute Working Paper No. 16-264. Kalamazoo, MI: W.E. Upjohn Institute for Employment Research.

O'Leary, Christopher J., Paul T. Decker, and Stephen A. Wandner. 2005. "Cost Effectiveness of Targeted Reemployment Bonuses." *Journal of Human Resources* 40(1): 270–279.

O'Leary, Christopher J., and Randall W. Eberts. 2009. "The Wagner-Peyser Act and U.S. Employment Service: Seventy-Five Years of Matching Job Seekers and Employers," prepared for the National Association of State Workforce Agencies. Washington, DC (January).

O'Leary, Christopher J., and Kenneth J. Kline. 2016. "Are State Unemployment Insurance Reserves Sufficient for the Next Recession?" Upjohn Institute Working Paper 16-257. Kalamazoo, MI: W.E. Upjohn Institute for Employment Research.

O'Leary, Christopher J., Robert G. Spiegelman, and Kenneth J. Kline. 1995. "Do Bonus Offers Shorten Unemployment Insurance Spells?

Results from the Washington Reemployment Bonus Experiment." *Journal of Policy Analysis and Management* 14(2): 245–269.

O'Leary,Christopher J., and Stephen A. Wandner, eds. 1997. *Unemployment Insurance in the United States: Analysis of Policy Issues.* Kalamazoo, MI: W.E. Upjohn Institute for Employment Research.

Poe-Yamgata, Eileen, Jacob Benus, Nicholas Bill, Hugh Carrington, MariosMichaelides, and Ted Shen. 2011. "Impact of Reemployment ad Eligibility Assessment (REA) Initiative." Employment and Traning Administration Occasional Paper 2012-08. Washington, DCU.S. Department of Labor.

Rothstein, ?sse. 2012. "Unemployment Insurance and Job Search in the Gat Recession." *Brookings Papers on Economic Activity* 1(Fall): 3–213.

USDOL. n.d. "Temporary Federal Benefit Extension bgrams." Table. Washington, DC: U.S. Departme of Labor. https://workforcesecurity .doleta.go\nemploy/spec_ext_ben_table.asp (accessed March 15, 2018).

———. 2013."Initial Determination in Miami Workers Center v. Florida De;tment of Economic Opportunity, Division of Workforce Servi;." Civil Rights Center Complaint No. 12-FL-048. WashingtonC: U.S. Department of Labor, Civil Rights Center.

———. 2016Comparison of State Unemployment Insurance Laws." Wasgton, DC: U.S. Department of Labor, Employment and Traininglministration, Office of Unemployment Insurance.

———. 2017aenefit Accuracy Measurement State Data Summary, Impro\Payment Information Act Year 2016." Washington, DC: Offi\f Unemployment Insurance, U.S. Department of Labor.

———. 2017b.\nemployment Insurance Outlook: President's Budget FY 20 Washington, DC: Division of Fiscal and Actuarial Services,ice of Unemployment Insurance, U.S. Department of Labor.

———. 2018. "St\nemployment Insurance Trust Fund Solvency Report." Washin, DC: Division of Fiscal and Actuarial Services, Office of Un\loyment Insurance, U.S. Department of Labor (March) https:,.doleta.gov/unemploy/docs/trustFundSolvReport2018.pdf (a\ed March 30, 2018).

Vroman, Wayne. 2016. "The Big States and Unemployment Insurance Financing." Washington, DC: The Urban Institute. http://www.urban.org/sites/default/files/alfresco/publication-pdfs/2000661The-Big-States-and-Unemployment-Insurance-Financing.pdf (accessed September 29, 2017).

Vroman, Wayne, and Vera Brusentsev. 2009. "Short-Time Compensation as a Policy to Stabilize Employment." Washington, DC: The Urban Institute. http://www.urban.org/sites/default/files/alfresco/publication-pdfs/411983-Short-Time-Compensation-as-a-Policy-to-Stabilize-Employment.PDF (accessed September 29, 2017).

Walsh, Stephen, Rebecca London, Deana McCanne, Karen Needels, Walter Nicholson, and Stuart Kerachsky. 1997. "Evaluation of Short-Time Compensation Programs: Final Report." UI Occasional Paper 97-3. Washington, DC: U.S. Department of Labor, Employment and Training Administration.

Wandner, Stephen A. 2010. *Solving the Reemployment Puzzle: From Research to Policy*. Kalamazoo, MI: W.E. Upjohn Institute for Employment Research.

———. 2012. "The Response of the U.S. Public Workforce System to High Unemployment during the Great Recession." Unemployment and Recovery Project Working Paper 4. Washington, DC: The Urban Institute. https://www.urban.org/research/publication/response-us-public-workforce-system-high-unemployment-during-great-recession (accessed September 29, 2017).

———. 2013a. "The Public Workforce System's Response to Declining Funding after the Great Recession." Unemployment and Recovery Project Working Paper 5. Washington, DC: The Urban Institute. https://www.urban.org/research/publication/public-workforce-systems-response-declining-funding-after-great-recession (accessed September 29, 2017).

———. 2013b. "Trade Adjustment Assistance Program." In *The American Recovery and Reinvestment Act: The Role of Workforce Programs*, Burt S. Barnow and Richard A. Hobbie, eds. Kalamazoo, MI: W.E. Upjohn Institute for Employment Research, pp. 151–172.

210 O'Leary and Wandner

———. 2015. "The Future of the Public Workforce System in a Time of Dwindling Resources." In *Transforming U.S. Workforce Development Policies for the 21st Century*, Carl Van Horn, Tammy Edwards, and Todd Greene, eds. Kalamazoo, MI: W.E. Upjohn Institute for Employment Research, pp. 129–168.

Wandner, Stephen A., and Jon Messenger, eds. 1999. *Worker Profiling and Reemployment Services Policy Workgroup: Final Report and Recommendations*. Washington, DC: U.S. Department of Labor, Employment and Training Administration.

West, Rachel, Indivar Dutta-Gupta, Kali Grant, Melissa Boteach, Claire McKenna, and Judy Conti. 2016. "Strengthening Unemployment Insurance Protections in America: Modernizing Unemployment Insurance and Establishing a Jobseekers Allowance." Washington, DC: Center for American Progress. https://cdn.americanprogress.org/wp-content/uploads/2016/05/31134245/UI_JSAreport.pdf (accessed September 29, 2017).

The White House. 2017. *America First: A Budget Blueprint to Make America Great Again*. Washington, DC: Office of Management and Budget.

Woodbury, Stephen A. 2014. "Unemployment Insurance." Upjohn Institute Working Paper No. 14208. Kalamazoo, MI: W.E. Upjohn Institute for Employment Research.

Woodbury, Stephen A., and Murray Rubin. 1997. "The Duration of Benefits." In *Unemployment Insurance in the United States: Analysis of Policy Issues*, Christopher J. O'Leary and Stephen A. Wandner, eds. Kalamazoo, MI: W.E. Upjohn Institute for Employment Research, pp. 211–283.

Chapter 6

Conclusions and Needed Reforms

Stephen A. Wandner
*W.E. Upjohn Institute for Employment Research
and The Urban Institute*

This book has carefully examined the Unemployment Insurance (UI) system and reviewed a number of recent proposals for UI reform. All of these proposals find that the UI program requires substantial reform. The reform proposals cover a wide range of needed changes, and they suggest alternative approaches for resolving some issues. Thus, a number of approaches should be taken into consideration to implement the key reforms discussed below, and many options for change have been discussed in the earlier chapters.

The main thrust of this book is the need for comprehensive reform that creates a robust, self-sustaining UI program that restores the ability of the system to reliably provide temporary adequate income replacement during the search for reemployment. Reforms should put the UI system in balance so that benefits and taxes are in equilibrium both in the long term and over the business cycle. The UI benefit system must be adequate and reflect current labor force behavior and current economic conditions. In addition, UI taxes need to be able to pay for a robust program of UI benefits and be distributed equitably. Finally, the objective of UI is not just to provide income support to unemployed workers, but to help them return to work, so reemployment services are required for all permanently separated workers.

KEY REFORMS

Below is a list of key needed UI reforms. The list is a broad summary of reforms and is not as comprehensive as some of the proposals discussed in the previous chapters, but it outlines a framework for a sustainable, adequate, and equitable UI system to provide adequate benefits for experienced, unemployed workers.

Bring Benefits and Taxes in Balance

Today, the UI system is out of balance. The federal tax base is inadequate, and many state taxable wage bases are also inadequate. Tax rates are not necessarily adjusted to accommodate adequate benefit payment levels, and benefit levels and maximums are adjusted upward over time in some states but not others.

Strategic balancing of UI revenues and benefits has been neglected throughout the program's history at both the state and federal levels. By contrast, Social Security has dealt with this issue repeatedly and has assured that both benefit levels and the taxable wage base keep up with the cost of living. The same should be done with UI.

Regular UI Benefits

The basic regular 26-week UI system should be changed. It needs to have adequate benefit levels and benefit durations as well as reasonable eligibility conditions for workers with past attachment to the labor force before they become unemployed. And the benefit provisions should be adapted to the substantial changes that have occurred in the United States in recent decades.

Adequate benefit levels

Given the wide discretion of states to shape their state UI programs, UI benefit provisions vary greatly across the country, and they are likely to continue to do so in the future. This variation is significant enough that it creates substantial equity problems, with unemployed workers receiving widely different duration levels, even after adjusting for state differences in average weekly wages.

Proponents have argued for a benefit amount standard for seven decades. They have reached a consensus that the original proposal is the most reasonable—to set the maximum weekly benefit amount at two-thirds of each state's average weekly wage.

Adequate benefit duration

There should be a minimum of 26 weeks of potential duration. It was not previously necessary to advocate for this in the past because all states had a minimum potential duration of 26 weeks from the mid-1970s until 2010. The spread of lower potential durations in the past few years shows that such a standard is needed.

Eligibility conditions

A small number of states have significantly narrowed benefit eligibility and harshened benefit administration. States should be encouraged to avoid punitive eligibility conditions that reduce benefit recipiency below reasonable levels.

On the other hand, as a social insurance program, unemployed workers should not be eligible for UI benefits unless they have exhibited recent attachment to the labor force. To achieve this goal, O'Leary and Wandner (Chapter 5) recommend setting eligibility for minimum benefit amounts with high quarter earnings of at least $1,000 and second highest quarter earnings of at least $500.

Adjust other benefit provisions to the changing American labor force

The American labor force has changed significantly in the decades since UI was enacted in 1935. The biggest changes over the past two decades have been more multiple earners within households, a long-term increase in the participation of women, and the increased participation of older workers over the past two decades. The program should adjust to this modern labor force by implementing the following changes:

- For two-worker families, UI should pay benefits when one spouse follows the other to a new job in a new location.

- The participation of women and older workers has resulted in a sharp increase in part-time work. The UI program should allow part-time workers to collect UI while searching for part-time work.

- Older workers often have to change career jobs or move to jobs that "bridge" their transition to full retirement. These transitions require job search methods that are different from traditional job searches for similar employment. They often result in older workers taking bridge jobs that involve a decline in wages, a change in industry and occupation, or a change from full-time to part-time work, so older workers should be provided with special reemployment services to help with the search for bridge jobs and new careers.

- Because many older workers are continuing to work after leaving their long-term career jobs, the federal pension offset provision should be removed.

UI Finance

Adequate, equitable funding

Today, low wage employers pay a disproportionate share of UI taxes. They may pay UI taxes on all or nearly all of their wages paid, while high wage employers may pay taxes on only a small portion of their wage bill.

- A higher taxable wage base is needed to spread the burden among low and high wage employers, as well as to raise adequate revenue.

- The UI taxable wage base must be increased considerably, such that it equals between one-third and one-half of the Social Security taxable wage base. It should also be indexed each year to increase at the same percentage rate as the Social Security taxable wage base. Alternatively, the UI taxable wage could be tied to the average wage in covered UI employment rather than to the Social Security wage base.

- To have a sound UI tax system, state tax schedules should be set such that no state is permitted to include a zero rate in any tax schedule so that all employers support UI system operating costs and each tax schedule includes at least 10 rates so that all employers pay UI taxes closely reflecting their unemployment experience.

- Employers tend to oppose increases in UI benefits and taxes because they pay the entire tax. UI research, however, indicates that the incidence of the UI tax falls, in part, on workers through reductions in their total compensation, that is, wages plus benefits. The UI tax should change from an employer tax to a joint employer-employee tax, with employees paying half or more of the tax so that employees have increased ownership in the UI program.

Countercyclical funding

- To have a countercyclical financing system, forward funding is needed. The Unemployment Trust Fund should have adequate reserves before a recession. UI taxes should not be increased at the beginning of a recession. State accounts in the Unemployment Trust Fund should be restored after a recession is over and before the next recession begins.

- States need to adhere to the appropriate tax schedule under their state law, without any legislative deferral of movement to higher schedules, subject to loss of UI offset credits. State tax schedules need to be selected annually based on maintaining or achieving adequate state system reserves.

- U.S. Department of Labor reserve requirements should guide states in attaining reserve adequacy.

- Building an adequate trust fund can be facilitated by either requiring states to reach an adequate level of reserves or by providing states with a financial incentive for building their reserves to a specified level. Both approaches have been recommended by UI reform proposals, and both would improve system solvency.

Administrative financing

The administration of the UI, Employment Service (ES), and other federal-state labor market programs is funded from the Federal Unemployment Tax Act portion of the UI tax. Federal funding pays for program administration, extended benefits, and loans to states—each with its own account. For many years, states have faced severe funding problems in the administration of these programs, and it has become more severe over time. The balances in the federal accounts have been inadequate, and Congress has appropriated a declining percentage of the tax revenues that are deposited into the administrative account.

Whereas the payment of UI benefits is an entitlement and does not require appropriations from Congress, the payment of administrative funds to the state agencies for UI and Wagner-Peyser Act programs is discretionary and must be appropriated. Congress should fully fund UI and ES administration. Appropriation levels for UI should fully reflect benefit payment, benefit integrity, and tax collection costs. Appropriations for ES should be greatly increased, bringing appropriations back to the 1984 level in real terms—a time when ES funding was more adequate.

Extended Benefits

- Although Congress will always want to have the final say about benefit duration extensions during recessions, it often is slow to take action. The United States needs an automatic system of benefit extensions that works in a timely fashion.

- Extended benefits (EB) are not insurable. They should not be treated like the regular 26-week program and should be funded from general federal revenues.

- Existing EB triggers don't work. They should be replaced with a new trigger mechanism that uses the total unemployment rate rather than the insured unemployment rate. The number of weeks of EB should vary with the unemployment rate, so that EB is sensitive to the severity of recessions.

- More specifically, recent EB program proposals reviewed in this book propose to improve the EB trigger mechanism by making use of the total unemployment rate and having multiple levels of EB durations from 7 to 54 weeks. EB should be paid 100 percent by the federal government, either from the Unemployment Trust Fund or from general revenue.

Reemployment Services and the Work Test

The work test is crucial for having the UI program remain as a social insurance program. The ES provides the work test under federal law, ensuring that UI recipients are able, available, and actively searching for work. The service also refers UI recipients to jobs and provides them with labor market information.

- Reemployment services are critical in a world with few temporary layoffs and many permanently displaced unemployed workers. The UI and ES programs need sufficient funding to provide displaced workers with intensive, in-person job search assistance.

- Job search assistance and other reemployment services have been shown to be highly cost effective in promoting return to work and shortening durations of UI benefit receipt. Nonetheless, UI claimants receive inadequate reemployment services both because of general underfunding of ES and because of inadequate and declining funding of UI reemployment services.

O'Leary and Wandner (Chapter 5) recommend restoring ES funding to its 1984 level in real terms.

- Other reemployment and unemployment prevention services can speed the return to work of UI recipients by expanding their use in short-time compensation and self-employment assistance programs, and by enacting a program of targeted reemployment bonuses. New federal legislation would be needed to make reemployment bonuses a legal use of Unemployment Trust Fund reserves.

CONCLUSION

Public policy toward the UI program has been neglectful for many decades. Much of the program is broken and requires major reform now. Both states and the federal government should adopt policies and legislation that can restore the program to be consistent with its original intent. Otherwise, the system will be inadequate in the future, particularly when it is needed during the next recession.

This book has reviewed a number of recent comprehensive UI reform proposals. The proposals present alternative approaches for improving the program. Policymakers should conduct a comprehensive review of the UI program and options for change, including the various proposals considered in this book.

Authors

David E. Balducchi is a research and policy consultant specializing in unemployment insurance and employment services programs. Among his recent projects, he was principal investigator for IMPAQ International, Inc., conducting an evaluation of employer participation in short-time compensation programs. Retired from the U.S. Department of Labor, his responsibilities included managing the research of public workforce demonstration projects, developing employment services policy, and analyzing unemployment insurance legislation. As a U.S. Senate aide, he drafted federal laws for national service and short-time compensation. Mr. Balducchi received the 2013 George Mills-Louise Noun Iowa Popular History Award for his article, "Iowans Harry Hopkins and Henry A. Wallace Helped Craft Social Security's Blueprint." He holds an MPA from Drake University and a BA in political science from St. Ambrose College.

Christopher J. O'Leary is a senior economist at the W. E. Upjohn Institute for Employment Research where he joined the staff in 1987. He holds a PhD in economics from the University of Arizona. He has authored many articles, papers. and monographs on aspects of unemployment insurance and workforce programs. In unemployment insurance research, he has evaluated many unemployment and reemployment programs and demonstration projects. He has edited and contributed to several books published by the W.E. Upjohn Institute.

Suzanne Simonetta is the Director of the Division of Policy, Legislation, and Regulations in the Employment and Training Administration, U.S. Department of Labor. Previously, Ms. Simonetta was the Chief of Legislation in the Office of Unemployment Insurance. In that position, she worked on a variety of initiatives, including the Middle Class Tax Relief and Job Creation Act of 2012, the American Recovery and Reinvestment Act of 2009, and Emergency Unemployment Compensation. She holds an MA in political science from Syracuse University and a BA in government from Cornell University.

Wayne Vroman is a senior economist at the Urban Institute. He holds a PhD in economics from the University of Michigan and has authored many articles, papers, and monographs on aspects of unemployment insurance, including taxes, trust funds, and benefits. He has written three books on unemployment insurance benefit financing that have been published by the W.E. Upjohn Institute.

Stephen A. Wandner is an economic consultant. He is a Research Fellow at the W.E. Upjohn Institute for Employment Research, a Visiting Fellow at the Urban Institute, and a Senior Fellow at the National Academy of Social Insurance. He holds a PhD in economics from Indiana University. He formerly worked for the U.S. Department of Labor, including as Director of Research for the Employment and Training Administration and Chief of Benefit Financing and Deputy Director of the Office of Legislation, Research, and Actuarial Services in the Unemployment Insurance Service. He has authored many articles, papers, and monographs on unemployment insurance and workforce programs. He has edited three books that have been published by the W.E. Upjohn Institute.

Index

Note: The italic letters *f*, *n*, or *t* following a page number indicate a figure, note, or table, respectively, on that page. Double letters mean more than one such consecutive item on a single page.

ACUC (Advisory Council for Unemployment Compensation), 13, 153

Advisory Council for Unemployment Compensation (ACUC), post-recession creation of, 13, 153

AHCM. *See* Average high cost multiple

AJCs (American Job Centers), 66, 78, 81, 94*n*35

Alabama, 126*t*
    action by, to improve UI program financing, 104*t*, 105

Alaska, 59*n*4, 126*t*
    action by, to improve UI program financing, 104*t*, 105

Alternative Trade Adjustment Assistance (ATTA) program, wage insurance for older workers under, 185

Altmeyer, Arthur, ES-UI partnership and, 67–68, 72, 90*n*4, 91*n*16, 92*n*19

American Job Centers (AJCs), as public offices for ES, 66, 78, 81, 94*n*35

American Recovery and Reinvestment Act (ARRA, 2009), 59*n*3
    ES funding from, 7, 94–95*n*39, 140, 174*n*4
    temporary *vs.* permanent federal EB payments to states with TUR triggers, 146, 149–150
    UI Modernization provisions in, 13–14, 47, 49–52, 134–135, 135*t*, 174*n*1, 181, 182, 193, 197

Apprenticeships, 195, 200

Arizona, 126*t*
    bonding by, to finance UI during Great Recession, 104*t*, 106
    changes to benefit duration in, 36, 37*f*

Arkansas, 108*t*, 126*t*
    duration of UI benefits in, 85, 95*n*43, 112, 113*f*, 114, 114*t*, 123*nn*9–10, 143–144, 174*n*6

solvency improved through legislation in, 104*t*, 105

ARRA. *See* American Recovery and Reinvestment Act (2009)

ATTA (Alternative Trade Adjustment Assistance) program, 185

Average high cost multiple (AHCM)
    forward-funding of UTF and, 153, 175*n*13, 181, 184, 188
    prerecession state RRMs, 104–107, 104*t*, 122*n*1
    as state solvency measurement, 28, 41–42, 42*f*, 46, 60*n*29

Benefit payments
    adequacy of, currently, 4, 10, 11–12, 42–43, 45*f*, 172–173
    adequacy of, in proposals, 47–52, 60–61*n*23, 132, 144–145, 174*n*8, 212–213
    alternative employment base periods for, 24–25, 48, 59*n*4, 133–135, 135*t*, 138, 189
    balance of, with taxes, 3–4, 11–12, 18, 132, 212
    borrowing by states to pay, 27, 40–42, 41*f*, 43*f*, 59*n*7–9
    changes to maximum weekly, amount in, 110–111, 123*nn*4–6
    duration of, 33–39, 35*ff*, 36*f*, 37*t*, 38*f*, 43, 47, 110, 112–115, 113*f*, 123*nn*8–9, 132, 143, 145, 174*nn*5–6, 212, 213
    eligibility for, 9, 14, 16, 24–25, 43, 47, 58*n*2, 59*n*3, 88–89, 132, 133–137
    eligibility for, in UI reform proposals, 177, 178*t*, 180, 181, 183, 189–193, 213
    financing, and policy recommendations, 133–150, 196–198

Benefit payments, *cont.*
  integrity of, 31, 56–57, 60*n*18, 187,
    201*n*3
  state UI, post-Great Recession,
    110–116
  UI recipients and, 1–2, 5, 6, 9, 19*n*1–
    2, 29–30, 38*f,* 39*f,* 60*n*13
  See also Extended Benefits (EB)
    program
Benefit standards
  UI, needed and federalism, 149–150,
    175*n*11
  UI reform proposals for, 178*t,* 180,
    181–182, 193–195
BLS. *See* Bureau of Labor Statistics
Bureau of Labor Statistics (BLS)
  data supplied by, 32–44, 60*n*19, 62
  WKTU ratio measured by, 116–117,
    128*t*
Bush, Pres. George W., ES grants cut by,
    82, 94–95*n*39

California, 126*t,* 165
  benefit payments in, 111, 123*n*7, 187
  FUTA tax credit offsets in, 104*t,*
    106–107, 108–109, 108*t*
  UI debts and loan payments to U.S.
    Treasury by, 107, 121, 122*n*3,
    144, 174–175*n*9, 174*n*7
Canada, STC programs in, 165
CAP (Center for American Progress), 14,
    86, 171, 177, 201*n*1
Capitalism, employment security
    programs in, 67, 90*n*4
Career services
  typically same as ES services, 79
  See also One-stop career services
Center for American Progress (CAP),
    nonprofit study of UI partnership
    and reform by, 15, 86, 177,
    189, 201*n*1
Center on Poverty and Inequality (CPI),
    Georgetown University Law
    Center, nonprofit study of UI
    partnership and reform by, 15, 86,
    177, 189
CGN (nonprofit consortium) and its UI
    reform proposal, 15, 86, 177

  differences from OW proposal,
    181–182
  particulars of, 178*t*–179*t,* 184, 189–
    200
  social welfare aims in, 182, 183, 185
Civil Works Administration, public work
    projects under, 68, 90–91*n*7
Clinton, Pres. William J., reemployment
    bonuses and, 170–171, 175*n*18
Colorado, 126*t*
  debts in bond market for UI financing
    by, 59*n*7, 104*t,* 106, 107, 122*n*3
  duration of UI benefits in, and bond
    debt payments, 144, 174*n*7
  ES funding delayed in, due to
    political issues, 70, 91*n*13
  tax base indexation adopted post-
    recession by, 104*t,* 106
Commission of Economic Security
    (CES), 69
  social insurance report by, 67–68, 72,
    90*nn*5–6, 92*n*18
Connecticut, 126*t*
  offset FUTA tax credits by, to
    improve UI program financing,
    104*t,* 106–107, 108*t,* 109
  UI program loan payments to U.S.
    Treasury by, 144, 174*n*7
Council of Economic Advisers,
    participation in White House
    meeting on UI by, 15–16
CPI (Center on Poverty and Inequality),
    Georgetown University Law
    Center, 15, 86, 177, 189

Delaware, 126*t,* 168
  tax base increases in, to improve UI
    program financing, 104*t,* 106
Discrimination lawsuits, UI recipients
    and, 136
Dislocated Worker programs, 169
  help for returning to employment
    with, 80, 159, 161, 171–172
  modest to nonexistent funding for,
    8–9
  public job training in, 76, 92–93*n*27
  WPRS as unfunded mandate of, 82,
    94–95*n*39

District of Columbia, 48
    action by, to improve UI program
        financing, 104*t*, 105
    UI recipiency rate in, 117, 126*t*
Domestic Policy Council, participation
    in White House meeting on UI
    by, 15–16

EB program. *See* Extended Benefit (EB)
    program
Economic rights, 83, 150
Education and training, research and
    policy recommendations for,
    172–173
Eisenhower, Pres. Dwight D., 75, 83
Eligibility review procedures (ERPs),
    163
    cost-effectiveness of, 161–162
    as ES function, 140, 187
Emergency Unemployment
    Compensation Act (1991), ACUC
    created by, 13
Emergency Unemployment
    Compensation (EUC) program,
    61*n*28, 89
    ARRA extension of, 13, 61*n*30
    effect on unemployment rate of,
        147–148
    Great Recession and, 54–55, 56,
        61*n*29
    as temporary measure, 133, 145, 146
    UI reform proposals and, 179*t*, 180,
        181–182, 195
Employers
    FUTA tax credits to, 27, 46, 59*nn*8–9
    integrity of, 31, 57, 60*n*18
    not at fault, and involuntary
        unemployment, 49, 61*n*24
    payroll tax on, as UI contributions, 2,
        26, 83, 151–152, 155–156, 180
    preventing workforce dispersal of,
        66, 90*n*2
    resistance to UI reform by, 11–12,
        60*n*22, 155, 215
    UI tax rates and, 153, 214–215
    work-sharing survey of, 165–166
    worker fired by, due to misconduct,
        49–50

Employment
    earnings from, and work history
        for UI eligibility, 24–25, 48,
        58*n*2, 175*n*12
    part-time, and UI adaptation to, 9, 47,
        49, 138–139, 214
    suitable work in policy
        recommendations for UI reform,
        135, 139–140, 174*n*3, 192
Employment and reemployment services
    background, 159–161
    research and recommendations,
        161–173
    See also Education and training;
        Employment Service (ES);
        entries beginning Reemployment;
        Self-Employment Assistance
        (SEA); Short-time compensation
        (STC); *under* UI recipients,
        helping, return to work; Worker
        Profiling and Reemployment
        services (WPRS)
Employment and Training
    Administration (ETA)
    data supplied by, 32, 43, 48, 54–55, 62
    Office of UI now within, 115–116
Employment Security Administrative
    Financing Act (1954), 76
    earmarking of FUTA receipts in,
        74–75, 92*nn*25–26, 158
    UTF deposits of excess FUTA
        receipts for state loans in, 156–
        157
Employment security programs
    capitalism and, 67, 90*n*4
    earmarking revenues for, 74–75,
        92*nn*25–26
    See also mention of ES-UI under
        Partnerships
Employment Service (ES)
    adapting to permanent layoffs by, 8,
        29–30
    evolution of federal, partnership with
        state UI programs, 17, 52, 61*n*27,
        65–90
    (*see also under* Partnerships)
    functions of, 66, 80–81, 90*n*1, 90*n*3,
        140, 161, 193, 217–*218*

Employment Service (ES), *cont.*
funding of, 6, 68–69, 76–77, 80–84, 87–88, 90*nn*9–11, 92*nn*21–24, 158, 164, 197–198
(*see also under* Wagner-Peyser Act (1933), ES-UI funding and)
job placements by, 73, 94*n*34, 135, 162–163, 175*n*12
older workers and, 9, 134
public offices for, 52, 61*n*27, 66, 68–70, 83, 91*n*10, 92*n*18, 140, 174*n*4
staffing levels in policy recommendations for UI reform, 140–141, 193
Entrepreneurial training, funding for, 169, 170, 199
ERPs (Eligibility review procedures), 140, 161–163, 187
ES. *See* Employment Service
ETA. *See* Employment and Training Administration
EUC. *See* Emergency Unemployment Compensation (EUC) program
Extended Benefits (EB) program, 19*n*1, 59*n*11
administration funding through FUTA, 6, 59*n*12
analysis of, in budget proposals, 52–55
Congress and, 5, 6, 13, 146
faulty trigger mechanism of, 10, 28–29, 52, 145–146, 217
as permanent measure with research and recommendations, 132, 145–150
UI reform proposals for, 178*t*, 180, 181, 182, 183, 195, 197, 216–217

Family units, 53
multiple workers within given, 213–214
uniform UI eligibility for, 88–89, 135, 135*t*, 174*n*1, 191–192
workforce definition of, 47, 48–49
Federal Security Agency, 90*n*4
Social Security Administration and ES transferred to, 74, 92*n*24

Federal-State Extended Unemployment Compensation Act (1970), 45–46, 59*n*11
Federal Unemployment Tax Act (FUTA), 45, 155, 196–198
earmarking revenues from, for employment security programs, 74–75, 79, 92*nn*25–26, 132–133, 141
general revenues mixed with, receipts, 76, 156, 167, 175*n*15
policy call to raise, taxable wage base, 87–88, 151–154, 175*n*14
state credit reductions post-Great Recession, 107–109, 108*t*, 128*n*4, 188
tax credits to employers and states under, 27, 59*nn*8–9, 188
tax rate on workers' earnings in, 25–26, 59*nn*5–6, 81–82, 94*n*38
UI administration funding through, 6, 51, 59*n*12, 60*n*13, 61*n*26, 197–198, 216
Federalism, UI benefit standards needed and, 149–150, 175*n*11
Florida, 108*t*, 110, 126*t*, 136, 174*n*3
duration of UI benefits in, 36, 37*f*, 85, 95*n*43, 112, 113*f*, 114, 114*t*, 123*n*9, 143–144, 174*n*6
FUTA. *See* Federal Unemployment Tax Act

Georgetown University Law Center, CPI, nonprofit study of UI partnership and reform by, 15, 86, 177, 189
Georgia, 126*t*, 174*n*3
changes to UI maximum weekly benefit amount in, 111, 114, 114*t*, 123*n*7
duration of UI benefits in, 36, 37*f*, 85, 95*n*43, 113*f*, 143–144, 174*n*6
FUTA tax credit offsets in, 104*t*, 106–107, 108*t*
Germany, STC programs in, 165
Great Depression, recovery from, 5, 68, 90–91*n*7, 91*n*8
Great Recession 2007–2009, 7, 82
avoiding problems experienced during, 4, 14, 54, 56

Great Recession 2007–2009, *cont.*
impact of, 40, 130, 144, 159
national recovery from
(*see* American Recovery and
Reinvestment Act [ARRA, 2009])
state responses to
(*see* State UI financing post-Great
Recession)

Hawaii, 1967–2007 regular UI
recipiency rate regression of, 126*t*

Idaho, 126*t*
bonding by, to finance UI during
Great Recession, 104*t*, 106
changes to benefit duration in, 36, 37*f*
Illinois, 126*t*, 170
debts in bond market for UI financing
by, 59*n*7, 104*t*, 106, 107, 122*n*3,
144, 174*n*7
duration of UI benefits in, 36, 37*f*, 85,
95*n*43, 144, 174*n*7
ES funding delayed in, due to
political issues, 70, 91*n*13
FUTA credit reductions as share of
UI tax revenue in, 108*t*
ILO (International Labor Organization),
83
Indiana
1967–2007 regular UI recipiency rate
regression of, 126*t*
changes to UI maximum weekly
benefit amount in, 111
FUTA tax credit offsets in, 104*t*,
106–107, 108*t*
UI program in, with debts to
Treasury, 107, 122*n*3
Insured unemployment rate (IUR)
as EB trigger, 28–29, 146, 149
ratio of, to TUR as UI recipiency
rate, 38*f*, 39, 39*f*, 136, 137*f*
International Labor Organization (ILO),
asserts rights of workforce to free
labor market information, 83
Iowa, 126*t*, 174*n*3
action by, to improve UI program
financing, 104*t*, 105
ES office closures in, 81, 91*n*14, 94*n*35

IUR. *See* Insured unemployment rate

Job creation, 200
federal law for, 31, 56, 161
Job Search Assistance program
cost of, 86–87, 95*n*44
funding of, and service levels, 66,
184
UI recipients and, 7, 80, 147, 150,
163, 217–218
Job seekers allowance, UI reform
proposal for, 185
Job training, 89
federal laws for, 76, 78, 82–83,
95*n*40
public, and dislocated workers, 76,
92–93*n*27
UI benefits receipt during, 194–195
Job Training Partnership Act (1982),
175*n*16
ES-UI cooperation required in, 78,
93*n*30
incrementalism in, 70, 91*n*12
research and policy recommendations
for, 140–141, 163–164

Kansas, 126*t*
acceptance by, of matching Wagner-
Peyser funds in its UI laws, 70,
90*n*11
duration of UI benefits in, 36, 37*f*,
85, 95*n*43, 113*f*, 114, 114*t*, 143–
144, 174*n*6
tax base increases in, to improve UI
program financing, 104*t*, 106
work-sharing survey of employers in,
165–166
Kentucky, 126*t*, 163
FUTA tax credit offsets in, 104*t*,
106–107, 108*t*
UI program in, with debts to
Treasury, 107, 122*n*3

Labor force. *See* Workforce
Labor markets
changed conditions in, as priority for
UI reform, 8–11, 85, 131–132,
182, 213–214

Labor markets, *cont.*
information about, 7, 83, 217
maintaining robust, in U.S., 65–66
Layoffs, 2, 159
STC and, 30–31, 60*nn*14–17, 166
switch from temporary, to permanent, 8, 217
UI payments during, 29–30, 60*n*13, 153
Louisiana, 126*t*
action by, to improve UI program financing, 104*t*, 105

Maine, 126*t*, 174*n*3
acceptance by, of matching Wagner-Peyser funds in its UI laws, 70, 90*n*11
action by, to improve UI program financing, 104*t*, 105
effective SEA program in, 168, 169
Manpower Development and Training Act (MDTA, 1962), ES-UI partnership and, 76, 92–93*n*27
Maryland, 127*t*
acceptance by, of matching Wagner-Peyser funds in its UI laws, 70, 90*n*11
action by, to improve UI program financing, 104*t*, 105
reemployment services in, 162, 168
Massachusetts, 127*t*, 174*n*5
2012–2015, not subject to FUTA credit reductions, 108, 108*t*
ES funding delayed in, due to political issues, 70, 91*nn*13–14
self-employment allowance experiment in, 168–169
MCTRJCA. *See* Middle Class Tax Relief and Job Creation Act (2012)
Means tests and social welfare, 133, 185
Michigan
1967–2007 regular UI recipiency rate regression of, 127*t*
acceptance by, of matching Wagner-Peyser funds in its UI laws, 70, 90*n*11
bonding by, to finance UI during Great Recession, 59*n*7, 104*t*, 106, 107, 122*n*3

changes to UI maximum weekly benefit amount in, 111, 123*n*7
ES grant suspended in, 91*n*14
UI benefit duration in, 36, 37*f*, 85, 95*n*43, 112, 113*f*, 114, 114*t*, 143–144, 174*nn*6–7
Middle Class Tax Relief and Job Creation Act (MCTRJCA, 2012)
implementation of, as USDOL study, 165, 166–167
STC encouraged in, 31, 56, 161, 165, 169
Minnesota, 127*t*, 164
ES funding delayed in, due to political issues, 70, 91*n*13
work-sharing survey of employers in, 165–166
Mississippi, 127*t*, 174*n*3
acceptance by, of matching Wagner-Peyser funds in its UI laws, 70, 90*n*11
tax base increases in, to improve UI program financing, 104*t*, 106
Missouri, 127*t*, 174*n*3
changes to UI maximum weekly benefit amount in, 111, 123*n*7
duration of UI benefis in, 85, 95*n*43
duration of UI benefits in, 36, 37*f*, 112, 113*f*, 114*t*, 123*nn*9–10, 143–144, 174*n*6
ES funding delayed in, due to political issues, 70, 91*nn*13–14
FUTA tax credit offsets in, 104*t*, 106–107, 108*t*
Montana, 127*t*, 174*n*5
acceptance by, of matching Wagner-Peyser funds in its UI laws, 70, 90*n*11
action by, to improve UI program financing, 104*t*, 105
suitable work as nonmonetary UI eligibility redefined by, 140, 174*n*3
Moral hazard, UI recipients' reemployment and risk of, 66
Municipal bonds
states issued, to repay Treasury for recession UI loans, 104*t*, 106

Municipal bonds, *cont.*
  states with debts in, market, 107,
    120, 122*n*3, 174*n*7

NAFTA (North American Free Trade
    Act), 169
NASI (National Academy of Social
    Insurance), 16
National Academy of Social Insurance
    (NASI), UI reform examined by,
    16
National Commission on Unemployment
    Compensation (NCUC), reports
    generated by, 12, 77, 93*n*28
National Economic Council,
    participation in White House
    meeting on UI by, 15–16
National Employment Law Project
    (NELP), nonprofit study of UI
    partnership and reform by, 15, 86,
    177
National Governors Association,
    principles of state-federal
    relations by, 88–89, 95*n*47
National Industrial Recovery Act, public
    work projects under, 68, 90–91*n*7
National Reemployment Service (NRS),
    in temporary offices, 68, 70,
    91*n*13
NCUC (Commission on Unemployment
    Compensation), 12
Nebraska, 1967–2007 regular UI
    recipiency rate regression of, 127*t*
NELP (National Employment Law
    Project), 15, 86, 177
Nevada, 127*t*, 162
  debts in bond market for UI financing
    by, 59*n*7, 104*t*, 106, 107, 122*n*3,
    144, 174–175*n*9, 174*n*7
  duration of UI benefits in, 144,
    174–175*n*9, 174*n*7
  ES-UI cost-effectiveness data from,
    81, 94*n*34
New Hampshire, 127*t*
  solvency improved through
    legislation in, 104*t*, 105
  tax base increases in, to improve UI
    program financing, 104*t*, 106

New Jersey, 59*n*4, 108*t*, 127*t*
  effective SEA program in, 168, 169
  reemployment services in, 163, 170
New Mexico, 127*t*
  action by, to improve UI program
    financing, 104*t*, 105
New York (State), 127*t*
  changes to UI maximum weekly
    benefit amount in, 111, 123*n*7
  effective SEA program in, 168, 169
  FUTA tax credit offsets by, to
    improve UI program financing,
    104*t*, 106–107, 108*t*
North American Free Trade Act
    (NAFTA), temporary self-
    employment allowances under,
    169
North Carolina, 127*t*
  changes to UI maximum weekly
    benefit amount in, 111, 123*n*6
  duration of UI benefits in, 36, 37*f*, 43,
    85, 95*n*43, 113*f*, 114, 114*t*, 143–
    144, 174*n*6
  FUTA tax credit offsets by, 104*t*,
    106–107, 108*t*
North Dakota, 127*t*, 174*n*3
  tax base increases in, to make UI tax
    law work, 104*t*, 106
NRS (National Reemployment Service),
    68, 70, 91*n*13

Obama, Pres. Barack
  2017 budget of, and UI reform, 14,
    17, 23–58, 171, 177
  one-time increase in ES grants by,
    82, 94–95*n*39
  White House meeting on UI reform
    called by, 15–16
Office of Unemployment Insurance
    (OUI), data supplied by, 32–44,
    64
Ohio, 127*t*
  ES funding delayed in, due to
    political issues, 70, 91*n*13
  FUTA tax credit offsets by, 108*t*
  offset FUTA tax credits by, 104*t*,
    106–107, 109

Ohio, *cont.*
   UI program in, with debts and loan
      payments to U.S. Treasury, 107,
      122*n*3, 144, 174*n*7
Oklahoma, 127*t*
   ES funding delayed in, due to
      political issues, 70, 91*n*13
   tax base increases in, to make UI tax
      law work, 104*t*, 106
Older workers
   in bridge jobs, 49, 61*n*25, 214
   emergence of, since mid-1990s, 9,
      136, 213–214
   UI eligibility of, and state
      restrictions, 134, 136–137
O'Leary, Christopher J., update of UI
      policy book by, 7, 131–132
O'Leary-Wandner (OW) UI reform
      proposal, 177–180, 178*t*–179*t*
   CGN and WHO *vs.*, 181–182
   eligibility recommendations in, 213
   major differences with other reform
      proposals, 182–185
   particulars of, 189–200
One-stop career center system, 161
   ES now included in, 52, 61*n*27, 140
   workforce development delivery
      consolidated in, 77–78, 93*n*29
Oregon, 127*t*
   action by, to improve UI program
      financing, 104*t*, 105
   effective SEA program in, 168, 169
OUI (Office of Unemployment
      Insurance), 32–44, 64
OW UI reform proposal. *See* O'Leary-
      Wandner (OW) UI reform
      proposal

Parental leave, as Trump proposal,
      186–187, 201*n*2
Parsons, Frank, USES and state ES laws,
      70
Part-time workers
   policy recommendations for, in UI
      reform, 138–139, 175*n*12, 190
   UI adaptation to, 9, 47, 49, 138–139,
      214
Partnerships
   cost-effectiveness of, 80–81, 93*n*34

EB program as, 145–147
employment security (ES-UI)
   programs as, and earmarked
      revenues, 74–75, 92*nn*25–26
ES and UI as interdependent
      programs, 77–80
ES-UI federal-state, and
   revitalization opportunity, 85–89
ES-UI federal-state, as failures,
   10–12, 65, 89, 145–146
financing and organizing ES-UI,
   73–74, 92*nn*21–22
origin and evolution of ES-UI
   program, 67–71, 90*n*4
political context of the 1937
   agreement on, 71–73, 91*n*16,
   92*nn*17–21
Pennsylvania, 59*n*4, 121, 127*t*, 168
   debts in bond market for UI financing
      by, 59*n*7, 104*t*, 106, 107, 122*n*3,
      144, 174*n*7
   duration of UI benefits in, 36, 37*f*,
      144, 174*n*7
   ES funding delayed in, due to
      political issues, 70, 91*n*13
   FUTA tax credit offsets as share of
      UI tax revenue in, 108*t*
   reemployment bonus experiment in,
      170–171
Perez, Sec. of Labor Thomas, work-
      sharing report to Congress by,
      167
Perkins, Sec. of Labor Frances
   Secretary-Board Agreement on ES-
      UI partnership, 71–73, 91*n*16,
      92*n*19, 92*n*21
   state ES laws and, 68, 70, 71
Politics, 88
   collaboration among government
      executive agencies and, 71–72,
      91*n*14, 92*n*19
   constraints of, on UI reform, 11–12
   cronyism in, 65, 70, 91*n*14
Public policy, 17, 65
   effect of elections on, 93*n*28
   evidence-based, recommendations
      for UI reform, 18, 131–189, 218
   need for, to ensure adequate ES
      funding, 83, 86–89, 95*n*41

Public policy, *cont.*
    UI program as, 1–2, 5–7, 11, 18,
        19*n*2, 132
Public Works Administration, public
        work projects under, 68, 90–91*n*7
Puerto Rico, 48
    UI program in, missing from RRM
        table, 104*t*, 122*n*2

REA program. *See* Reemployment
        and Eligibility Assessments
        (REA) program
Recessions, 6, 150
    1937–1938, and ES-UI partnership,
        69–71
    post-1974–1975, and UI reform, 12
    post-1990–1991, and UI reform
        attempt, 13
    preparation for, 28, 41–42, 44–45,
        59*n*10, 167, 218
    UI as stabilizer for U.S. during, 2,
        18–19, 146, 148, 174*n*2
    See also Great Recession 2007–2009
Reed Act. *See* Employment Security
        Administrative Financing Act
        (1954)
Reemployment Act (1994), proposed but
        never enacted into law, 172,
        175*n*18, 199
Reemployment and Eligibility
        Assessments (REA) program
    evidence of cost-effectiveness in,
        80–81, 93*n*34, 162
    reevaluation of UI durations and,
        187–188
Reemployment bonuses, research and
        policy recommendations for,
        170–172, 199, 218
Reemployment services, 6, 90*n*30
    analysis of, in budget proposals,
        55–56, 162
    availability of, 8–9, 18, 78, 91*n*12
    one-time increase in ES grants from
        ARRA, 94–95*n*39
    temporary offices for, 68, 70, 91*n*13
    UI recipients and, 7–8, 29–30, 52,
        61*n*27, 137, 217–218
    UI reform proposals and, 184–185,
        198

Reemployment Services and Eligibility
        Assessments (RESEA) program,
        86
    ES-UI cooperation required in, 78,
        93*n*31
    long-term unemployed and, 30, 55,
        61*nn*31–32
    research and policy recommendations
        for, 140, 158, 161–163
    UI reform proposals for, 180, 181,
        182, 187–188, 193
    See also Job Search Assistance
        Program
Reallocation allowances, CGN proposal
        for, 199, 200
RESEA. *See* Reemployment Services
        and Eligibility Assessments
        program
Retirement income, 4
    offsets of, as policy recommendations
        in UI reform, 136–137, 139, 202
Rhode Island, 111, 127*t*
    tax base indexation and increases in,
        to improve UI program financing,
        104*t*, 106
    work-sharing survey of employers in,
        165–166
Roosevelt, Pres. Franklin D., New Deal
        reforms by, 67, 68, 90*n*4
RRM (reserve ratio multiple). *See*
        Average high-cost multiple
        (AHCM)

Self-employment, state allowances in
        lieu of UI benefits for, 159,
        168–169, 180, 185
Self-Employment Assistance (SEA)
        programs, 160, 161, 179*t*, 180
    research and policy recommendations
        for, 168–170, 199, 200, 218
Short-time compensation (STC), 56
    research and policy recommendations
        for, 165–168
    as response to layoffs, 30–31,
        60*nn*14–17
    temporary *vs.* permanent programs
        for, 160–161
    UI reform proposals and, 179*t*, 180,
        185, 198, 218

230   Wandner

Short-time compensation (STC), *cont.*
  USDOL studies of, 165–166
Small Business Development
  Centers, entrepreneurial training
  recommended at, 170, 199
Social insurance, 217
  CES report on, 67–68, 69, 90*nn*5–6
  CGN beyond, to social welfare,
  182–183, 185
  UI as form of, 1, 16, 132, 173
Social Security Act (1935)
  amendments to, 80–81, 94*n*38, 131
  policy objectives of, 17, 65–66,
  70–71, 151
  public Employment Offices for UI
  payments under, 29, 60*n*13, 91*n*10
  Secretary-Board Agreement on ES-UI
  partnership, 71–73, 91*n*16,
  92*n*19, 92*n*21
  taxable wage base for, 4, 151–152,
  154, 158, 180, 182, 196, 214–215
  UI as form of social insurance in, 1,
  16
Social welfare, CGN UI reform proposal
  with, 182–183, 185
Solvency
  AHCM as state, measurement, 28,
  41, 42*f*, 60*n*20
  analysis of UI reform budget
  proposals, 44–46
  improvement in, through state
  legislation, 104*t*, 110–116
  minimum, standard in Trump UI
  reform proposal, 188, 201*n*4
  UI taxes and, 40–42
South Carolina, 127*t*
  acceptance by, of matching Wagner-
  Peyser funds in its UI laws, 70,
  90*n*11
  changes to benefit duration in, 36,
  37*f*, 112, 113*f*, 114, 114*t*, 123*n*8
  changes to UI benefit duration in, 85,
  95*n*43
  duration of UI benefits in, 143–144,
  174*n*6
  reemployment services in, 161–162
  tax base increases in, to improve UI
  program financing, 104*t*, 106

South Dakota, 127*t*
  initial resistance by, to ES-UI laws,
  69, 90*n*10
  solvency improved through
  legislation in, 104*t*, 105
  tax base increases in, to improve UI
  program financing, 104*t*, 106
State law and legislation
  day-to-day ES-UI administration by,
  1–2, 5–7, 11, 66, 110, 115–116,
  133
  inadequate UI benefits set by, 3–4, 6,
  9, 10, 11–12, 85–86, 88–89,
  95*n*43, 95*n*47
  trust fund restoration in, 17–18,
  26–27, 59*n*5, 104*t*, 107, 109, 215
  UI tax revenues vary in, 26, 59*n*4
  USDOL recommendations about ES
  or UI laws in, 10, 19*n*2, 68,
  91*nn*9–13, 133, 166, 169, 215
  See also names of specific states
State UI financing post-Great Recession,
  17–18, 59*n*7, 103–129
  FUTA tax credit reductions, 107–109,
  108*t*, 123*n*4
  program financing responses, 103–
  107, 104*t*, 122*n*1, 169
  recipiency rates in individual states,
  116–119, 125–129, 127*t*
  UI benefits postrecession, 110–116
  UI program nationwide, 119–122
STC. *See* Short-time compensation

Tax credits
  FUTA, offset to improve UI program
  financing, 104*t*, 106–107, 109,
  180, 181, 188
  FUTA, to employers and states, 27,
  46, 59*nn*8–9, 92*n*25
Tax Equity and Fiscal Responsibility Act
  (1982), tightened expanded
  access to UI benefits, 81, 93*n*37
Taxes
  balance of, with UI benefit payments,
  3–4, 11–12, 18, 132, 212
  federal and state structures for, and
  UI, 6, 25–27, 59*nn*4–6, 196

Taxes, *cont.*
  payroll, for UI program, 2, 92*n*25,
    151, 155–156, 179*t*, 197
  relief from, in federal law, 31
  (*see also* Tax credits)
  wage base for UI benefit adequacy
    and, 4, 10, 11–12, 45–46, 80–81,
    94*n*38, 104*t*, 131, 151–156,
    175*n*14, 214–215
Technological advances, 31, 48, 66, 167
  computing services, 57, 82
Tennessee, 128*t*
  changes to UI maximum weekly
    benefit amount in, 111, 123*n*7
  solvency improved through
    legislation in, 104*t*, 105
Texas
  1967–2007 regular UI recipiency rate
    regression of, 128*t*
  2012–2015, not subject to FUTA
    credit reductions, 108, 108*t*
  debts in bond market for UI financing
    by, 59*n*7, 104*t*, 106, 107, 122*n*3
  duration of UI benefits in, and bond
    debt payments, 144, 174*n*7
Total unemployment rate (TUR)
  duration and payments on regular
    UI, 34–37, 35*ff*, 36*f*, 37*t*, 38*f*, 43,
    47, 60–61*n*23
  as EB trigger, 29, 52–54, 146, 149,
    181, 182, 195
  as part of weekly (WKTU) ratio,
    116–117, 128*t*
  ratio of IUR to, as recipiency rate,
    38*f*, 39, 39*f*, 136, 137*f*
  state-level recipiency rate regressions
    and, 113–114, 114*t*, 125,
    126*t*–128*t*
  in states *vs.* national average, 32–33
Training opportunities, 161
  ARRA UI Modernization and, 134–
    135, 135*t*
  entrepreneurial, and funding, 169,
    170, 199
  ETA and, 32, 43, 48, 54–55, 62
  job, under federal laws and policies,
    76, 78, 82–83, 89, 92–93*n*27,
    95*n*40, 175*n*16

research and policy recommendations
  for, 172–173, 194–195
Truman, Pres. Harry, administrative
  reorganization and, 74, 92*n*24
Trump, Pres. Donald, 16
  2018 budget proposal of, 162, 173
  White House of, and UI reform
    proposals, 186–188
TUR. *See* Total unemployment rate

Unemployment
  current snapshot of, 32–33, 32*f*, 33*f*,
    34*f*
  (*see also under* Total
    unemployment rate (TUR))
  duration of, 9, 80, 82
  financing benefits for, policy
    recommendations, 150–156
  first federal laws to address, 65–66,
    90*n*2
  involuntary, and partial wage
    replacement, 49, 61*n*24, 66, 90*n*1
  levels of, 2, 28–29, 32–33, 69, 125,
    126*t*–128*t*, 129*n*1, 147–148
  long-term, 30, 33–34, 34*f*, 55
  regular UI claims to, as IUTU ratio,
    119–120, 120*f*
Unemployment Compensation
  Amendments
  (1976) as post-recession UI reform,
    12
  (1981) reduction of federal costs
    under, 13
  See also Emergency Unemployment
    Compensation Act (1991)
Unemployment Compensation for Ex-
  Servicemembers program,
  RESEA and eligibility for, 55,
  61*n*32
*Unemployment Insurance in the United
  States: Analysis of Policy Issues*
  (O'Leary and Wandner, 1997),
  update of, 7, 131–132
Unemployment insurance (UI)
  access to, 133, 175*n*12
  financing the administration of, as
    recommended policy, 158–159
  as form of social insurance, 1, 16, 27

Unemployment insurance (UI), *cont.*
  overview of, 24–31, 58*n*1
  public policy for, 1–2, 5–7, 11
UI program
  conceived as federal-state
    partnership, 10–12, 66, 131
  current snapshot of, 32–44, 122
  eligibility for
    (*see under* Benefit payments,
      eligibility for)
  evolution of ES with, 17, 65–90, 161
  failures of, and lack of updates, 5,
    7–8, 10–11
  financing postrecession, 17–18, 59*n*7,
    103–129, 214–215
    (*see also* State financing
      responses post-Great Recession)
  need to fix
    (*see* UI reform)
  system out of balance, 3–4, 11–12
  taxes for, 2, 6, 12, 13, 24–27, 40, 40*f*,
    104*t*, 150–156
  technological advances in, 31, 48, 57,
    66, 82
  White House meeting on, 15–16
UI recipients, 136
  benefit eligibility for, and policy
    recommendations, 135–141
  benefit payments to, 1–2, 5, 6, 18,
    19*n*1–2, 38*f*, 39*f*
  claims by, 36–39, 38*f*, 47, 57, 66–67,
    68, 73, 85–86, 95*n*45, 119–120,
    120*f*, 161, 217–218
  expanding benefits for, 51–52, 147
  helping, return to work, 2, 7–8, 19,
    29–30, 52, 61*n*27, 66, 147, 161,
    217–218
    (*see also* Dislocated Worker
      program)
  improper payments to
    (*see under* Benefit payments,
      integrity of)
  means tests for, 133, 185
  recipiency rates in individual states
    post-Great Recession, 113–115,
    116–119, 118*t*, 125, 126*t*–128*t*,
    129*n*1, 136

weekly beneficiaries to TUR, 116–
  117, 128*t*
work tests for, 80, 87, 92*n*33, 140,
  158, 187, 217
UI reform
  analysis of budget proposals for,
    44–58, 162
  changed conditions as priority for,
    8–11
  Obama 2017 budget and, 14, 17,
    23–58
  political constraints on, 11–12
  previous attempts at, 5, 12–14
  recent proposals for, 4, 14–16, 18,
    177–188, 189–200, 211–218
  sustainable and equitable keys for,
    18, 212
  Trump 2018 budget and, 186–188
  why needed, 1–19, 173–174
UI reform, evidence-based policy
  recommendations for, 18, 131–
    201
  administrative financing, 156–158,
    180, 182, 216
  benefit financing, 150–156, 179*t*,
    180, 181, 182, 183–184, 212,
    214–216
  benefit payments, 133–150, 170,
    212–213
  comparative summaries of UI reform
    proposals, 177–182, 178*t*–179*t*
  conclusion, 173–174, 211–218
  EB research and recommendations,
    145–150, 216–217
  education and training, 172–173
  eligibility, 137–141, 162–163, 213
  employment and reemployment
    services, 159–173, 217–218
  levels and duration of regular
    benefits, 141–145, 214–215
  major differences between UI reform
    proposals, 182–185
Unemployment Trust Fund (UTF), 218
  adequacy of, and state RRM, 104*t*,
    122*n*1
  deposits of excess FUTA receipts in,
    for state loans, 156–157

Unemployment Trust Fund (UTF), *cont.*
  forward-funding of state accounts in,
    28, 59*n*10, 151, 153, 155, 188,
    215
  impact of Great Recession on, 40,
    103, 144
  means to conserve reserves in,
    80–81, 216
  restoration of state accounts in,
    17–18, 26–27, 59*n*5, 104*t*, 107,
    109
  size of, as target for non-UI
    programs, 172
  state reserves in, accounts, 5, 6,
    17–18, 26–27, 59*n*5, 103, 120–
    122, 121*f*, 141
  taxes and, 11, 27, 45–46, 74–75
United States (U.S.)
  need to fix UI program in, 1–19,
    119–122, 173–174
  New Deal reforms in, 67, 68, 70,
    90*n*4
  UI recipiency rates in all 50 states,
    39, 39*f*, 128*t*
  *See also names of specific states
    within, e.g.,* Pennsylvania;
    Washington (State)
U.S. Congress, 150
  failure to act by, 5, 10, 12, 13, 14, 77
  permanent and temporary benefit
    extensions enacted by, 5, 6, 146
  programs underfunded by, 78, 216
  UI commissions and councils created
    by, 12, 13
U.S. Dept. of Labor (USDOL)
  data supplied by agencies within,
    32–57, 60*n*19, 60*n*21
  participation in White House meeting
    on UI by, 15–16
  projects proposed for, 199, 200
  recommendations to states about
    their UI laws, 10, 19*n*2, 49–50
  Secretaries of, 68, 165, 167
  state UI administration financed by
    grants from, 115–116, 156–158
  studies by, 165–167, 168–169
U.S. Employment Service (USES)
  public work projects and, 68, 90–
    91*n*7

  state ES offices and, 70, 91*nn*9–15
U.S. law and legislation
  annual deficits, 157
  economic recovery, 7, 13–14, 31, 68
  social insurance, 1–3, 17
  trade, 169
  UI taxes, 6, 12, 13, 74, 81
  UTF, 218
  workforce investment, 8–9, 92–93*n*27
U.S. Treasury
  programs with debts to, 45–46, 107,
    120, 122*n*3, 141, 174*n*7
  states issued municipal bonds to
    repay, for recession UI loans,
    104*t*, 106, 122*n*3
  UTF state reserves in accounts at, 5,
    75, 103, 120–122, 121*f*
U.S. Virgin Islands. *See* Virgin Islands
USDOL. *See* U.S. Dept. of Labor
USES (U.S. Employment Service), 68,
    70, 90–91*n*7, 91*nn*9–15
Utah, 128*t*
  acceptance by, of matching Wagner-
    Peyser funds in its UI laws, 70,
    90*n*11
  action by, to improve UI program
    financing, 104*t*, 105
UTF. *See* Unemployment Trust Fund

Vermont, 128*t*
  tax base indexation and increases in,
    to improve UI program financing,
    104*t*, 106
Virgin Islands, 48, 109, 121
  UI program in, missing from RRM
    table, 104*t*, 122*n*2
  UI program in, with debts and loan
    payments to U.S. Treasury, 107,
    122*n*3, 144, 174–175*n*9, 174*n*7
Virginia, 108*t*, 128*t*
  ES funding delayed in, due to
    political issues, 70, 91*n*13

Wages
  access to records of, 49–50
  insurance for, 55–56, 179*t*, 181, 182,
    185, 199
  replacement rates of, and UI benefits,
    110–111, 112*f*

Wages, *cont.*
   taxable base on, and FUTA, 45–46,
      59n6, 87–88, 151–155, 188, 196
   taxable base on, and UI benefits, 4,
      10, 11–12, 40*f*, 80–81, 94n38,
      131, 180, 181, 182, 214–215
Wagner-Peyser Act (1933), 17
   amendments to, 87, 90, 94n36, 95n46
   ES-UI funding and, 65, 68–74,
      77–79, 81, 83–84, 84*f*, 86–88,
      89–90, 91nn9–11, 92n14, 93n29,
      93nn32–33, 94–95n39, 95n46,
      95nn41–42, 185, 216
   policies needed to assure ES grants to
      states, 86–88, 95nn44–46, 140–
      141, 158
   WPRS referrals to, reemployment
      programs, 161, 164, 187–188
Wandner, Stephen A., update of UI
   policy book by, 7, 131–132
Washington, D.C. *See* District of
   Columbia
Washington (State), 58n2, 128*t*
   acceptance by, of matching Wagner-
      Peyser funds in its UI laws, 70,
      90n11
   action by, to improve UI program
      financing, 104*t*, 105
   changes to UI maximum weekly
      benefit amount in, 111, 123n7
   reemployment bonus experiment in,
      170–171
   reemployment services in, 161–162,
      168
   work-sharing survey of employers in,
      165–166
   work test data on UI claimants in, 80,
      93n33
West Virginia, 128*t*
   solvency improved through
      legislation in, 104*t*, 105
   tax base increases in, to improve UI
      program financing, 104*t*, 106
White House-Obama (WHO) UI reform
   proposal, 177, 178*t*–179*t*
   differences from OW proposal, 171,
      181, 183

ES and forward-funding requirement
   in, 184–185
   particulars of, 189–200
   publication of, 201n1
White House working groups
   on social insurance, 67–68, 90n5
   on UI reform, 15–16, 177, 186–188,
      201n1
WHO. *See* White House-Obama (WHO)
   UI reform proposal
Wisconsin, 108*t*, 128*t*
   ES-UI cost-effectiveness data from,
      80, 93n33
   first unemployment benefits paid by,
      71, 73, 91n17, 92n19
WKTU ratio. *See under* Total
   unemployment rate (TUR)
Women as workers, emergence since
   World War II, 9, 213–214
Work sharing. *See* Short-time
   compensation (STC)
Worker Profiling and Reemployment
   Services (WPRS) systems, 161
   ES-UI cooperation required in, 78,
      93n30
   incrementalism in, 70, 91n12
   research and policy recommendations
      for, 140–141, 163–164, 175n17,
      193
   spawned much worker development
      legislation, 160, 175n16
   as unfunded mandate, 82, 94–95n39
Workforce, 83
   changes in nature of, 9, 48–49,
      76–77, 85
   misconduct as cause for firing of,
      49–50
   organized labor in, and UI reform,
      11, 12, 131, 187
   part-time workers in, 9, 47, 49, 134,
      138–139
   preventing dispersal of, during slack
      demand, 66, 90n2
   UI tax proposed for, 155–156, 174,
      180, 215
Workforce Innovation and Opportunity
   Act (WIOA, 2104), 90, 170

Workforce Innovation and Opportunity
    Act (WIOA, 2104), *cont.*
    Dislocated Worker program under,
        8–9, 161
    effect of, on WIA, 79–80
    job training in, 82–83, 199
    predecessors of, 160, 175*n*16
Workforce Investment Act (1988), 78
    Dislocated Worker program under,
        8–9, 161
    one-stop career center system
        codified in, 52, 61*n*27, 78, 174*n*4
    predecessor and successor of, 160,
        174*n*16
Works Progress Administration, public
    work projects under, 68, 90–91*n*7
Wyoming, 128*t*
    acceptance by, of matching Wagner-
        Peyser funds in its UI laws, 70,
        90*n*11
    action by, to improve UI program
        financing, 104*t*, 105

About the Institute

The W.E. Upjohn Institute for Employment Research is a nonprofit research organization devoted to finding and promoting solutions to employment-related problems at the national, state, and local levels. It is an activity of the W.E. Upjohn Unemployment Trustee Corporation, which was established in 1932 to administer a fund set aside by Dr. W.E. Upjohn, founder of The Upjohn Company, to seek ways to counteract the loss of employment income during economic downturns.

The Institute is funded largely by income from the W.E. Upjohn Unemployment Trust, supplemented by outside grants, contracts, and sales of publications. Activities of the Institute comprise the following elements: 1) a research program conducted by a resident staff of professional social scientists; 2) a competitive grant program, which expands and complements the internal research program by providing financial support to researchers outside the Institute; 3) a publications program, which provides the major vehicle for disseminating the research of staff and grantees, as well as other selected works in the field; and 4) an Employment Management Services division, which manages most of the publicly funded employment and training programs in the local area.

The broad objectives of the Institute's research, grant, and publication programs are to 1) promote scholarship and experimentation on issues of public and private employment and unemployment policy, and 2) make knowledge and scholarship relevant and useful to policymakers in their pursuit of solutions to employment and unemployment problems.

Current areas of concentration for these programs include causes, consequences, and measures to alleviate unemployment; social insurance and income maintenance programs; compensation; workforce quality; work arrangements; family labor issues; labor-management relations; and regional economic development and local labor markets.